T0265666

The Unfinished Quest

The Unfinished Quest

*India's Search for Major Power Status
from Nehru to Modi*

T.V. PAUL

OXFORD
UNIVERSITY PRESS

Oxford University Press is a department of the University of Oxford. It furthers the University's objective of excellence in research, scholarship, and education by publishing worldwide. Oxford is a registered trade mark of Oxford University Press in the UK and certain other countries.

Published in the United States of America by Oxford University Press
198 Madison Avenue, New York, NY 10016, United States of America.

© T.V. Paul 2024

Library of Congress Cataloging-in-Publication Data
Names: Paul, T. V., author.
Title: The unfinished quest : India's search for major power status from Nehru to Modi / T.V. Paul.
Description: New York, NY : Oxford University Press, 2024. | Includes index.
Identifiers: LCCN 2023051075 (print) | LCCN 2023051076 (ebook) |
ISBN 9780197669990 (hardback) | ISBN 9780197670002 (epub)
Subjects: LCSH: India—Foreign relations—1947-1984. | India—Foreign relations—1984- | India—Foreign relations—China. | China—Foreign relations—India.
Classification: LCC DS480.84 .P39 2024 (print) | LCC DS480.84 (ebook) |
DDC 327.54—dc23/eng/20240116
LC record available at https://lccn.loc.gov/2023051075
LC ebook record available at https://lccn.loc.gov/2023051076

DOI: 10.1093/oso/9780197669990.001.0001

Printed by Sheridan Books, Inc., United States of America

This book is dedicated to my elder brothers, Mathew and Varkey, for their encouragement and inspiration throughout my academic career.

Contents

Figures

Preface

The rise of India with markers of a major power is a real possibility in the twenty-first century. As its economic, military, and technological capabilities increase, the desire for higher status recognition is rapidly growing in India. Yet this remains a project in the making, as India's status is truncated and still to be properly institutionalized by peer-group powers. The extant literature on Indian foreign policy is yet to be fully cognizant of the socio-psychological phenomenon of international status, or the conditions under which a new rising power such as India is accorded its due status in the international arena. This book attempts to unravel the historical efforts by India's leaders to obtain higher status in the international system and the constraints and opportunities they have experienced in that pursuit. Since its economic liberalization in 1991 and its emergence as the fifth largest world economy in 2022, India has come a long way in assuming higher international status as a rising power. In the changed geopolitical climate of the twenty-first century, India has a rare opportunity to become a leading power, yet the lack of inclusive economic development has hampered its pursuit. The rapid rise of China and its increasing rivalry with India have offered the latter opportunities in improving its relations with the United States, Russia, the European Union, Japan, and its immediate neighbors in South Asia and extended regions of the Indo-Pacific, in particular, East Asia, Southeast Asia, the Persian Gulf, and Africa.

Work on this project has taken several years, interrupted by other projects and the disruptions caused by the Covid-19 pandemic. Many individuals helped me during this journey. They include: Rajesh Basrur, Kanti Bajpai, Udai Bhaskar, Rudra Chaudhuri, K.P. Fabian, Erik Gartzke, Kai He, Selina Ho, Happymon Jacob, Andrej Krickovic, M. Matheswaran, Manjeet Pardesi, Miriam Prys-Hansen, Harold Trinkunas, Mahesh Shankar, George C. Verghese, C. Vinodan, Rahul Sagar, Aseema Sinha, Daniel Smit, T.P. Sreenivasan, Sunil Mani, Manjari Chatterjee Miller, Anit Mukerjee, Lawrence Prabhakar, Pushkar, Venu Rajamony, K.M. Seethi, and Constantino Xavier, many of whom organized book-in-progress seminars and provided valuable insights. The seminars were held at S. Rajaratnam

School at Nanyang Technological University, Singapore; Lee Kwan Yu School at the National University Singapore; School of International Relations and Politics at Mahatma Gandhi University, Kottayam; India International Center, New Delhi; German Institute for Global and Area Studies, Hamburg, Goa International Center; Center for Development Studies, Thiruvananthapuram; Center for Peace and Security Studies, University of San Diego; Brookings India, New Delhi; Carnegie India, New Delhi; Pardee School, Boston University; and the Peninsula Foundation, Chennai. Graduate students who helped me over time with valuable research support include Alice Chesse, Pengqiao Lu, Apoorva Malepati, Erik Underwood, Viktor Vucic, and Muhammed Yusuf Yilmaz. I also acknowledge the vital support and encouragement of my wife, Rachel, and her diligent copyediting, as well as the moral support of my daughters, Kavya and Leah, enhanced by the pleasant arrival of my cheerful grandson, Benjamin, in October 2022. The support of Don Fehr of Trident literary agency was significant. My editor at Oxford University Press, David McBride, showed much interest in the project and patience in its development. The two anonymous reviewers offered many insightful comments. Thanks also goes to OUP's production team, in particular, Alexcee Bechthold, Vinothini Thiruvannamalai, and copy editor, Dorothy Bauhoff. Funding for field research and graduate student assistance came from the James McGill Chair grant, Social Sciences and Humanities Research Council Canada (SSHRC), and the Fonds de recherche du Québec–Société et culture (FRQSC). Some portions of Chapters 3 and 6 are adapted from my published articles: "India's Soft Power in a Globalizing World," *Current History* 113, no. 762 (April 2014): 157–162 (with permission of University of California Press); and "When Balance of Power Meets Globalization: China, India and the Small States of South Asia," *Politics* 39, no. 1 (2019): 50–63 (with permission of Sage Publications).

1
Introduction

In May 2020, in the high-altitude Himalayan mountains of Eastern Ladakh, several Chinese People's Liberation Army (PLA) soldiers appeared, placing their tents in the barren borderlands surrounding the Line of Actual Control (LAC) claimed by both India and China—an area that has rarely been encroached upon for more than three decades. Caught unawares for several weeks, the Indian Army finally responded by sending a patrol party in June that engaged in a hand-to-hand battle in the frigid Galwan Valley. Some 20 Indian and an undetermined number of Chinese soldiers died, the first casualties since 1967 involving the two Asian giants. Subsequently, both sides used firearms in a threatening manner, again a first after four decades of non-lethal patrolling activities. As the winter months approached, both sides set up more permanent fixtures for stationing their troops in a terrain where nighttime temperatures can fall to −50°C. On February 11, 2021, after many rounds of behind-the-scenes negotiations, both sides agreed to withdraw their troops to the pre–April 2020 positions, but the prospects for durable peace were not favorable, given that intrusions continued in 2022.[1] In a near-repeat event on December 9, 2022, Chinese and Indian forces engaged in hand-to-hand combat involving sticks and iron rods in Tawang in the Northeastern section, injuring some 34 Indian and an undetermined number of Chinese soldiers.[2]

A more prolonged, but non-lethal, confrontation took place in the Doklam tri-junction of the India-Bhutan-China border in the summer of 2017. It resulted from China's road construction there, which India resisted by intervening militarily in the disputed territories. The Chinese temporarily withdrew from the immediate encroachment areas after a 73-day-long standoff. Subsequently, China has claimed to have occupied a border village inside Bhutan and to have built housing there for Chinese nationals as well as an alternate all-weather road, bypassing Indian defenses at Doklam.[3] These Chinese actions, presumably with the approval of the paramount leader Xi Jinping, surprised the Indian leadership, along with many international observers. The latest serious border incident occurred right in the middle of the Covid-19 pandemic that began in Wuhan, China, and spread around the world, with India being the second-most affected country after the United States. Was the 2020 incident simply a land grab opportunity, resulting from the Indian leadership's attention being deflected by the pandemic crisis as well as the weaknesses that the Indian economy had been facing following the national lockdown in April 2020? Or was it a response to an earlier Indian decision to remove the special autonomous constitutional status of Jammu and Kashmir, which includes the Ladakh territory, and then make it a full constituent part of India? It is also reported that along with building more military infrastructure, Indian troops have been patrolling the disputed areas more frequently in the recent years, provoking China.[4]

In this book, I contend that the upsurge in the Sino-Indian confrontation is only a manifestation of a larger contestation for international status that is playing out in the Indo-Pacific region. In this context, I define status as "collective international recognition of an actor based on its valued material and/or non-material attributes." The increasing tensions in bilateral relations are a direct result of status anxiety experienced by both sides vis-à-vis each other. The massive growth in the gross domestic product (GDP) of China has increased the Xi Jinping regime's apparent decision to bring back an "all under heaven" tributary model (Tianxia) of yesteryears to the Indo-Pacific and beyond. The Belt and Road Initiative (BRI), linking China with Asia, Africa, and Europe, is a clear manifestation of this policy, and is coupled with "wolf warrior diplomacy," which includes challenging borders with India, and the control of waters in the South China Sea, and East China Sea, as well as increased military pressures on Taiwan. Beijing's larger contestation is with the United States for dominance over the Pacific and the Indian Oceans, and eventually achieving global hegemony. Among all Asian states, the one power that has resisted joining the BRI or conceding to Chinese aggressive territorial moves is India. Could the sudden upsurge in territorial challenges by China not be due to any decline in Chinese security, but rather to put India, the presumably lower-ranking status challenger, in its place in China's hegemonic contestation?

India's status quest is a story of lost opportunities, mixed successes in the past three decades, and possible positive turning points for future enhancements due to some favorable geopolitical circumstances. Even though not on par with China's growth in aggregate economic numbers, the expansion of the Indian economy over the past three decades has been impressive. In September 2022, India became the fifth-largest world economy with \$3.5 trillion GDP, replacing the United Kingdom, the former colonial ruler of India, whose economy dipped to \$3.2 trillion.[5] Over the past millennia India rose and expanded, eventually becoming a leading Asian civilization. It was then conquered by Islamic rulers and later by European colonial powers, most significantly the British, who made it the "jewel in the crown" of their empire—a region that supplied enormous amounts of wealth, manpower, and resources to Britain. India's successful independence struggle was largely nonviolent, elevating its status among other colonized societies and liberal-minded Westerners, enabling it to play a significant role as a third force in international politics. However, major conflicts with neighboring Pakistan and China somewhat upended its regional status aspirations. The timing of independence in 1947 did not work in India's favor in improving its status ranking in the postwar international order. More specifically, the UN Security Council in 1945 and the Nuclear Non-proliferation Treaty (NPT) in 1967 both precluded India as a ranking member with privileged positions similar to the five permanent (P-5) member states. However, the end of the Cold War and New Delhi's subsequent economic liberalization partially "uncaged the tiger," unleashing an era of economic growth and global activism. India's rise from the "Fallen People"[6] status to the "rising power" category is an impressive yet partially fulfilled story. Along the way came China, India's larger Asian neighbor, whose status aspirations collided with India's in a larger contestation over the Indo-Pacific region. Increasingly, the international status quest has become part of the electoral politics in India, with the Bharatiya Janata Party (BJP) projecting Prime Minister Narendra Modi as the best option for enhancing India's image and status globally, while the opposition parties contest this position. Simultaneously, the BJP denigrated the Congress governments of the past for not improving India's status, especially in civilizational, religious, and nationalistic terms.[7] Currently, India is aiming at becoming a "leading power," not just an "influential power"—in other words, the equivalent of a twenty-first century great power.[8]

Today, India's status elevation is challenged more directly by a rising China, although the policies of other states in the South Asia region, as well as domestic and international factors, also constrain the full realization of its status ambitions. Looking first at the China challenge, the Sino-Indian rivalry is often discussed in terms of territorial conflict, ideology, power, and influence.[9] However, the rivalry has evolved into a larger contestation for international and regional status. Status has been a source of conflict and cooperation between the two nations since their advent as fully independent states in the late

1940s, but it has worsened over the past decade since the arrival of Xi and Modi as leaders. China simply does not consider India as equal in status, while the Indian elite thinks they are equals.[10] Much of the Chinese propaganda has been to show that India is a weak, post-colonial state, overly tied to the United States today, and that it should assume a secondary role in the Asia-Pacific region while accepting China's primacy. India's reactions to the rise of China range from admiration to deep suspicion, as memories of defeat in the 1962 War and the ongoing territorial challenges add to the mix of status anxiety. In the decades ahead, this contest is likely to worsen, as the status ambitions of the two giant Asian states are unlikely to be reconciled. The widening material discrepancy between the two will potentially accentuate the status rivalry, with status anxiety worsening for India. The opposite (i.e., narrowing of the gap in material capabilities) could increase China's anxiety in this regard. New Delhi's balancing efforts with the United States and Japan, if fully realized, could generate intense pressures for China to act in a hostile way toward India.

India's challenge to China's rise as a global power is multidimensional.

- India is a powerful "swing state," geographically located at the central point of contestation, the Indo-Pacific, and in the larger global competition between China and the United States. Its siding with the United States and its allies such as Japan and Australia can tilt the balance of power in the region, potentially upsetting China's claims and ambitions for regional and global dominance.
- In April 2023, India overtook China as the world's most populous country and thereby gained a demographic dividend of working-age population for a decade or more. The Indian economy is also poised to grow at a higher rate than China's for some time, and with sustained growth rates, it could reach close to China's economy by mid-century. However, India's status position is not institutionalized like China's as it is not a permanent member of the UN Security Council, and Beijing's lack of status accommodation of India will remain a sore point in their relations.
- The unsettled border with India and the Indian resistance, both on land and in the sea, challenge China's status as the emerging superpower, and could potentially drag PLA forces into a contest that will divert them from their central conflict with the United States.
- India's active opposition to the BRI and one of its key components, the China-Pakistan Economic Corridor (CPEC) linking Xinjiang with the

Arabian Sea, has hurt China's ambitions for a smooth dominance of the maritime space of the Indo-Pacific and beyond. Moreover, if the India–Middle East–Europe Economic Corridor (IMEEC), initiated on the sidelines at the 2023 Delhi G-20 meeting, becomes a credible competitor to the BRI, China's expected status boost in the Global South countries could erode.

- India's economic growth in the post-pandemic era could return to a level that upsets China's goal of reaching a hegemonic position in the Indo-Pacific region and wean away many of the smaller Asian states that China has managed to co-opt, via a deft infrastructure and debt strategy, into economic dependency relationships. A more powerful India would give such states more strategic autonomy as they can seek India's assistance simultaneously. Some, such as Sri Lanka, have fallen into a "debt trap" partially due to involvement with China's infrastructure projects. They face massive social and economic challenges and are seeking more aid from India.

- India's strategic relationships with Japan, Australia, and Southeast Asian countries, as well as regional states in Africa and the Middle East where India has traditional strengths, could upset the Chinese elite's dreams of re-emergence of a Tianxia world. India is increasingly aiming at reasserting its Global South leadership role, in addition to the balancing role it hopes to play in great power contestation.

- Both India and China are led by ambitious leaders claiming historical primacy in Asia, with their millennia-strong civilizational legacies and powerful presence in the world economic scene before the arrival of the European colonial powers in the eighteenth century. However, high levels of misperceptions and cognitive biases exist in each other's opinions of their civilizational value and historical significance.

- Global events such as Russia's sudden attack on Ukraine in February 2022 have affected India's status quest as India attempted its multi-alignment strategy of maintaining good relations with all great powers, especially its principal arms supplier, Russia. It does not want to push Moscow into forming a coalition with China and Pakistan, an outcome that would negatively affect India's security and status ambitions.

India's quest for status parity with China was deeply hurt in the aftermath of its defeat in the 1962 war with China, which Beijing launched to teach Jawaharlal Nehru's government a lesson.[11] Until the 1970s the economic capacities of the two were almost similar, although China had more successes in human development, despite some brutal famines and the catastrophic policies of Mao Tse-Tung. China's massive economic and military growth, as a result of its early liberalization from 1979 onward, distanced the till-then somewhat equal economic trajectories of the two states. India took over two decades longer to liberalize and still managed to achieve comparable growth rates for two decades, only to slow down subsequently since 2016. The economic growth in this period energized Indian ambitions for obtaining equal international status with China. The rising power paradigm of the 1990s gave India, Brazil, and Russia newfound status in the BRICS (Brazil, Russia, India, China, and South Africa) associational context. This occurred in the backdrop of the 2008–2009 global financial crisis when the rising powers assumed a significant role in stabilizing the world economy. However, the BRICS received a jolt when the Xi regime decided to proceed unilaterally by launching the BRI. Partners in BRI have a secondary role in its management, unlike the BRICS mechanism as well as its associated banks, the New Development Bank (NDB) and Asian Infrastructure Investment Bank (AIIB), where some form of formal equality is maintained.

Why, however, does India consider itself as a counterweight to China and a state with unique status claims? More importantly, why does India's elite perceive their country as a rising or great power, and why has the recognition by other significant powers been slow to come?

Many statements by Indian leaders since independence in 1947 attest to India's desire for higher international status, even if those aspirations are not matched by material capabilities. More recently, in September 2020, Prime Minister Modi, while addressing the UN General assembly, reiterated his claim for a permanent seat for India in the UN Security Council.[12] In May 2019, an ambitious pronouncement was made by Modi, who, after being re-elected for a second term with a strong majority in parliament, announced: "We must work as one society with one purpose in one direction to regain the rightful position of India in the world order. In the past, our country had that place. I am sure India will regain its importance in the world order."[13] More than seven decades earlier, India's first prime minister, Jawaharlal Nehru, quoted French Indologist Sylvain Levi to assert: "India has left indelible imprints on one-fourth of the human race in the course of a long succession of centuries, . . . from Persia to the Chinese Sea, . . . from the icy regions of Siberia to the islands of Java and Borneo, and from Oceania to Socotra," and "she has the right to reclaim in universal history the rank that ignorance has refused her for a long time and to hold her place among the great nations."[14] In his first address to the nation on the eve of independence, Nehru declared at the Constituent Assembly: "At this solemn moment when the people of India, through suffering and sacrifice, have secured freedom, I . . . dedicate myself in all humility to the service of India and her people to the end that this ancient land attain her rightful place in the world and make her full and willing contribution to the promotion of world peace and the welfare of mankind."[15] Nehru had visualized India as one of the four great powers of the postwar international system, along with the United States, the Soviet Union, and China.[16]

Since the 1990s, a series of U.S. leaders—Bill Clinton, George W. Bush, Condoleezza Rice, Barack Obama, and Hillary Clinton—have all acclaimed India as a rising power that deserves to be recognized as a lead actor in the international arena.[17] All permanent members of the UN Security Council except China have openly acknowledged the need to include India as a permanent member of the Council.[18] Yet, full status accommodation of India is yet to take place. India remains in an "almost great power" mode. In its seven decades as an independent state, India has achieved much progress in fulfilling the dreams of its leaders in obtaining higher global status, but the quest is still unfinished.

Some fundamental questions are: Why have successive Indian leaders believed that the country has a destiny to rise as a major power, despite its relative weaknesses in tangible hard power resources—military, economic, technological, and demographic assets—vis-à-vis other leading powers of the day? Or did they assume that intangible soft power indicators—culture and civilization, diplomacy, active participation in international institutions, and leadership roles among the developing countries on global collective action issues—would offer status in the short run until the material capabilities improved over time? Despite their stated and unstated ambitions, why haven't the larger bureaucratic and political elite worked hard enough to achieve the goal of making India a powerful developmental state and taking advantage of its demographic dividend, essential to becoming a major power in the contemporary world? What are the external and internal constraints in this pursuit and the opportunities that India may have both exploited and missed? Is there a mismatch between ambition and action, and a misreading on what markers are really needed to achieve major power status, especially in the twenty-first century? What are its domestic implications, especially in terms of minority rights and political freedom? Is global and regional status acquisition becoming a key issue of electoral politics in India? Finally, what does the future hold for India's status elevation, especially in the context of China's rise, increasing U.S.-China rivalry, and their implications for regional and global orders?

This book argues that India's external behavior in a variety of areas powerfully suggests that while security and prosperity are two key national goals, the more intangible status aspirations have been an underlying quest, irrespective of the political dispensations that ruled in Delhi. The key reference group of countries for status recognition that Indian leaders had in mind varied over time. While Nehru during the 1950s thought that India's status enhancement in the newly emerging countries would offer global recognition, a more confident India since the 1990s has viewed itself as a putative status equivalent of China, based on acceptance by other major powers. Obtaining status recognition by higher-status nations, especially the United States, became the key approach of Indian governments since the nuclear tests in 1998.

India's status quest, however, has been marred by a number of international, domestic, and societal constraints. At the international level, India missed the boat on two occasions—in 1945 and 1968—when the post–World War II pecking order was institutionalized largely by the established great powers. In 1945, in San Francisco, the victorious great powers of World War II principally determined the structure of the United Nations, with five permanent members (P-5) acting as the custodians of international security with veto power. India was under waning colonial rule at that time, and the British would not support permanent membership for India, even when all of the great powers supported China's membership, based on differing perceptions of importance they held of the two Asian states. Representation of the colonies was very limited in San Francisco.[19] However, surprisingly, British India and the Indian princely states had participated as fully accredited entities, similar to the British dominions of Canada and Australia, in the 1919 Paris Peace Conference and the League of Nations. This was despite the anomalous legal character of India at that time, comprising 11 provinces under direct British rule and some 500-plus semi-autonomous princely estates.[20] It may very well be that China was never fully colonized and that it was a sovereign republic since 1911, recognized by most other states, while India was viewed as an appendage of the British Empire, even though during this time the British were in serious negotiations to give India independence and treated the British Indian Army somewhat differently from the regular

British Army. On a second crucial occasion in 1968, India had yet to conduct a nuclear test when the NPT came into force, and India was bracketed as a non-nuclear state, thereby permanently barring it from gaining the status of a legitimate nuclear-weapon state, similar to the status accorded to the P-5 under this unequal treaty. China's atomic tests in 1964 helped in solidifying its membership in the NPT as a nuclear-weapon state, a crucial status differentiator. In fact, India's opposition to the NPT was largely due to the status deprivation it would entail in perpetuity, a point that is rarely acknowledged in the scholarly or policy worlds of nuclear non-proliferation.[21]

Pivotal global events were critical for New Delhi to make policy adjustments that helped or constrained India's status pursuit. The onset of the Cold War, which coincided with India's independence, affected the extent of India's autonomy, despite pursuing a policy of non-alignment, especially in the 1960s. Among the key factors, the East-West conflict, China's nuclear tests, U.S.-China alignment, the Soviet invasion of Afghanistan, the dismantlement of the Warsaw Pact, and the dissolution of the Soviet Union were critical in determining India's trajectory as a lead actor in the international arena. In the post–Cold War era, the arrival of intense economic globalization, the 9/11 terrorist strikes, the rise of China, the global financial crisis of 2008–2009, and the 2022 Russian attack on Ukraine have all affected India's status pursuit and prospects in varying degrees.

With the end of the Cold War in 1991, India rose in international status partly because of the economic reforms which began that year, which for over two decades made it one of the fastest-growing major economies of the world.[22] The economic liberalization allowed India's GDP to grow six-fold since 2000, and it stood at $3.5 trillion in 2022. The economy grew at an average annual rate of 6 percent during the past three decades; and in 2017, with a 7.5 percent annual growth rate, India was the world's fastest-growing economy, overtaking China's growth rate by a small margin during 2015–2017. Although the growth rate since then declined to some 4.5 percent in 2019 and to the negative range in 2020—following the outbreak of the Covid-19 crisis when the Indian economy entered into a recession, along with much of the world— the trend has been changing in the post-pandemic world. International agencies such as the International Monetary Fund (IMF), the World Bank, and Moody's have predicted that India may be the fastest-growing economy for several years after 2022.[23] Even with a modest annual growth rate of 5 to 7 percent (due to unpredictable events like Russia's war with Ukraine and subsequent oil price hike, as well as a global recession), it is projected that India will become the number two world economy by 2050 behind China, contributing to some 15 percent of world's GDP.[24]

Despite this impressive macro growth rate for some two decades and greater possibilities for the future, India has been trailing behind its nearest peer-competitor, China, on every developmental measure. These include GDP, per capita income, educational and health standards, infrastructure development, foreign direct investment, clean water, healthcare, and life expectancy.[25] In February 2021, China declared that it has eliminated mass poverty ahead of its targetted year of 2030.[26] India may take many more decades to achieve this coveted goal, despite claims otherwise by the political elite.

A Partially Self-Made Challenge?

While India's Cold War–era status position had been hampered by factors such as the U.S.-Soviet rivalry, post-independence national integration challenges, conflict with neighbors, and the lack of global economic prominence due to an autarkic economic strategy, India's post–Cold War–era weaknesses have been partially of its own making. Despite some significant achievements in raw indicators, the Indian state has not yet been able to obtain the necessary wherewithal and strength to catapult this pivotal country into a globally consequential economic and military power. Despite some recent advances, its grand strategy remains reactive, though at times bold. Limited diplomatic successes are shadowed by domestic challenges inhibiting the attainment of higher international status. India's record remains less than stellar in terms of creating an inclusive, developmental state, especially in wealth distribution and the provision of public services such as universal education and healthcare, as well as infrastructure development. As a result, in 2022 India's Human Development Index (HDI) ranking stood at 132 out of 193 countries, which is not reflective of its aggregate economic growth.[27] Even its smaller neighbors Bangladesh (127) and Indonesia (107) have done better in HDI compared to India. This means that India's status quest is yet to be embedded in a developmental model that can be emulated by others. The ill-planned and hastily announced national lockdown in March 2020 in the face of the coronavirus outbreak starkly revealed the economic divide as millions of poor migrant laborers had to trudge miles in the scorching heat without proper transportation to return to their villages, with fear of economic ruin and desperate struggles with no safety net.[28] As a result of the pandemic, some 155 million people who had come out of poverty from 1991 to 2014 were thrown back into extreme poverty, showing how fragile economic development has been for the masses in India.[29] The developmental path India has chosen, while making several billionaires and millionaires, has produced only a limited improvement in the pocketbooks of a large segment of the population that suffers from abject poverty and illiteracy. In 2022, 10 percent of the population held some 77 percent of total national wealth, and some 119 billionaires held over 40 percent of it, while the bottom 50 percent of the population possessed only 2.8 percent.[30] In 2022, the top 1 percent and top 10 percent of the population held 22 and 57 percent of the national income, respectively, and the bottom 50 percent of the population's share had declined to 13 percent.[31] According to Raghuram Rajan, a former governor of the Reserve Bank of India as well as a former chief economist of the IMF, India's billionaires have been able to generate such high levels of wealth due to their close proximity to the state.[32] Inequality is indeed a global phenomenon, but its impact is wider in this context, given that India began from a point of extreme inequality due to a number of historical and religious-cultural circumstances, which I discuss below.

The argument here is not to deny India its legitimate global institutional leadership role, as none of the existing great powers has solved all their domestic problems, but the markers have become harder for a newcomer's entry into the major power system and receive associated higher international status. While India has every right to demand proper representation and roles in global governing institutions—a right that is denied by the existing powers—if it does not address its huge developmental challenges, its status will remain on shaky ground, as status is in the eyes of the beholder, that is, others' perceptions of the attributes that keep one apart from other actors contending for the same status. An inclusive, developmentally-oriented, democratic, and pluralistic India will catapult its social, economic, and perceptual profiles in the global arena that it rightly deserves. Of course, diplomatic activism and a proper grand strategy will facilitate this process, as has always been the case for rising powers in the past. Status recognition in the contemporary world is due to not only military might, but also economic and social development, which brings a polity much wider attention and recognition. Adequate human development also increases per capita income and, as a result, enlarges and improves total GDP and all other parameters of a successful modern state on a sustainable basis.

India's Low Attention to Inclusive Human Development

Arguably, by 2021 India had obtained geopolitical conditions that previously had never been as favorable for its rise as a major power. The rise of authoritarian China has offered India, a subcontinental-size state, situated in one of the most important geopolitical crossroads of the world, a tremendous opportunity unparalleled for any other large state to achieve its status objectives in the contemporary world. The closest parallel case for India is Brazil, which is situated in the geopolitically less significant Latin American region, and Brazil heavily depends on soft power factors, which has placed it in an aspirational role for too long.[33] Yet, the full and deep status accommodation of India internationally is hampered by the internal status problems arising from the continued lack of adequate attention to human development, in particular the education and skill development of a majority of the population, especially those belonging to the lower castes and minorities. India suffers from a debilitating social inequality challenge, propelled by a unique caste system that privileges the upper castes, despite many constitutional and institutional efforts since independence to redress it.[34] The educational system still favors the small strata of upper and the middle classes, while large segments of the lower castes, women, and minorities, in particular Muslims, are unable to gain the fruits of modern education or economic development at a reasonable level. As a result, the depth of India's development is weak, despite the impressive aggregate economic numbers that derive from its sheer size. When a global crisis like the pandemic hit, India had only a limited cushion to shield its masses from both economic and medical catastrophes.

The reason for this persisting challenge is India's choice of an economic model that has not paid sufficient attention to inclusive human development. India finds itself developmentally behind many East Asian and Southeast Asian states (such as South Korea), which were in a weaker position than India in the 1950s. A developmental state needs to spend about 6–7 percent of its GDP on education, and a similar amount on health and human welfare, as well as a higher percentage on infrastructure development. Until recent years, India consistently spent less than 2 percent of its GDP on education, of which 1 percent was for higher education institutions and 1 percent for all others. This has hurt India enormously in multifaceted ways, in areas such as productivity, employability, quality of life, health standards, and overall capacity to innovate. Since 2014, education spending has gone up to 3.8 percent of GDP on average. However, in 2017, public health spending came down to 2.94 percent of the GDP, with significant variation across constituent states.[35] Of the three areas, infrastructure witnessed the highest increase to 9 percent of GDP in 2018. However, these are not sufficient to put the population on a competitive playing field in a society with deep-rooted poverty and inequality due to caste, class, gender, and shallow democratic values. In education, healthcare, and infrastructure, China has been outspending India for several decades (even during Mao's reign), and the results are visible.[36] China's status elevation, let alone rapid economic development, would not have happened if it had neglected the developmental aspect as India has done.

The question is why India has such great difficulty in spending on education and skill development of its greatest asset, human capital. While some Indian states like Goa, Sikkim, Tamil Nadu, Kerala, and Himachal Pradesh have a high proportion of their incomes going to education and healthcare, with many positive results, the embedded inequalities supported and maintained by the caste and communal system result in a reluctance to allocate resources needed for quality education of over 70 percent of the population, especially in the heavily populated Northern, Central, and Eastern states. These include Madhya Pradesh, Bihar, Orissa, Assam, and the largest state, Uttar Pradesh.[37] The emphasis from the beginning has been to develop a handful of elite institutions for the privileged bureaucratic and political class and provide low allocations for primary, secondary, and tertiary education. Barring a few, many Indian states followed this pattern. The justification was that economic development and international status will come only through science and high technology focused on select institutions. While this may have been the prevailing wisdom of the times, a simultaneous effort on mass education would have done wonders for India.

India's democratic system, despite its many positive features, has been unable to change the attitudes of the political and bureaucratic elite on inclusive development, which is required for deep transformation. The electorate does not seem to reward the developmental performance of political leaders, and often caste allegiances of candidates appear to be more important in the voters' calculations. Nor do they consistently demand improvements in public goods provisions by the governments, though at times they vote out non-performers.[38] The bureaucratic elite also imbibe the deeply held hierarchical notions of society and are reluctant to become active agents of change and modernization, unlike their counterparts in East Asia or many other rising powers in the past. The affirmative action or reservation system, although benefiting some, has not yet created the necessary skill sets for a large segment of the population, as quality education still eludes the lower strata of society. The strength of India's greatest asset, its human resources, has not yet percolated to economic and social development. Although inequality is a problem in much of the world, including the United States and China, the fact is that they entered the great power club before the new conceptions of higher status became prominent in the international arena. Inequality and poverty are also more visible in India, compared to all other existing great powers, as well as aspiring powers attempting to enter the higher status group, including Brazil.[39] Although in the past, European powers often attributed status ranking based on victory in wars irrespective of a state's internal developments, this option in the nuclear age is virtually closed for new aspirants. A rising power with global power ambitions must become a state of international consequence for the major powers as well as the global economy. To this end, it requires achievements in human development indices as well.

From a domestic angle, two powerful cultural and historical factors coalesce in India, hampering its attainment of full-fledged developmentally-derived major power status. The hierarchical caste ideas and the inherited British-era colonial class-based education system both reinforce inequality, especially in the country's heavily populated Northern states. Since independence, India continued the British-era policy of minimal spending on human development and education. For instance, until mid-1860, British spending on all forms of education in India was around 0.5 and 0.7 percent of government expenditure. In 1854, infrastructure development such as railways and roadways covered 9.5 percent of government expenditure. The main objectives of the British rulers were revenue collection and easing of movements of goods and commodities for trade, rather than the development of the Indian masses.[40] Following the 1857 mutiny, John Stuart Mill, the key British liberal thinker who served in the India Office, wrote a memorandum arguing for physical improvements in India while undercutting his own earlier emphasis on liberty and education. The annual publications, "Moral and Material Progress Reports," were a result of Mill's original report, which listed the number of "laws passed, then discussed finance, the post office, telegraphs, steamships, public works and the Indian geological department. This was a vision of the state as commander and builder, not a nurturer of human capacity and talent. Reports concentrated on law first, then physical infrastructure and public works, [and] only then education."[41] In writings, Mill argued that his liberal views were not applicable to "less advanced people" like Indians.[42] This attitude of the Raj persisted throughout British rule, and in 1947, when the British departed India, the literacy rate was abysmally low, at 16 percent of the population, with women at 8 percent.[43] As Sashi Tharoor states, "In his notorious 1835 Minute on Education, Lord Macaulay articulated the classic reason for teaching English, but only to a small minority of Indians. 'We must do our best to form a class who may be interpreters between us and the millions we govern; a class of persons, Indians in blood and color, but English in taste, in opinions, in morals and in intellect.' "[44] This attitude persisted throughout the British Raj.

Independent India sadly continued this legacy of low emphasis on quality mass education for a long time. In his seminal work on childhood education in India, Myron Weiner argued that India in comparison with other states—Germany, Austria, England, United States, Japan, China, Taiwan, South Korea, and even poorer Sri Lanka—did not promote compulsory primary education. Instead, various Indian governments allowed child labor to persist. Weiner attributed this sorry state of not putting resources to mass education as a vehicle for modernization, to prevailing cultural ideas held by "educators, social activists, trade unionists, academic researchers, and more broadly by members of the middle class" that "excessive and inappropriate education for the poor would disrupt existing social arrangements" and that the education of the poor would result in increased unemployment and that the "lower classes should work with their hands rather than with their heads."[45] There have been changes in the efforts of mass education since the 1990s, with India in 2021 achieving some 77.77 percent literacy rate, 84.7 percent for men and 70.3 percent for women. These data mask the huge regional variations between the heavily populated Northern states and Southern states, and until the laggards catch up, mass literacy will remain uneven in India.

Similarly, the British colonial rulers found caste as a very convenient way to manage Indian society, and thereby helped to solidify its preexisting caste structure. Nicholas Dirks has contended that under British colonial rule, caste "was anchored to the service of a colonial interest in maintaining social order, justifying colonial power, and sustaining a very particular form of indirect rule."[46] Leaders of independent India were aware of the power of caste. Bhimrao Ramji Ambedkar, coming from the lower caste himself, was a powerful voice for change and, as the chairman of the Constituent Assembly that drafted the Indian Constitution, did make serious efforts to undercut the caste system.[47] The reservation system of assigning some percentages of quota in education and jobs for lower castes was a concrete step that states in India undertook as a result of efforts by Ambedkar and other activists. Over time, Southern states in particular witnessed much resistance against caste oppression. Even beyond the South, empowerment did take place, as evidenced by lower castes taking political power in North Indian states such as Bihar and Uttar Pradesh. But voting along caste lines or even lower castes assuming power has not seriously undercut the domestic status hierarchy or improved the economic conditions of the subaltern castes sufficiently to uplift India's living standards on a mass scale. Positive results in this area are essential for advancing the status ranking of a country in the modern world.

The powerful merging of colonial and Indian cultural ideas thus treated inclusive human development as less important, despite rhetoric and some policy initiatives stating otherwise. Yet the question is, why have the hierarchical notions left behind by the British as well as millennia-old caste divisions continued, and what are their lingering impacts on development as such? Blaming the colonial rulers on this count has limitations, as the Indian elite at every level seemed to have harbored ideas of hierarchy, in particular caste and unequal economic development. Also, not sufficient efforts were made to break that social barrier system, enshrined in religious and cultural ethos. Since independence, there have been improvements in the living conditions of the masses, yet the pace has been less rapid than desired. Many poverty-reduction initiatives have only short-term benefits, although they have prevented the famines and mass starvation of the past. Following the economic liberalization of the 1990s, the Manmohan Singh government started several programs for poverty alleviation. One in particular, introduced in 2005, and currently called the Mahatma Gandhi National Employment Guarantee Scheme, offered 100 days of employment in public works to poorer unskilled workers.[48] Additionally, there has been subsidized rationing for the poor for essential goods like rice and kerosene in order to provide basic support. The Modi government has continued and strengthened these programs, especially their direct delivery to the poor, and this has been a major reason for the BJP's electoral successes. It also enhanced the prime minister's image. Although necessary to prevent starvation and mass suffering, these handouts to the poor are equal to band-aids, as they do not address the larger structural problems to alleviate recurring, deep poverty. They are not long-term solutions, as the poor are still unable to obtain the quality education that their children need in order to become productive members of a competitive workforce.

Major Powers and Their Key Assets

A country becomes a major power and/or a great economic power by utilizing its most significant assets to its advantage, with the effect that other countries, especially great powers, recognize its dominant position in the world arena. Even countries that are not recognized as major military powers have emerged as key economic players due to certain policy changes they have made. In the post–World War II era, those countries without many natural resources or endowed or conquered wealth have been able to obtain higher income and prosperity by focusing on human capital, technological advancement, international trade, and foreign investment. Both small and large states have shown that economic growth and human resource development are possible with careful national planning. The developmental states of East Asia, beginning with Japan and then Korea, Taiwan, Singapore, and China, are great examples of this phenomenon. These cases, except China, are relatively small states and hence may not carry high rank in terms of military clout, but they have a different ranking in global status. When a large state is judged as both economically and militarily superior, it can claim greater status, although formal recognition may not come immediately. Today, China's global status improvements are heavily linked to not only its economic, technological, and military strengths, but also its improvements in human capital, something the Chinese leadership has emphasized since the liberalization under Deng Xiaoping. In European imperial and colonial eras, great power status recognition relied heavily on military power, especially naval power, although race played a role as well, as the Europeans did not acknowledge non-European states as status equivalent. The examples of the Ottoman Empire and later Japan receiving hostile racial treatment in European status clubs are poignant.[49] Conquering others' territories and winning wars with other great powers were the way to achieve major power status and acquisition of wealth. Despite these prevailing notions, even the then-aspiring power Japan recognized the central role of human development for rapid economic and military growth. A fundamental shift has taken place since World War II, in particular as a result of the decolonization process and the widely observed norm of territorial integrity, making overt conquest of others' territories a difficult means of gaining international recognition. Due to powerful nationalism, great powers had much difficulty defeating weaker powers, as in the cases of Vietnam, Afghanistan (twice), and possibly Ukraine. On the contrary, a country can become rich and powerful by developing its population and domestic economy, while internationally it makes use of opportunities that accrue from geopolitical and economic changes. Spheres of influence still matter, but they are achievable through extensive economic partnerships and security alignments, without physically conquering territories. Countries also have to make use of their most valuable assets to further their status aspirations.

Human capital is where India has unparalleled assets that very few others have. With a population of 1.42 billion, India in April 2023 overtook China as the world's most populous country.[50] By 2036, 65 percent of its population will belong to the 15–59 age group, becoming the world's largest working-age population. In 2020, the median age of India was 28; China, 37; United States, 37; Western Europe, 45; and Japan, 49. India does not need to conquer new territories, as it has enough capacity to feed itself and to generate a powerful domestic market, given that one of the world's largest arable land spaces is in India. Its pivotal location in the Indian Ocean and at the crossroads of Asia, Africa, and the Middle East is ideal for global influence from a geostrategic perspective. However, it must dramatically improve its pitiful HDI ranking.[51]

Part of India's challenge is that many of its top technical educational institutions, like the Indian Institutes of Technology (IITs), do not promote research and development (R&D) adequately. They are predominently teaching institutions, and R&D is largely the domain of government institutions and a small number of corporations. The result is that India has a small segment of the population who are educated in its elite universities, many of whom go abroad to study in largely Western institutions and/or migrate to these countries due to better opportunities. The loss of the skilled segment of the Indian economy has been the gain of the multinational corporations, largely American. India has made only limited attempts to utilize this enormous human talent, unlike what China has done with its diaspora.[52]

The low levels of quality education and its uneven availability have affected India in many ways:

- Elevated population growth in the least-developed regions of the country, especially in the North. Those Indian states with higher levels of education have achieved population control, while the lower-ranking ones have high population growth.

- Low consumer base and participation in the market economy. This is due to low per capita income, which is not able to catch up with inflation. The un- and under-educated also end up in very low-paying jobs and do not effectively help the country's growth.
- Low levels of investment in R&D by the state institutions, universities, and corporations have not sufficiently promoted skill development.
- Health and hygiene understanding is not developing quickly enough, despite some recent improvements. High levels of calorie deficiency are partly due to non-availability of nutritious food for the poor, as well as their low educational levels.
- Infrastructure development is inadequate, as the number of skilled personnel who specialize in engineering and urban/infrastructural planning is limited. Moreover, many who work in this field are prone to corruption. A few exceptions, like airports and metro lines, have improved using public-private partnerships, but these have not been applied on a mass scale to other core sectors. The result is that India's roads, ports, electricity grids, and transportation are yet to reach global standards. Rural infrastructure especially is not developed or linked properly to urban infrastructure and as a result the contribution of the rural population to the economy remains low.
- The military strength of India is affected by the inability to develop domestic weapon systems, and in 2021 India remained the largest importer of weapons in the world, constituting 11 percent of the global total.[53] Granted that in firepower, due to imported weapons and increasing military spending, India is still a power to be reckoned with.

Despite its achievements in many of these areas—especially considering where it started in 1947—India still has miles to go in many measures of global status. For a rising power, insertion into international trade and investment is essential to obtain a quick rise in status, as China's experience shows. For this, India needs a massive shift to manufacturing industries and to expand its service industry offerings. Foreign companies are not yet willing to invest in India in a major way as they did in China, due to skill shortages, infrastructure bottlenecks, as well as political and bureaucratic hurdles. The *license raj* still persists, and exit rules are tough for investors. Even if corporations invest, they need to recruit the workforce that can compete with other countries, especially those of China and increasingly Vietnam. With China gradually becoming belligerent toward Western countries, many companies are leaving that country, and the question is, can India become the next factory for the world? The answer is "partially" and that too, if major advancements occur in quality education, infrastructure, and a corruption-free regulatory environment. Some sectoral improvements, especially in areas like information technology (IT) and pharmaceuticals, have happened, but the overall commitment of multinational corporations (MNCs) leaving China has not been to India, but to Vietnam, Taiwan, and Thailand.[54] There are indeed exceptions, like Apple, Google, and Amazon pitching India as their manufacturing base for some of their products. For instance, in August 2022 Apple announced its plans to produce its next-generation iPhone in India.[55] Market access may be a calculation of these companies, but this achievement needs replication in many other areas if it is to make a dent in India's economic prospects.

Historically, most rising powers have attempted to improve their domestic capacities along with their international standing and power positions. Some used the authoritarian route (such as Russia and Prussia), while others (e.g., UK, France, U.S.) still developed strong military and state institutions as well as infrastructural capabilities, within liberal democracies, to channel their energies into becoming or sustaining their positions as great powers. They had the added advantages as pioneering European states to exploit colonial expansion, which resulted in both ill-begotten wealth and the technologies of the industrial revolution. The ideas unleashed by the European Enlightenment, along with nationalism, mercantilism, and notions of racial superiority, helped in their pursuit of global domination, and war outcomes determined the fate of many of them. Rulers like Peter and Catherine realized that the only way Russia could emerge as a great power was to learn European ideas and technology and implement them in their empire while simultaneously expanding toward the East. The Meiji reformers in Japan realized that improvements in every walk of life were necessary to become a "rich country, strong army."[56] But these models produced extreme violence in the international system. How to avoid their conflictual paths is a challenge for aspiring powers, including India.

Along with military power and territorial acquisitions, some great powers pursued welfare state ideas for increased national cohesion and international status. Indeed, they were European colonial powers that had the advantage of colonial extraction to fund their welfare schemes.[57] For example, it was Otto van Bismarck who began the welfare state in Germany by adopting a health insurance law and retirement pensions in 1883. His assessment was that soldiers needed to be educated and fed to make them better fighting forces and to keep industrial labor from joining the Social Democratic Party.[58] Japan's Meiji restoration in 1868 was the result of its elite's perception that in order to achieve greater military and economic power and status, as well as avoid the fate of colonial domination that had befallen China and India, deep internal reforms were necessary. Through the 1935 Social Security Act, President Franklin D. Roosevelt introduced a limited welfare state as a means to help older workers save for their retirement. This would later cushion the effects of the Great Depression, absorb returning World War II soldiers, and promote U.S. power and prestige.[59]

China is the most recent example of a state that is making major strides to obtain dominant global power status through internal development, external trade and investment, improvements in living standards, and military modernization, although increasingly through authoritarian means. The Chinese case shows that however weak a potential rising power initially is, if the elite and the public are determined, they can transform it in a relatively short period of time. The window of opportunity provided by the U.S.-China rapprochement, which was initiated in the 1970s by Nixon, Kissinger, and Mao, accelerated during Deng's reform era in the 1980s. The end of the Cold War and the increase in economic globalization since the early 1990s were carefully used by the Chinese elite for this purpose. The Chinese Communist elite has recognized that building world-class infrastructure and making major strides in both civilian and military technological areas were essential for obtaining higher international status. This would sometimes entail copying both technological and organizational ideas from competitors, especially from the West and Japan. More importantly, poverty removal and the elevation of educational and employment opportunities for millions of Chinese have been part of a strategy that has paid enormous attention to human development, but not basic freedoms. India's efforts in this regard are haphazard. Barring a few, the mainstream Indian political parties and the bureaucratic elite have yet to show the necessary understanding of the need to bring up the lower strata of the society and to use the demographic advantage as an asset for nation-building and improved international status.

But not all is gloom and doom for India's status elevation. Despite its internal weaknesses, India has made considerable progress in the past three decades in obtaining higher international status, some by default. Since 2020, China itself has been regressing economically under Xi Jinping, showing what policy reversals can do to the prospects of a rising global power. Further incremental and peaceful accommodation of India is possible, but for this to occur, existing great powers have to include New Delhi in key international institutions as a major stakeholder. Some limited accommodations have taken place since 2005, especially in the nuclear arena. Still others, in particular, membership in the UN Security Council, remain closed to India.

Today, international status is rapidly becoming part of the domestic political discourse and contestation in India. Status politics has emerged as a key factor in the electoral fortunes of the BJP government, led by Modi. Even though, since the 1990s, the strengthening of Hindu nationalism has placed a dent in the democratic and secular credentials of India, one of the key goals of the religious right has been to make India a great power as rapidly as possible. Many of the BJP leaders and supporters seem to believe that India can obtain great power status even when it becomes a religious state, or by whittling down its secular characteristics. Modi's 2019 second-term electoral victory has been partially attributed to selling to the public the notion that India's status had improved considerably under his leadership.

During the first two decades after independence, the first Indian government, led by Nehru, realized the material weaknesses of India and adopted a soft-power strategy for status enhancement through creative diplomatic initiatives such as the promotion of Asian-African unity, non-alignment, decolonization, disarmament, and diplomatic activism, especially among the newly emerged states, to gain higher status in the world arena. But these strategies came to a standstill following a crushing military defeat at the hands of China in 1962, a country Nehru's India was trying to befriend. Because of the defeat, India's status aspirations received a severe blow in the short run, although India's status as the leader of developing countries was maintained during much of the Cold War era. As disillusionment with such strategies set in, India under Indira Gandhi's leadership progressively adopted more confrontational strategies of asserting status in the form of challenging the unequal nuclear non-proliferation regime, especially the NPT of 1968, which had created two categories, nuclear-weapon and non-nuclear-weapon states. The most visible challenge to the world nuclear order was the 1974 nuclear tests dubbed as "Operation Smiling Buddha," which was framed as a test for peaceful purposes.[60] However, India did not develop full-fledged nuclear weapons capability until the 1998 tests, which resulted in it becoming a target of sanctions by the established nuclear states and their allies, hurting its status quest temporarily. The fence-sitter mode that India adopted from 1974 to 1998 offered the great powers an opportunity to pressure India, hoping it would abandon its nuclear quest.

India's tilt in favor of the Soviet Union, partially in response to the U.S.-China-Pakistan triadic alliance in the early 1970s by Nixon and Kissinger, as well as the 1971 war with Pakistan, had both negative and positive effects for status elevation. In the short run, the victory in the war gave India a fillip to its dominant status in the region; however, this would not last, as the Soviet invasion of Afghanistan in 1979 elevated Pakistan as a key ally of the United States in South Asia. Pakistan, after an initial period of inaction, strengthened itself through a military regime that was bent on building nuclear weapons. Beginning in 1989, it initiated an asymmetric war in Kashmir, supporting the renewed insurgency against Indian control. As India's material capabilities have grown progressively in recent decades, there have been more efforts by a confident India in attempting a rapprochement with the great powers, in particular the United States, which also showed an interest in accommodating India as a rising power. The 2005 U.S.-India Nuclear accord gave India special status as a de facto nuclear state without signing the NPT. Statements by Presidents Bill Clinton, George W. Bush, and Barack Obama, as well as Secretaries of State Condoleezza Rice and Hillary Clinton, all showed that the United States had begun to view India as a major power. During his state visit to India in November 2010, Obama stated: "In Asia and around the world, India is not simply emerging; India has emerged." In the same speech he said: "Indeed, the just and sustainable international order that America seeks includes a United Nations that is efficient, effective, credible and legitimate. That is why I can say today, in the years ahead, I look forward to a reformed United Nations Security Council that includes India as a permanent member."[61] Then, despite the topsy-turvy politics of the Donald Trump administration, India became a key partner of the U.S. thanks to China's conflictual behavior. President Joe Biden strengthened the relationship, largely aiming at balancing China.

In the twenty-first century, the rise of China as a powerful actor with a creative and increasingly combative status-elevation strategy has once again posed a challenge to India, with new opportunities and constraints. After an initial inclusive institutional strategy, largely through BRICS, G-20 (Group of 20), and other international groupings, in 2018 China under Xi Jinping decided to break out of the mold with an intention to replace the United States as the leading global power. In that process, the Chinese strategy has progressively relegated India to a position of a less important actor in the

Indo-Pacific. China's foray into the Indian Ocean and its massive effort to advance its BRI across Asia further undercut India's aspirations. A "string of pearls" strategy by Beijing, built around several port facilities that could potentially be used for naval purposes in the Indian Ocean region surrounding India, appears to be in place. These Chinese initiatives have prompted India to make strategic counter-moves. The Chinese entry into the Indian Ocean has opened up more avenues for India to join hands with the United States, Japan, the Association of Southeast Asian Nations (ASEAN), and Australia to create a counter-balancing coalition. China's more aggressive strategies under Xi Jinping to challenge the Western-led rules-based international order have unveiled possibilities for India, as it is more of a rule-reformer than a rule-breaker and seeks institutional accommodation for status enhancement through peaceful means. The Quadrilateral Security Dialogue (Quad) of the United States, Japan, India, and Australia is slowly developing as a quasi-balancing coalition. The G-20, in which India is positioned as a lead player, is also rapidly emerging as a possible alternative to the UN Security Council in dealing with global issues in which India is positioned as a lead player. This could be a major status boost for India, as becoming a key participant in the great power balance-of-power games is essential to gain their recognition in moments of great power settlements. Explaining the status moorings and cravings of India as a rising power is essential to understanding the twenty-first century's international fault lines, especially in the central geopolitical region of the Indo-Pacific. It is also important to recognize the violence and internal repression that great powers and rising powers can undertake in the name of status achievement and redressal of humiliations. As war is a costly mechanism for status acquisition, India needs to pursue other options. These include rapid economic and technological advancements, but most importantly, significantly improving its human development. They are crucial elements for an aspiring state, even when it posseses many existing and putative markers of major power status.

2

The Pursuit

A formally recognized international status as a major power has eluded India since independence in 1947, although some significant gains have been made since 2000. For over five decades, India remained in the category of "aspirational power," but moved rapidly to "rising power" after its economy made steady gains in the 1990s and the first decade of the twenty-first century. The most significant event in this respect was the 2005 U.S.-India Nuclear Accord, which legitimized India's status as a de facto nuclear weapon state even though it had not signed the Nuclear Non-Proliferation Treaty (NPT). These partial gains were achieved on the basis of relative status markers, such as a strong gross domestic product (GDP) growth rate, external value as a swing state to balance China's growing power, and limited institutional recognition through membership in the Group of 20 (G-20) and the Quadrilateral Security Dialogue (Quad). The re-linking of the Indian and Pacific Oceans in the term "Indo-Pacific"—now a widely accepted pairing—gives India strategic prominence, as it is the most significant state in the Indian Ocean rim.

In this chapter, I outline the key motivations behind and the constraints on the Indian elite's international status quest. I first identify status as a socio-psychological phenomenon pursued by nation-states. The questions posed include the following: Why did India aspire to higher international status even before obtaining adequate material power? And what changed India's aspirations in this realm over time? Concisely, its increased material power in the post–Cold War era, especially its economic strength and geopolitically important "swing power" position, accelerated India's status quest and resulted in a limited accommodation by other powers. The Indian case exemplifies the importance of the internal–external nexus in obtaining greater status recognition, especially in peacetime (i.e., without a postwar settlement among the great powers, as in 1815, 1919, and 1945). Even when favorable international conditions are present, India's sustainable status attainment is intricately linked to its domestic achievements, especially the substantial improvement in the living conditions of 1.4 billion people, as well as the retention and strengthening of its secular/democratic credentials as a bulwark of a refined liberal order and as a counter to China's authoritarian-coercive model.

Why Do Countries Seek Status?

Is India unique in the search for greater international status? During the past decade, many key works have emerged that examine the status motivations of states, while some others treat status as a key source of conflict and competition in the international arena and a cause and contributor to the rise and decline of major powers.[1] For "status" I use the same definition as in my previous work on the subject: "collective beliefs about a given state's ranking on valued attributes" such as "wealth, coercive capabilities, demographic position, sociopolitical organization and diplomatic clout."[2] Like beauty, social status is found in the perceptions of others, although an actor, be it an individual, a social class, or a nation-state, can misperceive the amount of status it may hold. Simple favorable perceptions by others are not enough for durable international status of a country; they need to be legitimized by way of membership in leading institutions of the day, as well as recognition of its special rights by other peer-group states, such as control over spheres of influence (in the case of great powers). A state may seek higher status through benign or aggressive strategies, the latter attested by Russia's invasion of Ukraine in 2022. Moreover, some states, like certain individuals, may crave higher status, while others may be satisfied with what they already possess, partially due to their implicit recognition of their lack of a sufficient level of markers for high-status achievement. Possession of some significant status-generating assets, relative to others, and smart diplomatic strategies are needed for any state to achieve its full status recognition in the international arena.

Fundamentally, two major motivations can be attributed to higher-status quests by national leaders. One is socio-psychological, and the other is material advancement. The socio-psychological argument states that leaders as individuals seek higher status for themselves and their countries as a way to fulfill their social craving to be treated deferentially by others, especially their peer groups.[3] Moreover, individuals tend to prefer to be in higher-status groups as it "increases collective self-esteem and pride."[4] As members of the international community, positive social comparisons by others matter to states. A material value argument would hold that higher status is necessary to obtain economic prosperity and, in some cases, military capabilities that state leaders often desire.[5] Such motivations are based on the fact that increased status through membership in institutions offers a state special rights and leverage capacities in bargaining with others.[6] These may include preferential trading rights, improved social capital, and networking opportunities, which in turn can influence the foreign policy choices of others.[7] Yet others have argued that higher status, especially membership in international organizations, affords the status holder "opportunities to shape political, economic, and security arrangements in the world, in accordance with their own interests" and "can induce behavioral deference from lower ranked states."[8] Institutionalized status thus can be a source of power and influence in international politics.[9] Membership in higher-status groups offers members associational power that would not be available otherwise.[10]

Psychological studies, in particular evolutionary approaches, suggest that higher social status is an adaptive mechanism that provides the holder increased social influence, the capacity to "mobilize others on behalf of the self and for demobilizing potential adversaries," and often the ability to "win contests without having to fight."[11] A status-seeking state can thus be motivated by both socio-psychological benefits and material advantages, as they are not necessarily incompatible. In any event, the desire for upward mobility, especially by those who earlier were denied it by a rigid, hierarchically organized international system, is a natural desire as the state's wealth and other material capabilities increase. But rigid stratification could still continue in some fashion or other, denying it the status it clamors for.

Status quest also has long been a subject of philosophical explorations.[12] It was Machiavelli who powerfully pointed out that men are driven by glory, similar to power, and that lasting glory can be obtained only through the creation of a republic.[13] In modern times, international relations scholar Robert Gilpin has argued that states seek prestige, among other goals, which is somewhat equivalent to status quest as "prestige rather than power, is the everyday currency of international relations" and that relative prestige determines bargaining outcomes, often without the use of force, as it adds legitimacy to the position of the possessor.[14] Many of these works conflate terms like "status," "prestige," and "glory," as they are cognate concepts, despite some differences.[15]

In addition, through their efforts and attainment of higher status, political actors could accrue internal legitimacy and power enhancement. The electoral politics of democracies is the arena where political leaders can use status as a mechanism for domestic popularity and legitimacy. Former U.S. president Donald Trump, India's Narendra Modi, and Turkey's Recep Tayyip Erdogan typify this goal, although others tend to seek it more subtly. Modi in particular has claimed international status enhancements as a domestic legitimation strategy for his party, and won re-election in 2019 partially on the basis of a claim that under his rule India's status has become more recognized internationally. His Bharatiya Janata Party (BJP) manifesto claimed that "today India stands tall at the international level. The world recognizes India's immense potential, which is clearly reflected in a record rise in foreign investment."[16] Trump's unusual electoral victory in 2016 is attributed to "status threat felt by the dwindling proportion of traditionally high-status Americans (i.e., whites, Christians, and men) as well as by those who perceive America's global dominance as threatened, resulting in support for the candidate who emphasized reestablishing status hierarchies of the past."[17] In authoritarian systems, too, seeking or obtaining higher status can be a source of legitimacy. Russian leader Vladimir Putin and China's strongman Xi Jinping both have used international status as a mechanism for enhancing their domestic power base and legitimacy among the general public, as well as vis-à-vis their domestic adversaries. Putin is an extreme example of aggressive behavior for status enhancement and rectifying or avenging perceived status humiliation caused by adversaries, akin to the prickly leader that Machiavelli describes.

Peculiar cultural attributes such as the caste system can also affect the status aspirations and sensitivities of a state's elite. The high sensitivity to perceived status slights among the Indian bureaucratic class is attributed to cultural factors, as a majority are drawn from upper castes.[18] This may not be a particular characteristic of only the Indian elite. Many members of the Chinese and Russian elites show extreme sensitivity to external status slights, especially by their Western counterparts. Chinese leader Xi Jinping chiding Canadian prime minister Justin Trudeau publicly at the G-20 meeting in Bali in November 2022 for revealing to the media their earlier discussion on China's meddling in Canadian elections is one example.[19] The notion of "White privilege" implies that White Westerners may expect and receive higher status on the basis of their racial attributes, and the elite may carry such notions in their dealings in the non-White world. They may receive and they may expect better treatment at airports, public services such as hospitals, and dealings with police and law enforcement agencies.[20] The colonial-era idea of the "White man's burden" of a civilizing mission for the inferior races (à la Kipling) gave White colonizers "ontological status plus great power over much of the inhabited world."[21] Thus, privileged groups can receive better behavioral responses from others, and the same goes for countries. Such groups may view status slights perceived by disadvantaged groups as unusual or unnecessary, may disregard them as irrelevant, and if challenged, may react defensively or violently.

In international politics, status enhancement appears to be one of the key motivating factors of large and most powerful states (i.e., great powers and aspiring great powers) in their national strategies. Sometimes, smaller states can also make deft efforts at status enhancement using the particular hard- or soft-power assets they hold. For example, smaller European states such as Denmark and Norway have attempted to play a larger role in international mediation efforts by projecting their status as peace-loving social-welfare states.[22] However, status quest and competition are most consequential for great powers and aspiring great powers, as status acquisition and status loss can involve much violence and conflict among them.

This begs the question: Why does status quest produce conflict, and how? It is now well established that one of the key reasons for great power conflicts, in particular power-transition conflicts, is status discrepancies. When material capacities of a once-weaker state overtake those of a dominant state, it wants to move up among deference groups but is often blocked by the existing status hierarchy because material power does not immediately translate into status gains.[23] While some believe that status is a core cause of revisionism among rising powers, as "obstructed status ambitions unleash social, psychological, and domestic forces within rising powers that push them to reject and challenge the status quo order," others contend that status quest need not always lead to conflict.[24] It is not clear, however, how often states engage in military revisionism to assert their status aspirations. At times, states can use normative means to assert their positions through institutional innovations, or they can assume an institutional veto-player role. They can show dissatisfaction by closing their countries to others through the pursuit of autarchic policies. States can engage in discreet ways of challenging the order, not frontally, but through asymmetric, diplomatic, and normative means. It is also not always the revisionist powers that engage in wars for status. A powerful United States has engaged in wars for status, altering the status quo in the Middle East and vigorously opposing Russia and China in their efforts to depreciate U.S. status.[25] Status assertion toward weaker actors has been present in U.S. foreign policy for a long time.

There are still several unanswered questions regarding the status motivation of states and how much it matters, as well as how it is manifested and articulated in their foreign policy behavior. Moreover, states can misperceive their status ranking as well as potential, the effectiveness of their strategies, or the impact their efforts may have on targeted groups, especially states with higher status. States need not engage in vicious conflicts for status elevation until an ambitious leader emerges in order to generate pride among the population. Soft-power-based strategies for status elevation can work for a period of time until material challenges emerge from others, for example, by way of military threats. If a state has no capacity to withstand military challenges, it could lose much of the credibility accrued through soft power and normative means, as happened to India in the aftermath of the 1962 defeat by China. Sometimes, states can "punch above their weight," as in the case of Maoist China, which was perceived as one that could say "no" to others and still got things done, even though until the 1970s its material capabilities were somewhat similar to India's.[26] Exercising military power can be tricky, and either suffering defeat against another major power or losing to a weaker power will negatively affect the perceptions of the state's effectiveness and hence its status. Unless decisively defeated, established great powers often manage to recover their status by using different markers or overcoming the deficiencies in their particular assets, and also by using deft diplomacy and propaganda. For instance, U.S. losses in Vietnam, Iraq, and Afghanistan dented its status temporarily, but Washington managed to recover over time. Membership in leading international institutions tend to facilitate this process of status recovery.

Major Power Status Recognition

What does a "great power" or "major power" mean in the contemporary world? And how is it related to status rankings?[27] The conventional definitions of great power status emphasize military power as the key ingredient, i.e., great powers are those states with the most physical power to hurt, deprive, deny, or provide military security to others.[28] It should be noted that not all great powers hold the same level of capabilities, although nominally they may have the same status ranking in international organizations. Some great powers (e.g., today's Russia, Britain, France, and China) have institutional recognition through their veto power in the UN Security Council, but it is increasingly clear that they are different from the United States (or the Soviet Union during the Cold War era) in terms of their power capabilities and global status. Therefore, it will be useful to talk about global powers (also known as superpowers) and major powers as two categories within a hierarchical order. A major power may have many markers of global influence, but a truly global power or superpower is one that can influence security and economic outcomes in any corner of the world most prominently. In that sense, in today's world the United States is the only global power and China is working hard to gain that status, and Russia under Vladimir Putin is trying to re-enter through forceful territorial aggrandizement. However, without major economic and technological advancement, Russia is unlikely to regain the global power status of the Soviet Union during the Cold War era.

Since the 1970s, but most notably with the end of the Cold War in the 1990s, great powers have been conceived of as states that rank the highest "in the primary global structures—economic, military, knowledge, and normative—and that enjoy relatively low sensitivity, vulnerability, and security interdependence because of massive resource and skill differentials and relative economic self-sufficiency."[29] All these elements would require state capacity as an indispensable ingredient for great power status. However, possessing all the above attributes in amounts greater than the majority of other states need not confer full-fledged great power status on a state, which is a challenge for aspiring powers such as India. In India's case, the domestic constraints have been upending its international status, as recognition by others may depend on higher levels of developmental achievements internally than what it has today. International institutional rigidity in terms of entry and recognition by existing great powers could be another major impediment to the aspirations of a rising power. The existing powers gained their institutionalized status as a result of the post–World War II settlement; today, since war as a mechanism of change is unlikely, newcomers must devise other strategies to convince the major powers to accept them into their ranks.

Based on the above discussion, in a previous book, we have identified 10 key elements as essential for a rising power to claim major power status in the new millennium. These form the main ingredients of a *comprehensive national power capability*. Holding these elements at a superior or equivalent level to existing great powers would enable a state to achieve global influence and possibly higher status, as opposed to regional influence. Four ingredients—military, economic, technological/knowledge, and demographic—are hard-power resources, while the other six—normative position, leadership role in international institutions, culture, state capacity, strategy and diplomacy, and effective national leadership—are soft-power resources.[30]

Despite possessing many of these power attributes, a state may still not be viewed as a high-status ranking actor, as the status-legitimation process for a new state on the world stage can be very cumbersome and fraught with challenges. It should be noted that international status is obtained when others recognize the superiority of the state in question in these markers of status and assign it such a rank by granting membership rights through institutional bodies and deferential treatment in diplomatic exchanges.

It is still a puzzle as to how a state obtains higher international status, as well as recognition by others, and enters the major power club in the absence of a major war. The grand strategies of states (i.e., their organizing blueprint for "securing and maximizing interests") may shed light on the mechanisms through which states obtain great power status.[31] Up until the end of World War II and to a limited extent during the Cold War era, the traditional elements of status, especially military power, held sway. Victory in great power wars was the most prominent mechanism through which a state gained or lost status that had already been conferred on it. Owning overseas colonies was a crucial manner by which European great powers exhibited and recognized their major power status. Closeness to the Christian religious establishment was the key element in nineteenth-century Europe, based on the idea of "standards of civilization," which equated the two as synonymous. Even though Russia under Peter the Great had to win wars to be recognized as a great power, but he adopted Western standards of social behavior and societal organization in order to be accepted by the West.[32] During the interwar period, Poland tried to use civilizational and normative standards to obtain great power status but had no success in gaining recognition by European powers as it did not possess sufficient material capabilities.[33] In the nuclear age that began in 1945, victory in great power war has become almost unthinkable.[34] This means that rising powers have to use other mechanisms to obtain their great power status. China, for instance, has been employing asymmetric strategies, hybrid warfare, and non-military expansion, such as the Belt and Road Initiative (BRI), to gain global power status.[35] Obtaining symmetrical or superior military capabilities quickly may not be a wise course for a rising power as it will likely come into direct conflict with the established powers.

Today, there is a need for a broader definition of great power status. Is the notion of "great power" an outdated European-era concept? Some of the great powers that have declined, such as the United Kingdom and France, still hold on to this status, while rising powers with larger material markers are not given institutionalized recognition. Russia, which has been in a long period of decline, is meanwhile attempting to re-establish its superiority through brute force, but is facing stiff resistance from others. If achieving institutional status accommodation has a high bar to achieve, rising powers may have to develop their own institutions or attempt to gate-crash into older ones, probably with less success. If international institutions decline due to lack of adaptation, rising powers may gain status-enhancing opportunities that they will have to skillfully navigate. Unlike previous eras, a rising power[36] that can help create new institutions to challenge or transcend existing institutions may have a greater chance of emerging as a major power in the twenty-first century.

Legitimacy and peer group recognition are crucial for a rising power to obtain major power status.[37] Rising powers often seek recognition in international organizations by taking leadership positions on global collective action issues, sometimes vetoing or opposing preferences of others. Today's rising powers, unlike those of yesteryears, cannot obtain their status elevation by acquiring colonies or by engaging in massive territorial aggrandizement. This global aversion to outright imperial conquest is a boon for today's powers to rise peacefully. Still, superior economic, military, and technological capabilities matter, as does soft power, especially diplomacy and grand strategy and the capacity to navigate international institutions effectively.

The Puzzle of India's Status Quest

A question that needs an answer is why some countries crave major power status more intensely than others. Is it because, even if everyone desires it, only some can reach the top of a hierarchical order at any given time due to material weaknesses or limitations in the diplomatic sphere? Some states seek status largely because they believe they have the required material and cultural wherewithal, or believe they are bound to reach the capability threshold in the future because of certain intrinsic or potential attributes and advantages they possess. Or maybe, some countries are more likely to pursue higher status because they have certain properties/memories/leadership

attributes that put the issue of status in the front and center of their national narratives. They could believe in the strengths of their cultural glories,
which are temporarily blocked by other status-seeking or powerful actors or
circumstances that are beyond their control. State elites may look back to history and make the claim that their deprivation was an historical aberration
because of domination by external powers who diminished their power and
status. This dimension is greater when it comes to India.

With a per capita annual income of $300, the country was one of the
poorest in the world when it emerged as a free nation-state in August 1947.
The nearly 200-year-long British rule drained India of its wealth and prosperity, despite colonial rule's integration of the diverse regions of the country
under one entity. It is estimated that in 1700 AD, India contributed some
24 percent of the world's wealth (China over 26 percent), but when the
British left in 1947 it had shrunk to 3.1 percent.[38] In 1750, India contributed
24.5 percent of the world's manufacturing output, but in 1900 it had fallen to
1.7 percent. The corresponding numbers for the West were 18.2 percent in
1750 and 77.4 percent in 1900, leading Bairoch to conclude that "the industrialization of the West led to the deindustrialization of the world."[39] India's
non-participation in the industrial revolution, other than as a supplier of
cheap labor and raw materials, was a major cause of its economic decline—
something its colonial rulers forced upon it. In addition, the deindustrialization of India under colonial rule left it crushingly agrarian. An overwhelming
majority of Indians lived in abject poverty, and at independence the average
life span was 32 years. Yet, its leadership was craving for a higher status than
what those material conditions warranted. Many Indian nationalists, from
the right and the left, and in recent years, more stridently by the adherents of
the Hindutva movement, believe that India had a higher status as a civilization that a millennium of foreign invasions and domination deprived it of, in
particular by successive Muslim rulers, followed by the British.

There is some merit in these assertions, even when we recognize that the
invaders contributed to the composite culture of India, making it a unique
historical mix of cultures, religions, and belief systems.[40] However, India was
not alone in suffering from the onslaught of imperialism and colonialism;
almost all non-European states fell victim to the blitz of Western expansion since the sixteenth century. The modern international system has been
defined by European imperial great powers since the seventeenth century.
The colonized had no voice in this hierarchical order, which was based on
"superior race" and ethnicity, both ascribed by the Europeans themselves.

The Catholic Church–sanctioned "doctrine of discovery" allowed many European powers to conquer territories that were sparsely populated by indigenous populations and gain international recognition, as in the cases of the Americas and Australasia.[41] The scientific, technological, and economic advancements of the Western countries and their greater war-making capacities allowed them to relegate non-Western civilizations such as China and India as "objects" of international power competition, rather than as subjects themselves. By the nineteenth century, both China and India fell to the onslaught of the expansion of the West, the latter more directly, and lost their preeminence as material and civilizational powers. It has been argued that until the seventeenth century, Europeans did not consider the "inferiority of India," but in the eighteenth and nineteenth centuries, a new representation emerged that "rested upon accounts of specific institutions and practices that were symbolic of the general 'barbarity' and 'debased' conditions of "the East . . . Purdah, sati (a widow committing suicide after her husband's death), child marriage, and the harem became more or less equivalent symbols of the barbaric 'other.' "[42] Japan attempted through imitation to prevent falling to Western dominance and rapidly modernized as a military power after the Meiji restoration in 1868, which itself was motivated by the desire to avoid India's and China's fate of status loss.[43]

Why did the Indic world lose its international status and regional dominance in the modern era, especially since the eighteenth century? There is no question that Indian civilization has contributed immensely to the larger Asian world and beyond over the millennia, yet it had no centralized military structure to compete with Western imperial powers, which were predominantly maritime powers that entered the Indian subcontinent through crafty strategies, such as "divide and rule" of the myriad kingdoms of the region. The Mughal Empire, one of the most powerful and economically strong in its heyday, was primarily a land power. Although it had a navy, the threats from Western navies were not felt to be imminent. Moreover, the penetration of the Western imperial powers occurred over a long stretch of time.[44] There were many competing kingdoms in the periphery of the Mughal Empire, and after the death of its most aggressive ruler, Aurangzeb, in 1707 the empire declined rapidly, providing the British a major space to penetrate deep inside into the subcontinent.[45] The Western colonial powers, especially Britain, not only drained India of its wealth by hurting its traditional manufacturing, but also used it as a source of primary products and then as a market for mass-produced goods made in Europe, especially in the United Kingdom.[46]

Decline in material strength vis-à-vis the colonizer made India an appendage of the empire, and one without much of a status in the racially determined power hierarchy of the world as it existed until 1947.

The two postwar settlements, the 1919 Versailles Treaty and the 1945 San Francisco Conference that created the UN system, did not give India significant status enhancement. In San Francisco, the representation did not include any key leaders of the Indian National Congress or the Muslim League. According to M.S. Rajan, "Indian nationalist opinion was bitterly critical of the choice by the Viceroy-in-Council of members of the Indian delegation to the San Francisco Conference, namely Sir A.R. Mudaliar (leader), Sir Firoz Khan Noon, and Sir V.T. Krishnamachari (the last, representing the Princely States). K.P.S. Menon (who became Foreign Secretary in independent India) was the Chief Adviser."[47] Indian representatives argued that based on their war contribution in World War II, it was unfair to give China a seat but not India. It should be noted that some 2.5 million Indian soldiers served in the British Indian Army and were pivotal in Allied victory in many theaters across the world.[48] A small concession was the Indian statesman Mudaliar receiving authority to preside over the newly formed United Nations Economic and Social Council (ECOSOC), as leaders such as Nehru were still in prison. The prevailing racialized world order was a major constraint in giving the colonized world, especially the largest of all, India, a proper say in the formation of the United Nations and its institutional structures.[49] Although in the 1919 Paris Peace Conference, India was given similar status to Canada and Australia as a British Dominion, it made no difference for the post–World War II system as the League was replaced by the United Nations.[50]

India's struggle to obtain higher international status has to be seen in terms of these systemic constraints, as well as a racialized international order, remnants of which are still lingering. Contrary to much Western mainstream scholarship, material power is not the only determining factor that an aspiring power needs in order to acquire higher international status. A postcolonial state may have to climb many hurdles before it gains social recognition as an equivalent major power. Much of international relations scholarship on status or power does not take into consideration the lingering racial and other biases (both conscious and unconscious) that a newcomer would face in achieving higher status or power ranking. Dominant international relations scholars believe that material strength is the key to obtaining higher status, and that status recognition follows once a country has the wherewithal to make a difference in world order. For instance, Gilpin argues that the international hierarchy of prestige is mostly representative of economic and military power.[51] Paul Kennedy also gives prominence to economic power over all other assets, as wealth is needed to build stronger military power. Because material power is calculable and comparable, status comparisons then become easy to make. However, lingering racial prejudices or other social constraints, somewhat similar to those experienced by individuals in low-status social class, caste, or racialized groups, can hamper a new state's status elevation even after it obtains material power, as Japan found out in the 1920s. At the 1919 Versailles Conference, Japan's proposal for the inclusion of a "racial equality" clause in the League of Nations Covenant was rejected by the Western powers and, according to Emperor Hirohito, the leading cause of World War II for Japan was the rejection of the "racial equality proposal demanded by Japan."[52]

Righting Wrongs: The Moral Bases of India's Status Quest

Neither the material (increasing wealth and power) nor the socio-psychological cravings of leaders' motivations, such as glory, capture fully the early post-independence Indian elite's desire for higher status in the 1940s and 1950s, although arguably subsequent decades did see an increasing role for materialist considerations. An unexplored source of status quest could be the beliefs of a country's leadership that they have a moral right and responsibility to gain status because by doing so they enhance the moral causes that are dear to them. Taking a leadership role in the fight for moral causes not only rights the wrongs of an international order perpetrated by an unequal system, in particular by Western imperialism, colonialism, and racialism, but also can enhance a country's international status.

In the Indian case, this kind of moral pursuit appears stronger than personal/psychological craving or material goals in the first two decades of independence. India fought a half-century-long freedom struggle, nearly 20 years of which were led by Mohandas Gandhi, who challenged the world order of Western imperialism and colonialism through a unique nonviolent strategy. Gandhi drew on many Indian and Western ideas of civil resistance. Tolstoy's *The Kingdom of God Is within You* and Ruskin's *Unto this Last*[53] made a profound impact on his thinking as Gandhi crafted a nonviolent strategy for the nationalist movement, unparalleled in human history. Gandhi's chosen heir, Jawaharlal Nehru, held intense anti-imperial ideas and was acutely sensitive to India's moral responsibilities, status aspirations, and possibilities in the newly liberated postcolonial world as a voice of peace and justice. Thus, the nationalist leaders, inspired by the strength of their anti-imperial convictions, and drawing ideas from a more than three-millennia-old civilization, were aware of material weaknesses, but despite were serious about creating a new path for India and a leadership role for their newly emerged country.

This civilizational base of status-seeking behavior is a critical element in the case of India. Many Indian leaders believed that material strength was not the key basis of status, but rather that the civilizational contributions their society has made over the millennia should be treated equally or more prominently in status ascription. Leaders of all varieties have touted the nation's civilizational claims in their speeches, as a marker of its higher status in the international system. To the Indian leaders, their country was new in a Westphalian sense, but their civilization was old. This elite, immersed in their anti-colonial struggle, viewed themselves as inheritors of not only a grand civilization, but also a state that was a leading light for other suppressed nations in Asia and Africa that needed to be liberated through peaceful means. It also fell upon this elite to view their efforts in terms of preventing another round of imperial conquest and domination of their hard-won freedom, and joining the Cold War alliances they felt, would lead to such an outcome.

"Righting the perceived wrongs" and "injustices" as well as "humiliations" can thus motivate elites to pursue higher status. Past humiliations at the hands of alien invaders and religious ideologies can be a source of a continued sense of humiliation and obsession of the elite the wrongs through higher status acquisition. China, for instance, seeks higher status as a way to redress the "hundred years of humiliation," which also generates suspicions on the part of neighbors as to whether China will engage in aggressive policies to correct the past wrongs. Somewhat similarly, it is a perception of humiliation at the hands of alien conquerors for over a millennium that pervades the Indian, especially the Hindu nationalist, psyche in this regard, even when the challenge remains as to how they can rectify that in future years.[54] The problem is that past civilizational attributes can take a country only so far as glorious civilizations such as Egypt and Greece do not get any higher status in the contemporary international status hierarchy, largely because of their material deficiencies and shrunken size. India has the physical and demographic size, yet relative material deficiencies affect the perceptions of others toward its status and its civilizational claims, especially if those claims largely spring from religion, which the secular proponents of modernity do not view so favorably. Further, in the case of India, righting the historical wrongs would mean that the sizable Muslim and smaller Christian minorities would bear the brunt of such efforts. By extension, the efforts of the BJP in this direction have already posed major challenges to India's image as a tolerant multiethnic, multi-religious society. An internally divided India will not gain much higher status in the eyes of the world, and already many Western and Muslim countries have raised major concerns about the curtailment of the religious freedom of minorities in India.

Other Puzzles

Historically, there have been several means for status elevation by rising powers. These include categories such as pursuing social mobility (emulating the values of higher groups with an expectation of accommodation), social competition (efforts to undo an unacceptable order), and social creativity (by seeking acceptance based on one's positive attributes, such as culture or developmental model).[55] There may be other in-between mechanisms, such as partial challenge to an established status hierarchy while accepting some of its bases, as India did during much of the Cold War era. While the social identity theory offers a basic understanding of status-seeking mechanisms, we still need to go beyond these instruments to explain why states, as well as specific leaders of countries, vary in their pursuit of higher status. It may very well be possible that states choose strategies based on their understanding of the permeability and legitimacy of the prevailing status hierarchy, and their own key assets (as they perceive them) in the status domain.

Further, what determines the particular strategies that countries adopt at a given time? What forces them to abandon their strategies after attempting something steadfastly for a period of time? Does failure in wars, or other major crises, including impending economic collapse, encourage states to rethink their status strategies, along with their foreign policy goals? When do learning and adaptation take place in foreign policy? Or has this to do with improvements or decline in their relative material capabilities, which encourage the elite to pursue more daring status goals and strategies? Changing economic fortunes may very well be key markers that determines status pursuit and change in strategy. When a country is poor, or small in size, it may have to resort to normative and diplomatic tools, but when it becomes rich, it may change that strategy by including acquisition of expensive weapons and other symbols of higher status to impress others.[56] This is, similar to some extent, to neo-rich individuals resorting to conspicuous consumption. Moreover, the role that national identity and culture play in enhancing status aspirations of countries, as well as status ascriptions by others, needs to be recognized.

Status signaling is a pivotal process through which a state shows its specific status markers to the world with the expectation of receiving recognition for its accomplishments.[57] A rising power can resort to signaling through conspicuous consumption of acquiring weapons systems, such as nuclear arms and aircraft carriers or hosting high profile international events like the olympics.[58] The success of a particular status-signaling strategy depends on the availability and acceptance by others of global status attributes that become key markers at a given point in time. Sometimes, elites do not recognize that the strategy they use may be inconsistent with prevailing global markers for higher status. So, a question that arises is: Why do countries adopt strategies that might not be consistent with what the current order values? Could this be due to misperceptions, not having the resources to pursue the conventional path, or just being interested in signaling it domestically for electoral and nationalist purposes?[59] Vladimir Putin's Russia poses these questions. As in this case, an aspiring state need not properly send the signals, and the receivers do not recognize them.[60]

Status is in the eyes of the beholder, but the status-seeker need not recognize it that way. Donald Trump's policies are a good example of the discrepancy between expectations and the actual responses of the world. Trump's "make America great again" strategy assumed persisting higher status for the United States even if it engaged in unilateral and protectionist trade policies while undercutting associational links with allies. The obvious calculation was that others were free-riding on America's economic and military power, and unilateral policies by Washington would enable it to obtain more material wealth and increased status. A similar question may be pertinent in India: Can the country under the BJP rule perceiving the right attributes for status elevation in the twenty-first century? Are religion, civilization, and culture the key attributes of status elevation, or are they elements for electoral calculations that can ultimately diminish India's status claims internationally? Further, can domestic politics and the narrow focus of the elite to gain power undercut their own efforts at higher international status? While Prime Minister Modi has made a number of global moves to improve India's status aspirations, aren't some of his domestic policies working against the global norms and markers that value India's traditional strengths, for example, secularism, democracy, and tolerance of religious and minority rights?

As status is an ascribed attribute, it is primarily "located" in other people's minds. Therefore, in order to change one's status, others have to change their opinions of the status-seeker. It is also an inalienable resource, and conversion of others' views through force or bribe may not often be effective. Newcomers have to work hard to break into status clubs or status orders. In order to protect their higher status, status groups often "distribute negative status and thereby create underclasses and outcasts."[61] In most instances, they do not want too many members in their status groupings, lest they lose the value of their privileged positions. Historically, in traditional societies high-status groups attempted to make their position unbreakable by "linking status to knowledge" and "those with high levels of esoteric knowledge are admired."[62] Priestly classes, such as the Brahminical caste in India or Christian ecclesiastical groups in medieval Europe or Muslim imams in the Arab world, held on to their social status by monopolizing knowledge and spiritual power. In today's world, guilds like those in medical professions in some countries keep quotas to prevent too many new members from entering their domains, even when high demand for their services exists. Similarly, the Indian Foreign Service is known to be against expanding their numbers to keep their coveted status in place.[63]

This social problem of granting membership to new status-seeking actors, which can reduce the higher status of the privileged groups, is very applicable to international relations. This is a key reason for established great powers not wanting more members in their club unless they add to their own status. Generally, they fear a depreciation of their positions, as there is only so much top status that is available at a given time. Those who monopolize status will try their best to hold on to it as long as they can unless pressured through war or intense crisis, or if they perceive the need to add the newcomer to their status club to enhance their own status and power position, especially for balancing purposes. Status dilemma, similar to security dilemma (i.e., any increase in one's status causes a decrease in another one's status), is thus an endemic problem in international relations.[64]

Powerful classes and groups, including nation-states, can also attempt to edit out those attributes that may help the status enhancement of aspirants, while lower-ranking actors with aspirations can engage in editing out their attributes that do not allow them status achievement.[65] Textbooks can be edited showing only one side of history, with the hope that this will improve the status of the editor's identity group. For instance, Western historians in general portray the Mongols in an extremely bad light, despite the fact that they were the only Asiatic group that conquered many parts of Europe and had history's largest contiguous land empire. Some argue that the Mongols contributed general ideas to world order despite their barbarity, which was also characteristic of most Western imperial and colonial powers, which their history books often edit out.[66] In the current world order, North Atlantic Treaty Organization (NATO) member countries have attempted to belittle Putin's Russia as an inconsequential status seeker. Former U.S. senator John McCain captured this derision well when he stated, "Russia is a gas station masquerading as a country."[67]

Status is both *aspired* and *ascribed*, and there could be a discrepancy between the two, often generating tensions between states. This is partly because the elite and the general public of a country could believe that their state commands a higher status than ascribed and need not bring material rewards, as foreign audiences "may discount the alleged status and prestige that a particular state ascribes to itself, and so do not offer voluntary deference and accommodation."[68] India is a good example of this phenomenon. Many Indians, in particular, the Hindu nationalists and members of the diaspora, expect India to have a higher status for their country than what is ascribed by others in the global system. Or some may genuinely believe that India has already achieved a higher status, and national leaders make them imagine so. For instance, a 2023 survey by Pew Research Center showed that some 70 percent of Indians surveyed believed that India's global influence has become stronger, even though only 43 percent of the international participants in 23 countries looked at India favorably.[69] Nehru crafted the idea of normative leadership to transcend the material markers of his time and exerted much influence among the newly emerging countries. The superpowers often ignored those normative claims by India and its non-aligned companions, although in the long run their activism might have helped in the decolonization process, nuclear test ban negotiations, and the creation of a tradition of non-use of nuclear weapons.[70] Nuclear weapons did become status symbols for India as well, but since the 1970s, especially in the post-NPT era, it became a contested symbol, even though it can provide deterrence to large-scale aggressions. There has been an argument that in the globalization era, status has become less about hard military power, and increasingly more about both economic and soft power, or the skillful use of "smart power," as Joseph Nye calls it.[71]

In the twenty-first century, status markers are once again in flux as populist leaders in many countries, including India, have upended democracy, tolerance, and pluralism, claiming they are not pivotal ingredients for higher global status. Domestic politics may be both a factor in and a challenge to understanding the status-quest behavior of particular elites.[72] Nationalism is a powerful force that can upend many peaceful status-seeking mechanisms, especially for leaders with authoritarian streaks.

Yet another question in this context is whether a state has to bargain forcefully to obtain higher status, or will status accommodation be made for other reasons, such as the creation of balance of power coalitions? The question of who the salient others are in determining and fulfilling status aspirations of a rising state is also very important. If status is a potentially zero-sum attribute, will some peer competitor attempt to deny the status of the other state? For instance, it is now well known that China seeks to gain global power status, replacing the U.S., while the United States wants to deny that objective. India, on the other hand, does not seem to have such an ambition, and it is seeking status as one among the great powers in a multipolar order, partially due to material discrepancies vis-à-vis other powers. Some believe that India has been a reticent state in seeking higher status commensurate with its material strengths.[73]

Over the years, India's status ranking and status seeking have waxed and waned. In fact, external pressures were necessary for the Indian elite to change their strategies for obtaining increased status. It took the end of the Cold War, the onset of intensified globalization, and its own economic liberalization to regain some of India's reduced status in Western perceptions, although India had a higher status in the socialist world during the Cold War era. The rising power paradigm, especially the leadership shown by BRICS and G-20 during the 2008–2009 financial crisis and post-crisis recovery, gave India some amount of status elevation. Similarly, the rapid rise of China, and Beijing's aggressive policies have offered new opportunities and constraints, and India's decoupling with China has been occurring since 2017 under the Xi Jinping regime became more assertive. This has in some sense helped India's case with the West, but it might not yet be sufficient for full status elevation. Both material strength and diplomatic strategy vis-à-vis China will matter greatly in the future. While India has made much material progress, it becomes a natural tendency of those who make assessments of the relative status of rising powers to rank India unfavorably, even if unfairly, when compared with China.

There is, in short, rhetoric on status among the Indian elite aiming to convince Indians that the world thinks highly of them, but they have made inadequate efforts to mobilize Indian society in a way that would actually heighten India's status abroad. This is in contrast to the Chinese Communist leadership which, through propaganda, often reminds the Chinese population of the need for higher status, partially to rectify injustices for the "hundred years of humiliation" carried out by Western powers.[74] The Chinese Communist Party has placed much of its future and its legitimacy on the achievement of certain status aspirations in the global arena.[75] In the electoral politics of India also, status is increasingly becoming important, but elections can still be won in India without actually performing well on concrete developmental status markers, as propaganda, money, and caste politics tend to play a greater role in electoral outcomes of political parties contesting for power.

A natural question is: How do we know countries are driven more by status than by other considerations, such as sheer material ambitions? Although we can concur that status drive does not exclusively determine a state's foreign or security policy, one can examine choices that countries make that do not add to their security, but instead are motivated by status considerations. India's nuclear tests in 1974 are a good example. By choosing not to develop a functional deterrent capability, India lost the deterrent and security value of possessing nuclear weapons capability. While some would consider opaque nuclear capability as deterrent enhancing, it is difficult to see how others viewed such capabilities. India lost the security value of nuclear weapons for a time being, as it became an easy target of sanctions and isolation by the nuclear powers, affecting its economic prosperity for at least three decades. In the post–Cold War era, thanks to economic liberalization and increased aggregate national wealth, India gained increased status, from an aspirational power to a rising power. The contours of India's march toward greater status will be determined by the changes in the international system in the twenty-first century and how both established powers and non-great powers ascribe India greater status and role in the world order.

3

Hard Power

On August 23, 2023, India's lunar spacecraft, *Chandrayan III*, successfully landed its module at the south pole of the Moon, making India the first country to achieve this remarkable feat. Indians at home and abroad watched this event with pride, and it was indeed a status-elevating moment, as this generally poor country is now one among only four nations—alongside the United States, the former Soviet Union, and China—that have accomplished the feat of landing a craft on the Moon. The Indian achievement came a few days after Russia failed to land its Luna-25 spacecraft on the same mission. While the previous Indian attempt in 2019 failed, the new landing was flawless. *The Economist* put it cogently: "India did not just land its robot on the Moon. It did it with style."[1] Within some 10 days of this achievement, Indian space scientists launched a spacecraft named *Aditya-L1* to study the Sun from a spot 1.5 million kilometers from the Earth, where it will orbit at the same rate as the Earth, conserving its energy as a result, and studying the solar corona and its many effects.[2]

It took three years after the 2019 failure for Indian space scientists to perfect their spacecraft technology to launch a new vehicle to the Moon. In July 2019, India had launched the lunar spacecraft *Chandrayan II*, which crashed on landing. It nevertheless was lauded by Prime Minister Narendra Modi as a great achievement which would "be etched in the annals of India's glorious history."[3] Despite the fact that the mission cost only $142 million, a very low amount compared to similar missions by other space powers, *The Telegraph*, a British newspaper, carried an article questioning the huge expenditure on a space project that might at best bring limited tangible material benefits when the country had millions of undernourished people.[4] Western commentaries such as this, often miss the larger motivations behind spending on science and technology by aspiring states, which are not the immediate material benefits that it might bring, but the status and glory that the elite and the public presume that it might produce. Elites can also use these advancements for domestic electoral support, especially if their record in solving major domestic challenges remains weak. That even their poor country can achieve lofty goals that are generally reserved for advanced industrial states is a big morale booster for the Indian elite as well as the public at large, especially the growing middle class.

On every Republic Day on January 26, India parades its military capabilities and diverse culture on Rajpath, now renamed *Karthavya Marg* or *Duty Way*, the majestic street in New Delhi overlooking the presidential palace, Rashtrapati Bhavan, and the India Gate, a World War I memorial monument. This annual exhibition of both hard- and soft-power assets, depicted through floats of different cultural treasures from various regions and communities, is motivated by a sense of pride in India's accomplishments, and it is watched by millions on television and mass media. Increasingly, these parades include a display of nuclear missiles and space vehicles, in addition to newly acquired conventional arms. The parade is often viewed by foreign dignitaries, and it is indeed an attempt to exhibit and signal India's status as a major power in the international system. While one cannot reject the hard security motives of India's military acquisitions and technological programs, the contention here is that status motivations permeate many of these procurements and their exhibitions at parades like the Republic Day in Delhi. India is not alone in this sort of status pursuit, as all major powers and many regional states, especially in the Middle East and the Persian Gulf, acquire costly weapons for reasons of status or prestige. However, in the Indian case, the quest for higher status through the acquisition of hard-power assets has varied from leader to leader, and the pursuit itself has been haphazard, producing diverse results. Yet no leader since the Nehru era has fundamentally reduced India's hard-power asset acquisition, other than small-scale adjustments, showing how deeply the status quest, along with security calculus, has permeated the political system and ideological beliefs of its elite.

In terms of status markers, nuclear and space technology development assumed a larger portion of India's science and technology budget from the beginning, even when the country was suffering from high levels of poverty, illiteracy, and famine. In fact, India has not paid adequate attention to more applied sciences and technologies for agriculture and industry, instead favoring high-end status technologies such as nuclear and space. Even today, India suffers from many pathologies of poverty and illiteracy due to the lack of proper application of scientific ideas and innovations in its economic path. One can argue that the dearth of inclusive growth is partially the result of this skewed application of science and technology for the entire society, even though it may have brought scientific achievements and employment opportunities for a small segment of the population. The benefits are more palpable in technologies such as information, digital, and pharmaceuticals, which have both high-end and low-end utility. Yet from Nehru's days the desire for autonomous scientific capabilities in frontier areas captured the Indian elite's imagination. Enhanced international status and prestige—along with security, material power, and economic advancement—have been critical calculations in the pursuit of high-end science by the Indian elite. India's desire to be recognized as a leading power with the necessary hard-power wherewithal can be a source of this behavior.[5]

What are the pivotal hard-power markers for India's status-enhancement efforts? Traditionally, the key hard-power resources presumed to be needed for great power status are superior military, economic, and scientific/technological prowess and demographic strength. In fact, India's claim for higher status in the international system is largely based on the contemporary and putative capabilities it possesses in these hard-power realms. Here capabilities are viewed as essential resources for increasing status as well as power, showing the intimate link between the two elements. Does the Indian elite believe that increasing hard-power capabilities should offer it a higher international status than what it is accorded today? It is also important to know that capabilities need not immediately translate into increased status or influence in world politics. Status enhancement occurs when others, especially peer group powers, recognize one's position as a major power based on the capabilities one may possess, often for balance-of-power reasons. Further, a country with some threshold capabilities could still be reticent and not make the significant moves to advance its status at pivotal moments. According to Manjari Miller, India is in that category of reticent powers, often engaging in reactive rather than proactive foreign policy behavior.[6] Further, hard-power capabilities are expected to allow India to resist pressures by others to take foreign policy positions that it does not want.

Capabilities do indeed matter in changing status attribution by others, even though there could be a lag in the time required for status enhancement to a country possessing increased capabilities. The relationship between material power and status enhancement is a two-way street. The higher the material power of a country, the greater the chances of obtaining higher status in the international arena, although this process may cause much conflict with established powers. Conversely, the greater the status of a country, the higher its chances of acquiring additional material power, often using its high status itself, which can ascribe legitimacy to its efforts. The country can, like individuals who hold higher status, be entrusted with important resources, such as leadership roles in international institutions.[7] More importantly, the test question is as follows: Do the changing capabilities encourage the state to act more globally than regionally, both in security and economic domains? If the state expands its security domain to other regions beyond the immediate surroundings, there is indeed an assumption that its status goals have changed. In India's case, economic growth and increasing trade links have produced larger involvement in regions beyond South Asia. The limited naval expansion into the Indo-Pacific is a sign of its changing ambitions and recognition by key actors, such as the United States, Japan, and Australia, of its increased capabilities and role as a net security provider, especially to balance rising China. However, this expansion has been tepid at times, and as a result, more concrete and durable status attainment is yet to occur.

Below I take up the key hard-power markers—military, economic, technological, and demographic—and analyze the achievements India has made, as well as the challenges it has faced in its status quest.

Military Capabilities and Search for Status

Military capabilities matter in the status acknowledgment and expectations of the state elite and the general population of other significant states with which a rising power is aspiring to be coequal or superior. India's aspirations to become autonomous in terms of military capabilities are driven partially by status reasons, even though security motives are powerfully present. In military terms, in 2022 India has the world's second-largest standing armed forces, with 1.46 million personnel.[8] With a nuclear force of 160 weapons, that include inter-continental-range (ICBMs), intermediate (IRBMs), and short-range missiles, and conventional forces, including scores of imported modern fighter aircraft, tanks, and artillery, India is indeed a major military power, as evident in the 2023 Global Firepower Ranking Report which, using 50 factors, places India as having the fourth most powerful military in the world, behind the United States, Russia, and China.[9] Yet in terms of comprehensive power capabilities, India was placed fourth in Asia for 2021 by the Australian think tank, Lowy Institute, behind the United States, China, and Japan.[10] India's nuclear forces include aircraft delivery systems such as Mirage, Jaguar, and Rafael, land-based missiles, *Pritvi* and *Agni* series, with ranges from 250 to 5,000 kilometers, and sea-based missiles, *Danush* and *K-15*, with ranges from 400 to 700 kilometers. Longer-range missiles with ICBM range of 6,000 kilometers or more are in the developmental stage.[11] These capabilities would allow India to strike many urban targets of China and Pakistan, although both Beijing and Islamabad hold more nuclear weapons in their arsenals. In the conventional weapons arena, in addition to the active force of 1.46 million (Army 1.23 million, Navy 70,900; Air Force 139,850), it has a reserve force of 1.15 million. In 2018 India announced an Army doctrine, the creation of "'integrated battle groups' and improved cyber, information-warfare and electronic-warfare capabilities." And in 2017 India announced a "Joint Armed Forces Doctrine," created a "nuclear command and control, and envisaged an 'emerging triad' of space, cyber and special-operations capabilities complementing conventional land, sea and air capabilities." "With some 17 submarines, 3690 main battlefield tanks, 10 Destroyers, 17 frigates, and several squadrons of MiG-21, Mirage2000, Rafael DHSU-30MK, and domestically built, *Thejus* aircraft, India has a formidable force for an Asian power."[12]

In terms of military spending, at $76 billion in 2022, India's defense budget was the third highest in the world, even though it was at a relatively modest 2.21 percent of the GDP (see Figure 3.1). The Indian Army has one training command and six operational commands, which control 14 corps in total, with 40 divisions. The Indian Navy has three commands and the Air Force,

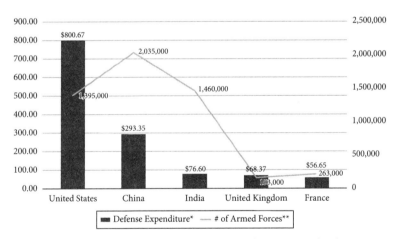

Figure 3.1. Top five military spending countries, the percent of military spending in their GDP, and the size of their armed forces.

* Current U.S. million dollars.

Source: The International Institute for Strategic Studies (IISS), The Military Balance 2022 and Stockholm International Peace Research Institute (SIPRI), Arms Transfers Database, 2022.

Compiled and adapted by Muhammed Yusuf Yilmaz and Daniel Smit.

seven.[13] India's power projection capability beyond the region is increasing, but not to the extent of an ambitious power like China. Military prowess as a status marker is useful if the forces have global reach, but in India's case, they are tied down largely by border conflicts and internal security threats and are not geared for major global missions in the foreseeable future. Active border disputes with Pakistan and China prevent a big change in expanding the military's missions in the near future. India's military effectiveness has also been hampered by weak civil-military relations, constraining it in the areas of weapons procurement, the ability of the different services to operate together."[14] In 2019, India announced a major reorganization of the armed forces affecting "high-level defense management, the military-command structure and the defense industry," including the appointment of a Chief of Defense Staff (CDS) coordinating the three wings of the armed forces. These changes, once implemented fully, are expected to make the armed forces more agile and modern.[15]

The key game changer is building a globally significant naval strength, which India has been slowly undertaking in response to China's naval expansion in the Indian and Pacific oceans. The Indian Navy is increasingly becoming stronger, with aircraft carriers, nuclear-powered submarines, and modern frigates in its arsenal in recent years, and some projects in the pipeline that will expand its operational domain beyond the Indian Ocean in response to China's naval expansion in the Indian and Pacific Oceans. Yet, India spends most on its Army and Air Force; only in 2022 did the Navy receive a boost, with 31.23 percent of the capital budget, in view of the increasing threat level felt from China.[16] India's inadequate allocation to the Navy has a historical background, as all major military threats came from the north and northwest, leading Indian empires, especially the Mughals, not to develop a strong navy. The Tamil Kingdom of Chola in the first millennium was an exception.[17] The rise of China as a major naval power is bound to change this dynamic, as status competition with China will require a strong navy; also military cooperation and status accommodation by other Quad members will call for a vibrant navy, including naval bases in and beyond the Indian Ocean region. India has been developing its naval facilities in the Andaman and Nicobar Islands in the Bay of Bengal, allowing it key capacities in the strategic Strait of Malacca navigational route in the Indo-Pacific, whose control will be crucial in any future military conflicts in the region. In September 2022, India commissioned its first indigenously built 43,000-ton aircraft carrier, *Vikrant*, which can carry some 30 aircraft. It is in addition to the already acquired Soviet built 44,500-ton aircraft carrier, *Vikramaditya*. According to the International Institute of Strategic Studies (IISS), "when both the current carriers are fully operational, they will potentially significantly add to India's ability to undertake both sea control and power projection missions not only in the Indian Ocean but also further afield, . . . increase the Indian Navy's ability to act independently as a long-range blue-water navy," and expand "India's potential contributions to multilateral naval formations with partners, including France, Japan, the UK and the US."[18]

In 2010, South Asia analysts Stephen Cohen and Sunil Das Gupta published a book titled *Arming without Aiming*, which questioned India's weapons acquisitions as lacking a central purpose or doctrinal justification.[19] While the puzzle they raise is interesting, they ignore the less than tangible status goal in high-ticket weapons acquisitions by all countries, in which the United States, China, and Russia lead the pack. Examples include the costly aircraft carriers that are sometimes called "sitting ducks" for enemy missile or drone attacks. The extraordinary number of nuclear weapons held by the United States and Russia today, beyond needed for deterrent purposes, are also driven partially by status motives. Differentiating status motivation from genuine security calculations is difficult in the area of conventional weapons acquisitions, especially high-ticket items. On many instances of weapons acquisitions or indigenous tests of weapons, delivery systems, or rockets for civilian purposes, the Indian elite have expressed the achievement in terms of enhancing the status and prestige of India. A 2001 study by David Kinsella and Jugdep S. Chima examined 136 articles justifying weapons acquisitions or tests in India's leading news magazine, *India Today*, and found that 91 "mention India's enduring conflict with Pakistan and China," and 21 comment on "India's dependence on foreign suppliers of weapons or spare parts and implications for the country's war fighting capacity." However, symbolic reasons appeared in half of the articles, categorized as: "India's autonomy in foreign affairs (35 articles), India's international status and prestige (39 articles), and India's self-image (34 articles)."[20]

This focus has not always been the case. While general scientific achievements were characterized in prestige terms, Prime Minister Nehru was reluctant to place weapons acquisitions as an important sinew of national status or prestige. Nehru's decision not to spend much on defense (less than 2 percent of GNP until 1962) in the first decade of independence[21] or to acquire expensive weapons systems was partially motivated by the desire to project India as a peace-loving country that wanted to give international

institutions, especially the United Nations, a leading role in security management and conflict prevention. His referral of the Kashmir dispute to
the United Nations was the result of this conviction. When this proved to
be a chimera, in particular due to the reverses in the 1962 war with China,
India under his successors went on an arms buildup spree, often acquiring
weapons from all big supplier nations, in particular the Soviet Union. Hard
learning was evident from this experience, that is, without hard military
power, a quest for status, let alone basic security, is not maintainable in an
environment of active military hostilities.

Since the times of Indira Gandhi, beyond security and economic
calculations, status and prestige appeared to be key reasons for developing
indigenous military systems, in particular, nuclear and space. Modi's BJP
government has extolled the weapons acquisitions as major symbolic and
status achievements, often giving them religious-nationalist coloration. The
Congress Party–led governments also gave symbolic meanings, evident in
the naming of weapon systems based on Sanskrit/Hindu mythological terms
such as *Prithvi* (earth), *Agni* (fire), and *Naag* (snake). India's aspirations to
become autonomous in terms of military capabilities were driven partially
by status reasons. The setting up of the Defense Research and Development
Organization (DRDO) and many new weapons programs under its aegis
were initiated to strengthen autonomous capabilities, thereby lessening dependence and increasing status and prestige. However, India's desire for autonomy in arms acquisition has faced many challenges from the start. For
many reasons, Indian scientists were more successful in space and nuclear
technologies than in developing conventional weapons capabilities. Weapons
manufacturing activities faced huge delays and major cost overruns. Barring
small arms and a few systems that India developed collaboratively with
foreign companies, the achievements have been underwhelming at best.
During the 2016–2020 period, some 84 percent of weapons were imported,
and in 2018 India emerged as the leading weapons importer of the world.[22]
However, according to SIPRI, during 2016–2021, despite India's accounting
for 11 percent of the global imports, there has been a steady decline of
imports by 21 percent.[23] Modi's "Make India" (Atmanirbar) plans have made
modest advances in reducing foreign dependency.

However, the continued high dependency on imported weapons is a dent
in India's status elevation given that one of the hallmarks of a great power
is self-reliance in military systems. In February 2022, when Russia invaded
Ukraine, India abstained from both UN Security Council and General

Assembly resolutions condemning the attacks for fear of irking Moscow, the main supplier of weapons and spare parts to India. A country aspiring to be a leading power is marked by its ability to produce its key military hardware requirements autonomously. It is again something that challenges the Indian science and technology community. India, however, has had made some modest success in exporting weapons; in 2021 this export was worth $1.71 billion and India plans to export weapons worth $5 billion by 2025. The exported weapons "include missile systems, LCA/helicopters, multipurpose light transport aircraft, warships and patrol vessels, artillery gun systems, tanks, radars, military vehicles, and electronic warfare systems."[24]

Economic Capacity

More than military power, the rapidly growing economy has been the major marker of India's rise, perhaps more than any other hard-power resource. In October 2022, with a $3.2 trillion GDP (in nominal dollar terms), India became the fifth largest economy in the world (see Figure 3.2).[25]

In terms of purchasing power parity (PPP), this amounts to $6 trillion, and as a result, India became the third largest economy, behind China and the United States (see Figure 3.3). It is estimated that with a growth rate of

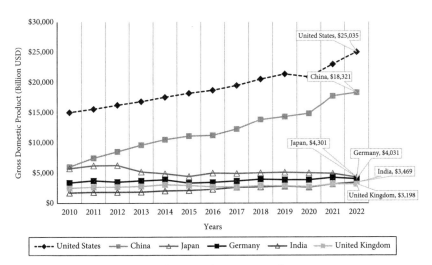

Figure 3.2. Top six countries by gross domestic product, 2010–2022.
Source: IMF, World Economic Outlook Data (October 2022). Compiled and adapted by Muhammed Yusuf Yilmaz and Daniel Smit.

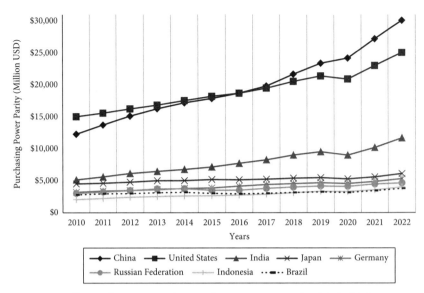

Figure 3.3. Top eight countries by purchasing power parity, 2010–2022.
Source: IMF, World Economic Outlook Data (October 2022). Compiled and adapted by
Muhammed Yusuf Yilmaz and Daniel Smit.

5–7 percent annually, by 2030, India will become the third largest economy
in nominal dollar terms, after China and the United States, and potentially
number two by 2050. In a 2022 report, Morgan Stanley projected that by
2027, India will surpass Japan and Germany and become the third largest
economy. This report also projects that by then the Indian stock market
could become $10 trillion strong. Among factors helping India's growth are
global offshoring by multinational companies, digitalization, and transition
to new energy sources.[26] The economic reforms since 1991 produced sustained growth, barring brief periods of downturns. By 2022, the economy
has produced an estimated middle-class population of 460 million and some
520 million lower middle class, while the rest still live below the poverty line,
considered as $2 daily income.[27]

It was indeed the reforms that were spearheaded by the former Prime
Minister P.V. Narasimha Rao and Finance Minister Manmohan Singh that
catapulted India's economic growth and status recognition by others. In
July 1991, reeling under a major foreign exchange reserve crisis and facing
the prospects of a debt interest payment default, they introduced a series
of reforms, sometimes in a stealthy fashion, which were then picked up by
their successors, realizing the economic growth and the international status

that could accompany it.[28] It also generated self-confidence in the Indian
elite that they could achieve more by way of international standing if they
persisted with economic growth policies.

Unlike previous great powers that amassed wealth through mercantilism, colonial expansion, and imperialism, today's rising powers, including India, have gained much through international trade, facilitated
by infrastructure development, smart regulatory policies, foreign direct
investment (FDI), and the overall global economic prosperity. Their participation in intensified globalization since the early 1990s was pivotal
here, and India has been a partial, but significant example of this trend.
The economic figures give much enthusiasm for those who believe that
India is a rising power and deserves status recognition sooner, rather than
later. Not only in growth, but also in the areas of foreign trade and investment, India has made some major strides. During the 2020–2021 period,
India received $87.973 billion in FDI, which was eighth among major FDI
recipients in the world.[29] Trade also showed growth, despite the impact
of the pandemic. In the 2021–2022 fiscal year, India's foreign trade was
$1.028 billion, with exports constituting $418 billion and imports, $610.2
billion (with a trade deficit of $192.4 billion).[30] There have been steady
improvements in high-tech manufacturing export beyond traditional items
such as cotton textiles, garments, gems, jewelry, and leather products. In
2021, automobiles, pharmaceuticals, mobile phones, electronic equipment,
and aerospace parts constituted some 9 percent of the total exports.[31] But
by 2028, manufacturing exports from India are targeted to grow to $1 tril-
lion.[32] These figures show improvements from previous years, although
India has still miles to go, as an export-driven manufacturing boom is yet to
take place in the country.

It must be acknowledged that forecasts can be rosy, as they assume
steady growth, with no major catastrophic events or domestic and international stagnation caused by prolonged periods of protectionism, tariff
wars, nuclear war, pandemics, or serious climate crisis. They also assume
growth-friendly economic policies pursued by successive governments.
The 2020–2021 pandemic crisis drastically cut India's economic prospects
in the short term, and such imponderables are major blows to India's status
aspirations, partly because of the relatively shallow roots of the economy.
Similarly, the Russian offensive in Ukraine in 2022 has produced a new Cold
War and a rise in oil prices. In particular, the new great power rivalry somewhat upends the economic globalization that has benefited India along with

other rising powers. India's hopes can be dashed if an intense international crisis persists for an extended period of time. In fact, the 2020 coronavirus crisis pulled down India's growth to minus 6.6 percent, although it was able to reverse the trend by 2022. Manmade catastrophes, such as a nuclear war or massive climate-induced disasters, could unravel India's prospects in a huge way.[33]

While India's raw economic numbers may be impressive, they mask the much deeper challenges that India faces in the economic arena, more than any other rising power.[34] As will be discussed in Chapter 6, it is the absence of proper distribution of wealth that is affecting human development in India. Historically rooted distributional inequalities make India's economic growth story a skewed one. While military capabilities are important markers of status, economic assets matter more than traditionally appreciated, especially in recent times. In the contemporary world, states without economic power cannot easily build strong militaries or develop their population into productive members of society and thereby strengthen their status position in the world system. While Indian leaders from Nehru to Modi have acknowledged the role of economic development and poverty removal, their economic strategies varied and often created conditions that did not help India's status elevation. Several domestic and ideational constraints worked against speedy and equitable economic development. Indeed, India's status elevation took place after the reforms of 1991 with two decades of continuous high economic growth. Without that economic change, the limited but crucial status change would not have materialized in the manner in which it has happened. This is often stated as the reason why the United States began to look at India seriously, although security motivations are intertwined here as well. Economic modernization and liberalization could be viewed not only for improving living standards, but also as a status-enhancement mechanism in terms of institutional recognition. In India's case, its improved institutional roles in the IMF, World Bank, BRICS, G-20, and ASEAN Regional Forum (ARF) have all been influenced by its growing economic position. It is also courted for bilateral and multilateral trade agreements in Asia and beyond because of the market size. India's annual dialogues with the European Union and ASEAN are concrete examples of status enhancement due to economic growth. Great powers are expected to be less sensitive to economic downturns, restrictive policies of others, and world economic pressures. In that sense, the still largely domestically rooted Indian economy may have an advantage.

Science and Technology

A third area of hard-power resource necessary for higher status in international politics is scientific and technological advances of a state relative to its peer competitors.[35] A state seeking higher status often will place much importance on technology, and India's behavior since independence has been motivated by the objective of improving its status as a technologically advanced state. It was in fact in the areas of science and technology, in particular two dual-use technology domains, nuclear and space, where India faced the biggest status contestation from established powers. It is also in these domains that India's status accommodation thus far has been partially accomplished, largely due to India's persistent efforts in the face of much international opposition, especially by the United States and its Western allies. India's status accommodation was partially achieved following its acceptance as a de facto nuclear power by the United States and other states since 2005.

Nuclear Weapons and India's Status Quest

When the first atomic bomb was tested on July 16, 1945, in Alamogordo, New Mexico, American nuclear scientist Robert Oppenheimer, quoting Lord Krishna from the Hindu epic Bhagavad Gita, said: "If the radiance of a thousand suns were to burst at once into the sky. . . . Now I am become death, the destroyer of worlds."[36] Atomic energy would capture the imagination of the Indian elite from the early days. There is no other area in which India has fought the most consequential status battle with other great powers, especially the United States, than in the area of nuclear weapons and dual-use nuclear technology acquisition for both civilian and military purposes. Important questions arise as to why India emerged as the lead challenger to the unequal nuclear order established by the great powers since the 1960s. The key reason is status related: nuclear weapons can act as "great equalizers" in the relations between great powers and non-great powers. Their diffusion could blur the line between a major and a minor power when it comes to existential security, as "one of the attributes of major power status has been the ability to intervene in the affairs of minor powers without punishment to their home territory in return."[37] Great powers are often eager to maintain their status as top-ranking states by possessing monopoly rights on the acquisition and use of the leading weapons of the day. The ability to intervene in the affairs of the non-great power is the hallmark of a great power. If a non-great power state succeeds in obtaining operational nuclear weapons, it will make the great power reluctant to intervene militarily, as deterrence can work asymmetrically between an otherwise weak and strong power. This consideration is behind the violent conflict that the United States pursued with Iraq and the active coercive diplomacy Washington has conducted toward North Korea and Iran. Status quo great powers and their allies often devise normative justifications for preventing the spread of certain coercive capabilities that distinguish status hierarchy in the world order of the time.

For a non-great power with ambitions and potential for higher global power status, accepting an unequal treaty or agreement that perceptually closes the door to great power status can be a major source of status anxiety. The Indian behavior in the nuclear arena and the responses of the other great powers toward it show the presence of these tendencies very powerfully. As George Perkovich, who wrote the definitive work on India's nuclear program, points out: "India has been torn between a moral antagonism toward the production of weapons of mass destruction, on one hand, and on the other hand, an ambition to be regarded as a major power in a world, where the recognized great powers rely on nuclear weapons for security and prestige."[38] India has also been driven by the notion of status equity, which implied that "India would not stop or abandon its nuclear weapon and missile programs without concomitant nuclear disarmament by the five 'major' powers."[39] Nehru earmarked substantial efforts at nuclear energy, even when it was not clear what immediate economic benefits it would bring. The creation of the Bhabha Atomic Research Center (BARC) at Trombay, near Mumbai, and other scientific research institutions was motivated by long-term capability building aimed at status enhancement. Even though Nehru did not initiate a weapons program, his calculation was that in the future it might become necessary, and India should have the capabilities for doing so. Perkovich argues that the main early incentive to develop a nuclear program was not only China's nuclear program, but also "Bhabha's and Nehru's beliefs that nuclear technology offered India a shortcut to modernity and major power status. By mastering nuclear science and technology—and in the process, acquiring the potential to make nuclear weapons—India could transcend its recent colonial past."[40]

However, it can be argued that two competing status goals motivated India's nuclear choices in the 1960s. The Chinese nuclear tests generated much discussion and debate in India, and status and security anxieties permeated those debates. A competing status goal of a peace-loving non-nuclear state was also part of the debate and won the day temporarily, with Lal Bahadur Shastri, the successor to Nehru, perhaps one of the last national leaders who held strong Gandhian moorings, deciding not to initiate a competing weapons program. While security was a primary discussion point, the desire to maintain India's status as a peace-loving state also affected the choices, as evident in Shastri not approving a nuclear weapons program. This shows that the status quest of a country can be contested internally between two diametrically opposed views on material markers such as nuclear weapons for status and security.

In fact, over time, one viewpoint gained prominence: a realpolitik-oriented approach won, over a more idealistic, normative perspective on status acquisition. The desire for pursuing a "morally superior approach," especially in terms of not imitating the militarized behavior of powerful states, was the normative dimension here. Yet, the dilemma India faced was that accepting their nonproliferation policies assigned for non-nuclear states would have been equivalent to "anti-modernism."[41] The Nuclear Non-Proliferation Treaty (NPT) that came into effect in 1970 created two classes of states: nuclear weapons states and non-nuclear weapon states. Those who tested nuclear weapons before January 1, 1967 (i.e., the P-5 states) were accorded legal rights to keep their nuclear weapons, and all others were asked to forgo their ambitions in return for vague promises of civilian nuclear energy support, even without an ironclad security guarantee of non-use against them. The fact that India was in the forefront of opposition to this discriminatory treaty showed that the Indian elite perceived permanent damage to India's status aspirations if it were to sign the Treaty. In opposing the NPT, Indian representatives argued against it on the basis of the two classes of states it created, nuclear haves and have-nots.[42] An earlier proponent of a non-discriminatory NPT, India clamored, along with other status aspirants such as Brazil and Argentina, and frontally challenged the legitimacy of the Treaty.[43] To V.C. Trivedi, the Indian representative at the Geneva-based Eighteen Nation Disarmament Committee (ENDC), "there should be no enshrinement or perpetuation of a privileged status of nuclear powers."[44]

The Indian opposition did not succeed in stopping the Treaty, as a majority of the Non-Aligned Movement (NAM) countries signed the NPT, in some cases under pressure from the United States and other nuclear-weapon states. However, most believed that such a treaty would enhance their security interests, as they had no chance of acquiring those weapons on their own while gaining civilian nuclear benefits. They also did not want to see their neighbors acquiring nuclear weapons. But India's call for universal disarmament and a nuclear test ban resonated in NAM declarations. The normative stand was a status booster initially, only to decline as India conducted its solo nuclear test in 1974, even though it did not develop a nuclear deterrent until the late 1980s.

In May 1974, India conducted a single nuclear test, codenamed "Operation Smiling Buddha," and declared it was only for peaceful purposes. This demonstration event, challenging the unequal nuclear order upheld by the great powers, was a status assertion. There are those who believe that Prime Minister Indira Gandhi decided to go ahead with the test after it was proposed by a small group of scientists and without even consulting her cabinet. The main purpose appeared to be sending a message to Western countries, China, and domestic audiences, demonstrating India's capability and determination to be recognized as a powerful state.[45] In her inner circles, only a small group was aware of the decision, as the lead scientists were the core group of influencers. As Raja Ramanna, then director of BARC, recalled, when her advisor P.N. Dhar objected to the testing as it would be very costly, "Mrs. Gandhi decreed that the experiment should be carried out on schedule for the simple reason that India required such a demonstration."[46] Mrs. Gandhi, in an interview with Rodney Jones, an American scholar on South Asian security, stated that even though the villagers would not understand PNE (peaceful nuclear explosion), "they would understand India's achievement and that it was done despite the big powers trying to prevent India."[47] Newly declassified documents from the US Interagency Intelligence Memorandum in June 1974 ascribed "prestige" as a key motivator for the nuclear test. In its words: "New Delhi probably believes that its demonstrated capability to explode nuclear devices has enhanced its position in the Third World and reinforced its position in Asia." It added: "In terms of strategic considerations, India wants paramountcy in South Asia, a major voice in decisions affecting the Indian Ocean, and security from pressures from China."[48]

But no subsequent tests were conducted, nor was a weapon system developed until the late 1980s. As the deterrent capability was not obtained, it must be viewed as a status-signaling device, at least in the short run. Ashish Nandi's interviews with India's strategic elite group showed that status considerations of inclusion and exclusion were pivotal in their decision to reject the nuclear order, especially the NPT, although only 38 percent wanted India to develop a nuclear arsenal, while 58 percent opposed such a move.[49]

The 1974 tests unleashed an intense status competition with the established nuclear powers, especially the United States, a development the Indian elite did not foresee. India's testing of a single nuclear device without building an arsenal brought no significant outside sympathy, let alone an improvement in its ability to push its disarmament agenda. On the contrary, "India became something of a renegade from the standpoint of the major power imposed-norm of non-proliferation and felt increasing pressure."[50] The fence-sitter mode inflicted much harm on India, both in terms of status and power competition, as the great powers and its regional rivals, Pakistan and China, interpreted it in highly oppositional terms. The tests indeed catapulted intense status challenge from established powers. The United States emerged as the largest champion of punishing India for its parvenu status assertion. The actions of the Nixon and Ford administrations were limited,[51] but it was the liberal-leaning Carter administration that in 1978 passed the Nuclear Non-Proliferation Act, and a series of technical and other sanctions and hurdles were created by other countries, including Canada, which had supplied the first CANDU reactor that produced the fissile materials for the tests. The Act declared that the "proliferation of nuclear explosive devices or of the direct capability to manufacture or otherwise acquire such devices poses a grave threat to the security interests of the United States and to continued international progress toward world peace and development."[52] In addition, the Nuclear Suppliers Group (London Club) was created to regulate and curtail nuclear exports, with India becoming a key target of their activities. A major propaganda campaign against India's claims was unleashed in the West, and Indian scientists were excluded from global scientific research collaborations.

For over two decades, India remained an opaque nuclear state without an actual nuclear weapon force. The decisions by subsequent governments showed the status ambivalence the Indian elite perceived in the nuclear arena. This was also the result of a lack of confidence—if India openly pursued a weapons program, it might not be able to withstand economic sanctions that the nuclear weapon states were sure to impose. Indian leaders were also divided over which status path to follow—one driven by Gandhian ideals and nuclear renunciation, or a realpolitik version of nuclear capability assertion. However, many top scientists continued the scientific work needed for fission capabilities, believing that India would inevitably have to obtain nuclear weapons. These calculations began to evolve into a pro-bomb strategy in the late 1980s in response to the nuclearization of Pakistan and the support of

China for that program, which India viewed as a major challenge to its security as well as its regional status.

Status Quest and the 1998 Tests

Both hard security and status considerations mattered in the decision by Prime Minister Rajiv Gandhi to develop nuclear weapons in 1989. It was Pakistan's development of nuclear weapons, in collaboration with China, that prodded Indian enthusiasm for developing an operational nuclear capability. Pakistan, a weaker regional power contender, would have become a nuclear weapons state before India did, which was both a key security and status issue for the Indian elite. It is somewhat clear that after the 1974 solo test, the Indian nuclear program went into a hibernation stage, and not much effort was made to develop an operational deterrent capability until the late 1980s. That China was colluding with Pakistan in the nuclear area suggested that the duo was treating nuclear weapons in the hands of Islamabad as a great equalizer and a balancer against India. Even after developing the weapon capability, some five successive Indian prime ministers from various political parties (V.P. Singh, Chandra Shekhar, P.V. Narasimha Rao, H.D. Deve Gowda, and I.K. Gujral) decided not to test openly, partly for fear of retribution by the nuclear powers. One of them, Gujral, later revealed in interviews that "since Rao's time, the nuclear file was on our table all the time."[53]

During the 1990s, status conflict between nuclear weapons states and India would move to the forefront with the negotiations for the extension of the NPT in perpetuity in 1995 by the UN conference and the conclusion of a Comprehensive Test Ban Treaty (CTBT). India resisted signing these treaties, as they would have forced it to give up its nuclear weapons program without concurrent commitment to do so from the recognized P-5 nuclear powers. According to Jaswant Singh, foreign minister under the Atal Bihari Vajpayee government, "The moralizing tone of India's stand on disarmament may have held currency earlier but became meaningless after 1995. To compound this irrelevance, the CTBT tacitly sought to make the nuclear club a pre-entry, closed shop."[54] The negotiations on CTBT generated intense nationalist opposition in India more than in any other country.[55] Arundhati Ghose, India's ambassador to the Geneva disarmament forum, summarized the status and security concerns in a speech opposing the pressure on India to sign the proposed treaty. In her view, the "CTBT as drafted reaffirmed the perpetuation of nuclear apartheid," and the indefinite extension of the NPT in 1995 "sought to legitimize indefinite possession of nuclear weapons by five countries."[56] The Congress government of P.V. Narasimha Rao almost tested nuclear weapons in 1995, only to abandon the decision at the last minute, as U.S. satellites detected unusual activities in the Pokran test site in Rajasthan and the U.S. ambassador Frank Wisner showed the Indian officials satellite pictures and persuaded them to abandon the tests.[57] The arrival of the BJP-led coalition government under Vajpayee in March 1998 changed the equation, as it viewed nuclear weapons acquisition as critical for asserting India's status aspirations.

The top officials of the five nuclear states met at Geneva and London and declared that "India and Pakistan do not have the status of NWS according to the NPT" and urged them to stop testing and to adhere to the NPT and CTBT.[58] In May 1998, the Vajpayee government tested five nuclear devices in the Pokhran site, after eluding detection by U.S. satellites. The gamble that India took worked well, despite short-term sanctions and denouncements by the great powers and their allies. Why did the 1974 tests generate intense hostility, while the 1998 tests and India's coming out of the nuclear closet produce a different outcome? As the Cold War wound down, U.S. policymakers began to view India as a potential status challenger to China, as well as a balancing power. India's steady economic growth, its impeccable non-proliferation record, compared to Pakistan's nuclear black-market trade via the A.Q. Khan network, and India's democratic credentials all gave it a new role in U.S. strategic calculations. Some U.S. policymakers, especially in the George W. Bush administration, including Secretary of State Condoleezza Rice, began to call India a rising power. Pakistan's reckless land-grabbing in the 1999 Kargil incursion under nuclear cover, and India's decision not to escalate the war were also eye openers to the world, differentiating India's nuclear status from that of Pakistan. India has also attempted to gain status as a responsible nuclear power by not exporting weapons and materials or by brandishing its weapons in a threatening manner, and it also has not produced more weapons than its adversaries, Pakistan and China. This nuclear restraint by India has been status driven to an extent for creating a "distinctive nuclear identity and social role."[59] However, the post-NPT status gradation in the nuclear realm continued, despite some level of acknowledgment of India's nuclear status by the United States and most other great powers.

Space technology is yet another area where India has made distinct marks that have boosted its international status.

Space Technology

On September 24, 2014, India's Mars mission, called *Mangalyaan* (Mars Vehicle), reached the orbit of the red planet and was successful on its first attempt, an achievement unmatched by any other nation. Costing $74 million, it was one of the least expensive missions of this nature; a former chairman of the Indian Space Research Organization (ISRO), U.R. Rao, compared the amount spent "to the amount Indians spend on Diwali crackers for one day."[60] India's space accomplishments include three *Chandrayan* missions to the Moon that they have touted as "frugal missions." The successful landing of the *Vikram* spacecraft under *Chandrayan III* in August 2023 at the Moon's south pole (the first of its kind by any country) was the most significant achievement thus far. With a budget of $1.94 billion annually, India's space program is one of the most frugal with many milestone achievements to its credit. India has mastered the designing, manufacturing, and launching of different satellites, varying in sizes and payloads.[61]

By October 2022, India's ISRO had launched 381 satellites for 34 countries, mostly developed countries, a creditable achievement for a developing country's space program.[62] The 2013 launch of a satellite to orbit Mars, was the first by an Asian country, and in September 2016 "it achieved its most technically complex launch ever, putting satellites into two different orbits during the same flight."[63] On February 15, 2017, India's Polar Satellite Launch Vehicle C37 was able to launch "104 satellites into the heavens in pairs, the highest number ever attempted in one mission. One Indian space analyst on television likened the complicated maneuver to dropping children at different bus stops. . . . The total number of satellites far outstripped the previous record—37 simultaneously sent into space by Russia in 2014."[64] In 2023, ISRO announced some impressive plans for a manned mission to space—"Gaganyaan."[65] Ten days after the successful soft landing on the Moon, on September 2, 2023, ISRO successfully launched a spacecraft to study the Sun, code-named *Aditya-L1*, as noted earlier. After a four-month journey, it will park in a spot some 1.5 million kilometers from the earth and orbit the sun for some time at the same rate as the earth.[66] It carried "payloads to observe the photosphere, chromosphere and corona in different wavebands."[67]

If there is a second frontier technology where status motivation is clearly present, it is in the case of India's space program. It has long been argued that such programs are cases of conspicuous consumption for a poor country. Yet India has invested tremendous resources over the years in its space program and has made much progress, at relatively lower costs than competing programs elsewhere, and has even been successful in earning foreign exchange, enhancing its status in this area globally. The space program has also allowed the development of different military satellites, remote-sensing capabilities, missiles of varying ranges, and an anti-satellite technology (ASAT) capability that India tested in March 2019. In the ASAT test, dubbed *shakti* (strength), a domestically developed ballistic missile interceptor hit and destroyed an Indian satellite, cruising at 17,000 miles per hour, producing less space debris than China's ASAT test in 2007.[68] Objectives for the active space program had to do with military applications, and the general desire for self-reliance on that front, to the extent that space technology could be translated into missile development for conventional and nuclear weapons delivery systems. However, beyond that, it is apparent that status-related concerns have driven this program.[69]

The origins of the Indian space program can be traced to a period when the United States and the Soviet Union (as well as a few other countries) were engaged in the space race, and as an aspiring power it is likely that India viewed the possession of a space program as a necessary symbol of being recognized as a technologically advanced country, a marker of major power status. As a bureaucratic organization, the ISRO has also been able to sell the idea of the space program to the political leadership by pointing to both the military application and the status benefits of having such a program. As the program has become more successful (which took a substantially longer period of time, partially due to external sanctions), and has finally begun to show some financial benefits, political leaders have displayed even more interest in taking pride in the program and using it as another illustration of how India is not a "typical" developing country and deserves more credit and status than have been ascribed to it. Leading space and nuclear scientists were given direct access to successive Indian prime ministers, overriding bureaucratic hierarchies, which showed the importance political leaders placed on space and nuclear arenas. Furthermore, as China's space program has advanced in recent years, there is greater incentive for India to augment its space program. Indeed, as the United States and Russia maintain their dominance in this area, countries like India and China have begun to see it as an opportunity to stand out, and an essential capability for developing cyber technologies. For India, status competition with China is driving the program in some areas.

The space arena also became a source of friction and status denial by established powers. Indian's civilian space program was being developed in tandem with its missile program, attracting the ire of the established powers. The missile technology control regime (MTCR) was established in 1987 by the G-7 advanced countries, partly to prevent India and other aspirants from developing their own capabilities. Along with nuclear sanctions, Indian space scientists were also barred from joint research with U.S. scientists in particular. The search for missile development continued apace, and one of the lead developers, A.P.J. Abdul Kalam, who became president of India in July 2002, had achievements in missile technology that were often regarded as elevating India's status. He was a key proponent of India gaining higher status through space, missile, and nuclear development.[70] Western countries have increasingly recognized India's space credentials and have used ISRO's relatively cheap program for launching a large number of satellites.

Space is an area where India has been able to adopt a program very successfully for the purpose of status, making necessary investments and delivering a high degree of success. The contrast here with conventional weapons development is particularly striking and instructive in that India has made more development in science and technology fields, where it has invested less than in the conventional weapons indigenization program. The contrast points to areas where India has fallen short in signaling its status on this front. Finally, even in this area of success, India will need to go further to obtain higher status achievement. While the fact that there is recognition of India as a player in the space game, and the economic returns to the program are increasingly lucrative, there are domestic and international applications, such as weather forecasting and disaster management, that need to be seriously explored for the Indian program to stand out as truly exemplary.

Information Technology, Pharmaceuticals, and New Technologies

Some specific technological areas where India has made major progress are information technology (IT) and the pharmaceutical industry. The credit for early IT achievements goes to former Prime Minister Rajiv Gandhi, who in 1988 initiated a major telecommunications and fiber optics program with the help of management expert, Sam Pitroda.[71] This would substantially help India's later achievement in IT industries. In 2021, with a revenue of $200 billion, IT employed some 5 million personnel.[72] Software companies and many multinational corporations are present all over major urban centers, and some cities like Bangalore and Hyderabad have become "mini Silicon Valleys." Internet access and mobile phone ownership have both expanded rapidly. In 2020, some 600 million internet and 448 million cellular phone subscribers made India the number two country in this technology area. The country is a big arena for major global players, such as Apple, Samsung, and Google, for the development and marketing of cell phones, and India is slowly entering the AI and 5G arenas of the fourth industrial revolution. Cell phones are one technology that India's poor have widely adopted. The 5G spectrum has emerged as a source of contention in India's efforts to retain its autonomy. In the face of China pursuing its 5G strategy, India joined many Western countries in prohibiting 5G trials in India by Chinese companies like Huawei and ZTE, showing that India clearly fears security and status challenges from China in this area.[73] India's use of online banking and other systems and, more significantly, the biometric digital identity technology called *Aadhaar*, developed under the leadership of the industrialist Nanadan Nilekani, have shown that a poor country can make much headway in the digital revolution.[74] This low-cost comprehensive digital identity, payment, and data-management system is a major innovation by India.[75] In an upbeat report in 2022, Morgan Stanley forecast that in the post-Covid world, India's outsourcing industry will even grow larger, as many Western companies are looking for cheaper sources. The global outsourcing industry is poised to grow from $180 billion to $500 billion by 2030, and India is likely to benefit the most.[76]

Similarly, pharmaceutical industries have boomed in India, facilitated by patent releases by major multinational corporations and the availability of cheap drug manufacturing facilities available, which have encouraged companies to set up firms in India. With some 3,000 pharmaceutical companies, in 2021 India ranked first in generic drug manufacturing and third in the world for pharmaceutical production. It also produces 60 percent of the world's vaccines.[77] The growth of this sector to a $49 billion industry in 2020 has been a substantial achievement. India supplies medicines to some 200 countries, giving it the nickname "pharmacy of the world." India's aim is to grow this industry to $130 billion by 2030.[78] India supplies 50 percent of Africa's and 40 percent of the United States' generic drugs and 25 percent of all medicines in the United Kingdom. The Pune-based Serum Institute is the world's largest producer and supplier of vaccines for both developing and developed worlds. Some 170 countries and about 60 percent of the world's children receive a variety of vaccines produced by this Institute.[79] During the Covid-19 crisis, the Institute, in collaboration with the AstraZeneca and Oxford University, co-developed the Covishield vaccine against the virus.[80]

Beyond IT and pharmaceuticals, there are many areas where technology is changing rapidly in India; AI, cyber capabilities, and solar power are among the areas in which India has made modest achievements in collaboration with international partners. Still, India needs to foster more innovation if there is a hope for wider status recognition as a technology power. As Nitin Pai argues, India has yet to develop a strategy to make use of its skilled workforce in the context of U.S. sanctions on chip makers from China. It has a window of 5–10 years, after which China will likely have caught up to the United States.[81] By 2022, India's efforts in renewable energy sectors such as solar, bio-power, windmill, and small hydro power units had seen some growth, but not to the extent of significantly changing its massive reliance on fossil fuels.[82]

Despite the emphasis on science and technology, Indian universities and research institutions lag behind their global competitors. A clear manifestation of this is the low ranking of Indian universities and scientific establishments in global ranking lists. While India has a large number of technical institutions such as the Indian Institutes of Technology (IITs), and a highly competitive system to enter them, their actual research productivity is low. India, however, has increased its patent applications in 2021 after being a laggard for several years. The total of 488,526 applications is still low compared to China's whopping 9.45 million.[83] The areas where China has made consistent improvements are its universities, patents, and technological innovations. India has ambitious plans, but the proof is in the pudding. Indian corporations are takers of technology, and not often developers. According to the Indian government agency Niti Ayog's India Innovation Index for 2021, with .07 percent of the GDP in R&D spending, India's is one of the lowest in the world.[84] There have been hopes for India pursuing the strategy of frugal innovations, making a large number of easy-to-use, simple, and cheaper systems for mass consumption the world over, replicating its success in supplying patented drugs to the world market.[85] This shows that proprietary products are one way to proceed, but creating value chains of existing models is another way. The direct benefit of IT would have been manifold had the entire population benefited from it. The low human development of some 40 percent of the population is the reason why the country is yet to fully utilize the potential of science and technology. Yet, India's achievements cannot be minimized, and the effort to leapfrog from the first industrial revolution to the fourth industrial revolution is active and ongoing in India's developmental and status-seeking endeavors.

Demographic Dividend

Among all the hard-power resources an aspiring power should possess for status enhancement is the appropriate mix of working-age population. In this area, India has plenty of positive and negative assets. In April 2023, India surpassed China as the leading state in terms of total population. This population asset is one of the putative strengths of India for its availability for both civilian and military purposes. India has the largest population within the age group of 20–55 in the world. In 2020, the 15- to 24-year-old group constituted 34.35 percent of the total population, while China and other Western countries all saw drops in this age group. Most observers therefore see India as a beneficiary of this demographic dividend.

Or is this a true asset for both economic development and status advancement? India has a not-so-stellar record in making use of its population, especially those of working age. India has not yet become a manufacturing hub, except for pharmaceuticals and software development. A broad-based manufacturing boom driven by export industries and additional domestic capabilities, such as solar energy, could bring many more jobs to India. Due to the inadequate skill development of the youth, as well as a number of bureaucratic and regulatory reasons, this has not happened adequately. The demographic dividend is thus not properly utilized as of yet, thereby slowing down India's status advancement. Low-quality education, especially technical education, except in its elite institutions, has made India's workforce largely less productive than its counterparts in most major advanced countries and emerging countries, especially China. Larger structural problems connected to globalization and the technological revolution exist both as constraints and opportunities for India. Service industries have been booming in India, making services the core employment sector and contributor to the GDP's growth. It must be recognized that India has indeed made some major strides in demographic development, largely due to the economic liberalization since the 1990s, which brought millions out of poverty and helped them to join the middle and lower middle classes. But population growth is happening disproportionality in states where economic growth, skills development, and inclusive human development have been lagging. This will not help India's status advancement until these states also substantially improve their human development indices.

Conclusions

Hard-power markers are essential for status enhancement, accommodation by established powers, and recognition by non-great-power states. Changing capabilities matter in identity formation of a rising power, even though a myriad of domestic and international factors can shape how that identity is expressed or evolved,[86] for example, whether it will resort to violence to achieve its goals or seek peaceful accommodation. However, the important question for an aspiring great power is whether its hard power is of consequence to other leading actors in the international arena. More concretely, can Indian capabilities deny or enhance the security and economic interests of the leading powers, or not? Similarly, in the civilian area, are the technologies that India has developed important for the well-being of other states and large segments of humanity? In the economic arena, is the Indian economy of consequence to world economy, especially to the economic interests of the leading powers of the world? Are they sufficiently intertwined? How inclusive is the Indian economic model of development? What are the emulative aspects of these economic developments and growth?

The answer to all these questions is that India is a project in the making. It has made some major strides in key markers of status and capabilities in the post–Cold War era, largely thanks to its economic liberalization and insertion into economic globalization, but it seems the trajectory is slow, except in space, IT, and pharmaceuticals, especially in comparison with its peer competitor, China. India is gradually becoming consequential, mostly in the economic arena, due to the sheer size of the economy, and is slowly emerging as a globally important economy in terms of trade, investment, and stock markets. The bottom line is that India still remains a second-tier power in comparative terms when it comes to material assets for status in the international arena. Status quest here is a long-term project, with the assumption that if India can sustain high growth trajectories for the next two decades, it may eventually reach a higher status threshold. In the next chapter, I turn to soft-power indicators and demonstrate how India has claimed higher status on the basis of these indicators. Significantly, both hard- and soft-power status markers are emerging as powerful vote catchers in the electoral contestation in India, especially for the BJP, showing the intricate relationship between status and the domestic politics of a rising power.

4

Soft Power

In a glowing tribute to India's civilizational impact on the Asia-Pacific region, the founding president of Indonesia, Sukarno, wrote in 1946:

> In the veins of every one of my people flows the blood of Indian ancestors and the culture that we possess is steeped through and through with Indian influences. Two thousand years ago, people from your country came to Jawadvipa and Suvarnadvipa in the spirit of brotherly love. They gave the initiatives to found powerful kingdoms such as those of Sri Vijaya, Mataram and Majapahit. We then learnt to worship the very Gods that you now worship still and we fashioned a culture that even today is largely identical with your own. Later we turned to Islam; but that religion too was brought by people coming from both sides of the Indus.[1]

Today, India's civilizational influence, as described by Sukarno, is pronounced in many Southeast Asian countries. This is evident in their religions (in particular Hinduism, Buddhism, and Islam), culture, and even cuisine, although other nations have adapted the culture and rightly made it their own.[2] Although India's cultural impact in the extended region is powerful, the natural question is how this dimension works as soft power for India in its aspiration for major power status, by way of greater social recognition and acceptance. The answer is unclear, as modern-day geopolitics and economic relationships hold a powerful sway in shaping the perceptions that others hold of India and its status in the international system.

From the beginning of its independent existence, the Indian elite's pursuit of status has relied on soft-power markers, based on an expectation that the intangible non-material attributes that India possessed should elevate its status ranking in the world system. Several of those components have been presented from early on as India's unique position in the global status hierarchy. The pluralistic cultural and religious ethos and civilizational factors matter considerably in this milieu of calculations of soft-power markers of status, both for Indians and for others who treat India as a potential global power—that is, a large subcontinental state that has contributed immensely to human civilization and that, despite its material weaknesses and periodic declines, can and will re-emerge at the right time. India's nonviolent struggle for independence under Mohandas Gandhi elevated its status in some key dimensions, especially among liberal-oriented world public opinion. The strategy of nonviolent resistance was adopted by many other social movements in the world, most prominently by Martin Luther King Jr. in the United States in the civil rights struggle during the 1960s for racial justice for Black Americans.[3] India's leadership in organizing the emerging Afro-Asian states also gave it higher stature for a period of time during the 1950s and early 1960s. India's support for decolonization and disarmament offered a higher level of status among the new states in Africa and Asia, even when India's position pitted it against the interests of the dominant Western powers.

In fact, India is an interesting case study of a state that initially attempted reliance on soft power before obtaining the necessary hard power to emerge as a leading state, showing the limitations of such a bifurcation for status elevation in the long run. The expectations of the Indian elite and informed public on soft power as a status marker offer an interesting contrast from what India has obtained in the international status realm. Affirming the historical significance of the Indian civilization in the global hierarchy of leading actors forms part of India's status-seeking strategy. While the Congress Party and liberal forces believe that India's secular-liberal democratic system gives it higher status, the BJP expects status to accrue through its Hindutva (Hinduness) agenda. There is indeed a disjunction in how the world looks at India in both these dimensions. India's periodic elections have generated praise over the years, and the peaceful transfer of power attracted international attention and occasional compliments. But the democratic order is often plagued by slow-moving and corrupt political processes and increasingly communal and caste politics that undercuts its soft-power value. More importantly, in recent years, Western liberal media and intellectuals have decried India losing its higher status as an inclusive and pluralistic democratic state as it has become quasi-authoritarian and religiously intolerant. To be sure, the decline of the quality of democracy is worldwide, and India still retains some democratic ethos and values. Yet, according to Freedom House, India in 2022 was only in the "partly free" category.[4]

For over 70 years, the organization of India as a secular, federal, and liberal democratic state gave it a higher stature among the post-colonial developing states in the liberal West, although this recognition has been tempered with questions of its survival and the actual liberal characteristics of its political system. Scholars have coined terms like "Indian exceptionalism" to explain the persistence of democracy in a large multiethnic and overwhelmingly poor country.[5] The effectiveness of the polity to address the developmental challenges has also been an issue that has confronted India and its status perceptions abroad. As the Cold War intruded, Western countries often ignored India's liberal-democratic credentials and embraced Pakistan and China, the two non-liberal adversarial neighbors of India, for strategic purposes. This to some extent shows that geopolitics often trumps democracy for many Western countries, despite their claims otherwise.

The translation of soft-power indicators to actual status elevation is a matter of contention. It is not clear which soft-power markers get the attention of others or what markers can sustain status on a durable basis. It is also questionable whether soft power without hard power can bring sustainable status to a state. Further, do these soft-power markers change over time? What are the soft-power indicators that India has often touted as the lead source of status distinction?

Soft-Power Markers and Status

Soft power of a state, or power built on attraction rather than coercion, results from intangible indicators such as culture, civilization, literature, philosophy, institutional involvement, diplomacy, political organization, and state capacity. As defined by Joseph Nye, soft power "is the ability to get what you want through attraction rather than coercion or payments. It arises from the attractiveness of a country's culture, political ideals, and policies. When our policies are seen as legitimate in the eyes of others, our soft power is enhanced."[6] Soft power can draw the policies of others into congruence with the influencing party's preferences, as the latter has something valuable to offer that is also worth emulating. This may help improve its status in terms of social recognition by others. However, the mere possession of soft-power resources does not automatically result in higher status on the world stage, as status is social recognition and not simply influence on others' choices. When soft power assets are translated into social recognition and appreciation, then only one can say that soft power is materialized. The translation of assets into status and influence requires well-calibrated national strategies that assess and reassess one's abilities in the changing global context and make timely policy adaptations. The current era of intensified globalization and the presence of social media offer a powerful window of opportunity for emerging powers such as India to actualize their soft-power resources more effectively as status markers. However, the reverse is also possible, as a country can be exposed by critics for its failings more effectively than before through social media.

Soft-power assets have emerged as important factors in the globalizing world for a country seeking higher status and influence. Even when a country has high material capabilities, without soft-power assets, its status will remain skewed, and the respect it may receive will be limited. Contemporary Russia shows the former tendencies, although in some soft-power areas like diplomacy, strategy, and culture, Russia is still treated as a dominant state, commanding higher status. Vladimir Putin's aggressive war on Ukraine in 2022 has undercut some of Russia's soft-power assets, although it is yet to be seen how this will affect Russia's status in the long run. It is likely that the lack of appreciation by the West of Moscow's status cravings has caused Putin to opt for an aggressive approach. The United States remains the most powerful state globally because of its comprehensive status ingredients that include soft power. Even here, the rise of populism and illiberal leaders like Donald Trump has trampled U.S. soft power, with the potential for further status depreciation. If the populist turn in U.S. politics continues, American soft power, especially its credentials for a functioning liberal democracy, may suffer irreparable damage over time.

China has been attempting to acquire both hard and soft power, with the aim of becoming the most powerful state by the mid-twenty-first century in both status and material terms. The 2020–2022 coronavirus crisis dampened Chinese soft power to an extent, as many countries suffered and the global economy was in near depression partly due to China's inability to contain the virus spread from the original location of Wuhan in the Hubei province. China's turn toward authoritarianism under Xi Jinping, coupled with the adoption of "wolf warrior diplomacy" and the stoking of territorial conflicts in the South China Sea, and with Taiwan, Japan, and India, have undercut the attractiveness of its model for many in the Indo-Pacific. The U.S., Russian, and Chinese cases show that status based on soft-power assets can depreciate rapidly as regimes engage in policy choices that undercut their previously accepted soft-power credentials and become more conflictual.[7] In the long run, the institutionalized status position could allow them to recover to their status ranking, but that will require deft diplomacy and investment in their soft-power assets (as they are perceived by others). In terms of soft power, India has some of the highest possibilities among rising powers, although translating soft-power markers to actual durable status and influence is always a challenge, especially for a rising power.

A key question arises in this context: Can soft-power resources alone earn a country more status in the global system? Does a nation need hard-power resources to harness soft-power resources effectively? Contrary to some assertions, I argue that soft-power resources alone will not bring influence or status, defined in terms of social recognition to a country. It is the confluence of hard- and soft-power resources that offers a country a leadership role and status in the global arena with an enduring footing. A country relying solely on soft power without hard-power assets for status and influence can be exposed easily, as happened to India in 1962, when China inflicted a humiliating military defeat, tarnishing India's hard-won soft-power status in the world, especially among other developing countries. India had also shown under Nehru's leadership that diplomacy had much power, and that despite limited hard-power resources, it could be used in global institutional forums for mediating conflict among the major powers to an extent. Yet, all these came crashing down in the Himalayas as the military conflict with China exposed the limitations of India's soft power, making Nehru's active global engagement a casualty in that process. Despite these pitfalls, soft power can still enhance reputation, credibility, and legitimacy to a state's status in the global system if it is developed and exercised in conjunction with hard-power resources.

As India's hard-power capabilities have accelerated, especially in the economic and military realms following its economic liberalization since 1991, and as it has made increasing efforts to acquire global power status, the value of soft-power resources as tools of grand strategy and foreign policy for this emerging power has attracted scholarly attention.[8] Soft power in this milieu provides legitimacy and credibility to a state's leadership role in the world, and more effectiveness to the exercise and wielding of its hard-power resources. Legitimacy of power implies that other states accept the status of a country as rightful and worthy of recognition through formal and informal mechanisms, which may include assigning additional leadership roles in global institutions. In many ways, soft power falls under the category of a means of "social creativity" to achieve prestige and status by promoting new norms or a developmental model, in contrast to "social competition," which attempts to attain preeminence through competitive or coercive means. It is also useful for staking out a distinctive position without directly challenging the dominant powers in the international system.[9] As Joseph Nye argues:

> The countries that are likely to gain soft power in an information age are: 1. Those whose dominant culture and ideas are closer to prevailing global norms (which now emphasize liberalism, pluralism, and autonomy); 2. Those with the most access to multiple channels of communication and thus more influence over how issues are framed; and 3. Those whose credibility is enhanced by their domestic and international performance.[10]

Obviously, all these markers have direct and indirect impact on a country's overall status in the international system. How do these factors apply to the Indian case?

India's Soft-Power Assets

In the next section, I discuss India's deep multiethnic culture, its grand civilizational assets, and their potential for producing and projecting soft power and increased international status.

Culture and Civilization

In April 2018, I visited Angkor Wat in Cambodia and marveled at some 72 temples with many hundreds of ruins partially submerged in a jungle territory constituting some 402 acres. It is a UNESCO Heritage Site and a must-see attraction in one's lifetime. One imagines, thousands of Hindu and Buddhist priests and builders passing through the Indian subcontinent and Southeast Asia by foot and animal, coming regularly to this oasis of Hinduism and Buddhism built by Khmer King Surya Varman II (reigned AD 1113–1150). Also noticeable was the defacing of many thousands of tiny Lord Ganesh statues on the walls, which may very well be the result of Surya Varman adopting Buddhism, as the Hindu gods were not helping him![11] Yet, amazingly, the defacing looks more like little acts of vandalism than anything meant to inflict serious damage to the structures, as if they still wanted to keep the original works intact in some form even while expressing discomfort!

During an earlier trip to Bali and Ubud in Indonesia in 2010, I was won-derstruck by the natural beauty of these places, their architecture, religious practices, art forms, and dance, which carry quite a resemblance to those found in South Indian villages. It is amazing how the Hindu/Buddhist culture and religion reached this place some 2,800 miles away from India via a com-bination of boat and foot. In the midst of the beautiful paddy fields are roads that are very busy with incessant traffic that can unnerve anyone. My taxi driver acted like nothing was unusual about this place, and said individuals are taught meditation and peacefulness from childhood, which enables them to react to difficult situations calmly. One should recognize that Indian civili-zation was adapted by the various cultures in Southeast Asia and syncretized with their own local values and ideas. Even Islam in Indonesia maintained some of these ethos. The challenge is to understand if these civilizational influences give India a higher status in the minds of the population there.

Civilizations and their inherent cultures are the core of much soft power in modern and ancient times. Empires that left lasting impressions are those with prominent civilizations. In today's world, such imperial civilizations are hard to establish. It is the multicultural and pluralistic civilizations that are most valued in a globalized era, as people from different ethnic and re-ligious backgrounds have to live together peacefully, even if they do not share key attributes and values on what constitutes the proper goals of so-cial life. As Peter Katzenstein argues, certain civilizations have been suc-cessful in promoting a kind of "magnetism" and prestige by achieving "multiple networks" and "distant connections." And they are "zones of at-traction" that invite students and visitors from distant lands, and "send out teachers and missionaries, both to civilizational peripheries and other civilizations."[12] India is considered one of those "zones of attraction." It is referred to as one of the seven leading world civilizations that contributed immensely to humanity throughout the millennia.[13] During several histor-ical eras, India was a zone of attraction for students and travelers, in partic-ular a large number of Buddhist missionaries. The spread of Buddhism to the rest of Asia, initially by Mauryan Emperor Ashoka and his emissaries in the third century BC and later by Buddhist monks in ancient and medieval times, was an amazing feat, considering that it occurred largely peacefully. I recall waking up in the middle of the night at a hotel room in Hiroshima in 1999 only to find a Buddhist text with many Sanskrit words in it to read! My visits to many cities in Japan and China always left me wonderstruck how this Indic religion spanned this distance peacefully, even when its native land largely abandoned it. From the fifth to eleventh centuries AD, the Buddhist universities of Nalanda and Takshashila (the Ivy League schools of their time) attracted thousands of students from all over Asia, who would carry their ideas to China and then to Japan and beyond.

India's cultural links with Southeast Asia are indeed very deep. Trade links brought India's languages, Sanskrit in particular, religious texts like Ramayana, and religious ceremonies associated with kinship to both the ruler and the ruled, as well as the daily lives of the people of the region. Lord Rama is a powerful figure in Thai, Indonesian, and Cambodian art and literature. The Thai epic *Ramakien* is heavily derived from the *Ramayana*.[14] It was the arrival of the colonial powers—Portuguese, Dutch, and English—that disrupted the relationship. The Cold War widened the gap in India's relations with Southeast Asia.[15] Moreover, the supplanting by Islam in Indonesia and Malaysia in particular and by Communism in Cambodia have affected India's civilizational impact and the perceptions of people in those countries toward India.

The multidimensional civilizational assets of India have great actual and potential soft-power significance. Foremost is the unique peace-generating ethos inherent in Hinduism, Buddhism, and other minority religions like Islam, Jainism, Sikhism, and Christianity as practiced in India.[16] India is both a mosaic and a melting pot in civilizational terms. Despite being a highly religious society, India has an immense tradition of intellectual "dialogue" and skepticism.[17] Three world religions emanated from India—Hinduism, Buddhism, and Sikhism—in addition to the smaller religion, Jainism. Christianity reached the Indian shores in AD 52 (believed to be with when St. Thomas arrived in Kerala) even before it was accepted in Europe. Likewise, persecuted religious minorities, such as Jews, Zoroastrians, and Baha'is from Palestine and Iran, found India receiving them with open arms. While Islam in the North arrived largely through invading Muslim rulers and latter-day conversions, in the South and beyond to Southeast Asia, it came via Arab traders, and its spread has been largely through peaceful means. What is unique about this religious mix is their relatively peaceful coexistence, despite some significant aberrations during the reign of the Mughal rulers such as Aurangzeb, and since the 1930s, especially during the partition of the subcontinent in 1947.

Minority religions, even foreign-originated ones like Islam and Christianity, have developed eclectic forms of ideas in conjunction with Indian ideals, largely emanating from Buddhism and Hinduism. Christian weddings in Kerala have some Hindu features, and some of the Hindu festivals have become national festivals as people of different religious communities observe them. The peace-generating ideals were promoted by India's ancient and modern heroes, four of whom are most prominent: Lord Buddha, Asoka the Great, Akbar the Great, and Mahatma Gandhi (two Buddhists, one Muslim, and the fourth a Hindu). They are all remembered for instilling peaceful values in India and beyond. Buddha's teachings, even without reference to God, reached millions over the millennia, and this feat may well be ancient India's greatest soft-power diffusion and contribution to world peace. Nehru states this aptly: Buddha's "message was one of universal benevolence, of love for all. For, 'never in this world does hatred cease by hatred; hatred ceases by love.' And 'let a man overcome anger by kindness, evil by good.'"[18]

Even within religions, medieval India produced movements like *Bhakti* (Devotion) and versions of Sufism, known for their peaceful, eclectic ideas, and practices.[19] Similar to Buddhism, Jainism also bore many ideals of peace, including aversion to animal killing. What is unique about Indian civilization is that it received and naturalized diverse cultural forms. The idea of "a 'composite civilization' captures the many religions, starting with Hinduism but continuing with Islam and Christianity, which found a home in India, and suggests that all are acceptable."[20] Shashi Tharoor, the Indian academic-turned-politician, states that "In India everything exists in countless variants. There is no single standard, no fixed stereotype and no 'one way.' This pluralism is acknowledged in the way India arranges its own affairs: all groups, faiths, tastes, and ideologies survive and contend for their place in the sun."[21] Since India's independence, violence-generating behavior has come from fringe elements of these religions, yet they contain powerful strings of harmony and peace in a deeper and sustainable manner. Some modern-day meditation gurus, like Deepak Chopra and Maharishi Mahesh Yogi, have articulated the elements of this peace, but it has not been fully utilized as a soft-power resource by India. Scholars have increasingly talked of India emerging (or resuming) its role as a bridge-building civilization. Kishore Mahbubani argues that one such example is Bollywood movies, which are watched equally passionately by both Hindus and Muslims, the latter in many Asian, Middle Eastern and African countries. Some of Bollywood's leading actors and actresses are Muslims, although the Indian film industry is increasingly featuring anti-Muslim themes.[22] The unique art, dance, architecture, cuisine, literature, and languages of India are all part of its composite culture and civilizational offerings to the world and are, therefore, soft-power assets. These assets can bring about global influence and status if they are accepted as valuable and worthy of emulation by different societies in the world. How a changing political narrative, especially from a composite, pluralistic culture to a religiously monolithic view, would affect India's soft-power markers and its status is yet to be seen.

Among the different cultural attributes, Prime Minister Narendra Modi in particular has been promoting *yoga* globally as a soft-power tool. International yoga day was adopted by the United Nations in 2015 almost unanimously, and it is now observed on June 21 globally with events in most major cities and urban centers. There has been some success in this area, as yoga's popularity is increasing and is practiced by millions across the world, a trend that had started even before this renewed effort. Yet, it is difficult to see if people pursuing yoga associate it with India to raise its status.

India's traditional and modern art have slowly become internationally accepted as powerful soft power assets. Visitors to any major art museums in the world where Asian art is exhibited will see India's contributions in this regard. Today, Indian artists are slowly making headway in the global scene through auctions and exhibitions. Different art forms, such as classical and modern-day dance, are yet to become global brands. *Bharatanatyam*, *Kathak*, *Kuchipudi*, *Kathakali*, and *Mohiniyattam* are prominent classical dance forms of India. Leading Western artists, such as The Beatles, Michael Jackson, Madonna, and Shakira, have adopted and appropriated elements of Indian dances or music in their performances, and the idea of fusion holds much promise for globalizing Indian dance forms. However, colonial-era cultural circulations have helped Western countries acquire cultural artifacts as millions of visitors throng to their museums and art exhibitions where colonial exploitations are still portrayed.

Likewise, Indian *cuisine* has already made tremendous impact globally, as evident in countries like the United Kingdom, where it has now become favorite international food. Globally, more and more people are adopting vegetarian diets due to health benefits and/or ecological values. With its multitude of vegetarian food options, there is much room for India to insert itself into this arena.

The *literature* of India in the English language has become global, especially those written by Indian expatriate authors. In fact, many prominent authors in English literature today are of Indian origin, and their themes are related to India or Indian diaspora. The long list includes: Salman Rushdie,

Arundhati Roy, Abraham Verghese, Rohinton Mistry, Vikram Seth, Amitav Ghosh, Aravind Adiga, Kiran Desai, and V.S. Naipaul.

Similarly, apparel design and fashion of India have made some impact globally and possesses tremendous soft-power potential. *Music* of India often has a particular soothing and calming characteristic. More upbeat dance and music forms, such as the *Bhangra*, are now popular in many wedding parties and other festivities in North America and other English-speaking countries. A substantial number of Indian musical traditions, such as *Hindustani, Carnatik*, instrumental (especially using flute, *tabala*, and sarang), and *ghazals*, have some global presence. Eminent figures like Pandit Ravi Shankar have done much to popularize Indian instrumental music in the West since the 1960s.

Films from India have already made a major mark in the global arena. Bollywood produces the largest number of films by any country and is now increasingly viewed as second to Hollywood in terms of its global reach. These movies are popular for entertainment and as such they have made major impact in Asia, the Middle East, and Africa, and slowly are spreading to the Western countries. Here again, quantity without a focus on quality is a drawback. In recent years, Indian films and Indian film stars like Amir Khan have become popular in China. Films such as *Three Idiots*, *Dangal*, and *Secret Superstar* have been very popular in China, and in 2017 *Dangal* (translated as *Shuai Jiao Baba* in Chinese), grossed some $189 million, higher earnings than the majority of Hollywood films during this period, and ran as the top box office movie for 16 days.[23]

Cultural and civilizational contributions do give India unique soft-power prominence, but is it enough to gain international status and legitimacy as a rising great power? India has possessed these attributes for a long time, and their globalization has added to India's appeal and status in a broad sense. Parallel negative trends, however, take away some of these achievements. The decline of India's democratic and secular political system is perhaps the most poignant of these contemporary challenges. Yet, among all the rising powers, India has a much larger set of soft-power assets, sometimes as a competitor to Western soft power, making it a potentially important factor for status enhancement, along with major increases in hard-power markers. If and when India obtains adequate hard-power markers of status, the soft-power assets could help its status become more durable and deep-rooted. However, human rights of all citizens and humane treatment of minorities will be essential for a state to acquire legitimacy rather than stigma internationally, if that claim is based on noble civilizational claims. As Yong Deng argues, "China's human rights stigma has no doubt contributed to international mistrust toward its intentions . . . as the logic went, a regime egregiously violating the rights of its citizens should not be trusted to respect the rights and interests of other countries."[24]

Civilizational attributes have been the claim for higher status by all Indian governments since independence, especially by Nehru and Modi. However, the BJP has increased the claim for international status based on religious/civilizational attributes. The Modi government has attempted to "render India into a 'world guru' (visva guru) using the soft power of its cultural and religious inheritance to achieve" its policy objectives, convinced "that India needs to recover its national pride or dignity (samman) and ensure that others recognize and respect its civilizational heritage and historical influence."[25] Yet any new achievements in status recognition due to the civilizational attributes that Modi touts are unclear due to his government's increasingly illiberal policies.

The Political System

Apart from civilization and culture, a well-functioning *political system* of a country can be a source of soft power and can help advance its global status. It can be viewed as a model for others to pursue, and the management of a multiethnic society, including peaceful power transfers through the ballot box as opposed to violent means, can be a major asset. India has had partial success in this soft-power asset, which may be altering now. In India's case, these arise from four institutional structures decided since independence: democracy, secularism, federalism, and the three-language formula. These institutional ideas also derive from India as an inclusive civilization, despite some deep hierarchical challenges arising from the caste system and endemic corruption among the political-bureaucratic elite. In spite of all its pitfalls and messiness, Indian democracy has survived, and some social science theorists have labeled it "Indian exceptionalism" (meaning that it is non-replicable). Since independence in 1947, power transfers have been generally nonviolent, and to this day Indian democracy stands as an imperfect, yet vitally important model for the governance of a multiethnic and multi-religious society. The generally peaceful conduct of elections and the massive logistics involved in this process have attracted much international attention.[26] Barring few exceptions, the institution of election commissions has acted without bias. Much of the credit for instilling democratic ethos goes to Nehru, as well as constitution makers such as Dr. Ambedkar.[27] Yet the decline of democracy under Modi has generated much consternation internationally given that India's soft-power status marker in this area has come under serious stress.[28]

Similarly, secularism has offered India soft power for a long time that many in the developing world, especially in its immediate neighborhood, could not replicate. The frequency of violent religious clashes in the aftermath of the bloody partition had subsided by the 1980s, despite occasional aberrations like the Delhi riots against Sikhs (1984), the destruction of the Ayodhya Muslim mosque (1992) by a Hindu mob claiming it was the birthplace of Lord Rama, and the Gujarat riots against Muslims (2002), as well as the occasional mob lynching of Muslims by Hindu cow-protection vigilante groups for possessing or consuming meat. There has been a population increase of minorities, unlike the minority populations in India's South Asian neighbors, especially Pakistan and Bangladesh, and their allegiance is to the Indian nation. The integration of the Muslim population in India and their low participation in global Jihadist organizations like al-Qaeda has been noted as an asset.[29]

Hindutva critics of Indian secularism have argued that it favors minority communities and promotes Muslim sectarianism, as it retains civil codes of religious communities. To them, India is a "Hindu country . . . and that as a result it would be culturally quite wrong to treat Hinduism as simply one of the various religions of India."[30] Adherents of Hindutva believe that India's soft-power credentials lie in a society dominated by Hindu values and ethos, where minority religious groups—especially the Abrahamic religions of Islam and Christianity—should remain secondary. This notion of Hinduism is rooted in the nationalist ideas propagated by the Rashtriya Swayamsevak Sangh (RSS) and its founder Vinayak Damodar Savarkar, who argued: "Thirty crores [300 million in 1923] of people, with India for their basis of operation, for their Fatherland and their Holyland with such a history behind them, bound together by ties of a common blood and common culture can dictate their terms to the whole world. A day will come when mankind will have to face the force."[31] The ideological underpinnings of Hindu nationalism draw partially from the European nationalisms of the nineteenth and early twentieth centuries,[32] based on myths of homogeneous ethnic groups.[33] From the point of view of the BJP, which draws much of its ideology from RSS:

India is composed of an essentially Hindu society. Therefore, the state should reflect the values and ambitions of the Hindus, just as Western states reflect the values and ambitions of their Christian populations, the Muslim states reflect Islam, and Israel embodies the values and aspirations of the Jews. The Hindu revivalists argue that India must act in the world as a Hindu civilization state. Non-Hindus are welcome to live in India, but only if they accept the fundamentally Hindu nature of the country.[34]

Contrary to the RSS/BJP vision, the Indian constitution makers were driven by both pragmatism and tolerance in their approach to secularism. The founding fathers, in particular Nehru and Ambedkar, recognized that as a composite culture, both Hindus and Muslims contributed immensely to India's development. They were also driven by instrumental reasons of pacifying a society scarred by the partition, which was one of history's brutal episodes of religious violence. It is very difficult to see how Hindutva can be a source of attraction or a status enhancer from the perspective of outside powers or societies. Except for the non-secular Hindu diaspora, there has been little evidence of any international recognition of India's status elevation based on the Hindutva ideology. Hindu values are recognized as an asset when they allow tolerance, inclusiveness, peacefulness, and non-aggression (Ahimsa). Gandhi extracted some of these values and made them into the much-admired strategy for India's freedom struggle. In fact, this achievement of Gandhi's is impressive given that there is a simultaneous warrior tradition in Hindu mythology and traditions. The two epics, *Ramayana* and *Mahabharata*, are all about the right side winning brutal wars against the wrong side, and in the latter, divine Krishna in the chariot advising Arjuna to fight despite his reluctance to wage a bloody battle against his cousins as part of his Dharma (duty).[35] Yet, simultaneously, virtue and righteousness are often themes that have resonated in Indian traditions. Aggressive promotion of a version of the religious ethos is unlikely to bring much soft-power value, as this dimension of the Hindu ethos has little capacity to persuade others to conform. In fact, it has hurt India's standing in various Gulf countries, as is evident in their strong condemnation against growing Islamophobia in India. The challenge here is that millions of Indians live and work in these Muslim countries, and if India loses its secular credentials, this will hurt India's economic and political clout as well. In other words, soft-power depreciation can undercut hard power and international status itself.

The major challenges to the Hindutva vision and its implications for India's status are the following. First, over 14 percent of the population is Muslim, and India's composite culture is Muslim as well, as they ruled many significant parts of the subcontinent for about a millennium and brought many cultural and civilizational attributes of present-day India. Second, neighboring states that have gone the religious route have all become illiberal and are extremely difficult places for minority rights. As exemplified in Pakistan, they have not increased their international status or material wealth due to their extreme religious ideology. Third, Hinduism is a polyglot religion, as there is no single version of it. Different castes and communities of Hinduism may not share the same ideals. The BJP has had difficulty establishing itself in the Southern states, except Karnataka, partly because the majority Hindu electorate does not share the Northern Indian notions of Hinduism that the BJP propagates. Fourth, other civilizations, such as Egyptian, Iranian, Greek, Roman, and Turkic, have contributed immensely to human progress. Many of these original states have shrunk, and it is impossible to resurrect their old glory on the basis of past civilizations. Other attributes are needed for a modern state to use its civilization for status elevation.

In fact, the modern state is judged for its performance and competence, especially in sustainable and inclusive economic development. How would India gain more international status if the governments at the center and in the states fail to develop and manage Indians of all religious hues and pursue discriminatory policies toward minorities? The electorate keeps re-electing the BJP governments in non-Southern states largely because of the welfare schemes, the weaknesses of the splintered opposition parties, and Modi's yogi-style appeal. Hindutva has contributed to their electoral successes internally, but there is little evidence that it has been translated into any international status enhancement. Finally, minority Christians, who constitute some 2.5 percent of the population, have immensely contributed to the educational and health sectors of India. Some of the best-run schools, colleges, and medical institutions are Christian, and the elite who preach Hindutva themselves educate their children in these institutions. Hindutva groups have not been able to create educational institutions that can compete with the top Christian colleges and schools in India.

Brendan O'Leary argues that a *Staatsvolk* (a national or ethnic people) is necessary for the creation and functioning of a stable democratic federation,[36] but there is a danger of majoritarianism and authoritarianism affecting the federation. In India's case, the dominant ethnic group is not as unified, nor do they share the same ideals. India's heterogeneity of populations, even under umbrella Hindu religious identity and a powerful Muslim minority, suggests that power sharing similar to a consociationalism model is necessary for democracy, peace, and national unity. This model gives some power representation to minority groups, thereby not marginalizing them completely.[37] Democratic theorist Arend Lijpart contends that it was such a consociational arrangement that offered a stable democracy in India under Nehru.[38] From a soft-power standpoint, the transformation of the BJP into a more moderate party is necessary for India's status enhancement globally. The party can attempt to promote India's Hindu civilizational values, as European Christian parties promote European values, but not in the manner of the aggressive Christianity of the Middle Ages.

The federal setup of the Indian constitution has allowed provincial governments to function reasonably autonomously—in some cases, more effectively than in others. The manner in which Kashmir was forcefully integrated in August 2019 generated questions on the role of federal units in determining their political future. India's "two plus one" language policy (Hindi, English, plus local language) has brought tremendous peace in this area, an issue that still bedevils even advanced countries like Canada, the United States, and Spain. By the mid-1950s, India was on a developmental path unparalleled in history, and despite much turmoil, it did not fall apart as Churchill had warned (and probably hoped). However, India's asset in this regard is also its bane. As discussed in Chapter 7, the Indian state is a *soft* or a quasi-*weak state*, exhibiting some strengths, while showing many signs of weakness.[39] The reason that India's political system has not received the credit it may deserve is because of its chaotic nature and the inefficiency of the Indian state at every level—central, state, city, municipality/village—to deliver public services effectively. The inability to create an inclusive developmental society, even after seven decades of independence, has undermined India's soft power and status aspirations. India also has not propagated democracy and secularism to other states or made freedom promotion part of its foreign policy. World rankings of India's democratic performance also generate questions about its virtues. For instance, in 2022 the Freedom House publication, *Freedom in the World Index*, gave India 66th rank out of 100 and termed it "partially free."[40]

Many in India and abroad associate the political system with India's weaknesses in infrastructure and public services. Part of the challenge here is the lack of recognition that democracies too can be effective, and that the majority of authoritarian models, including those in India's neighborhood, have not performed any better in providing public goods. According to a recent study, historically, democratic great powers in general have been more effective than their autocratic counterparts in sustaining durable global power because of their stronger economies, better diplomacy, and higher-quality military.[41] China may be an exception in some of these elements, but only history will tell if Xi Jinping's turn toward authoritarianism will undercut China's prospects in the twenty-first century, as it is attracting more enemies and generating less economic growth due to its drastic policy shifts. In fact, the American decline in international status may partially correlate with its democratic decline as U.S. society becomes more fractionalized into ethnic and racial identities, producing a lack of consensus on crucial domestic and foreign policy issues.

The increasing challenge of the spread of illiberal values, especially among Indian youth, is likely to negatively affect its soft power and the durability and sustainability of its international status ranking. Individuals become tolerant of different perspectives only when they obtain contending viewpoints, especially of a historical nature, in their school and college curricula. If history is taught in a very partisan way (editing out unsavory parts) that belittles the contributions of minority religions and groups, students (and later as adults) will become intolerant over time. When changes are made to the curriculum, it has long-term implications. India needs compulsory liberal arts education, as sometimes well-qualified Indian engineers and doctors, especially in the diaspora, exhibit a high level of intolerance toward other faiths and belief systems, partly due to their minimal exposure to contending philosophical and political viewpoints of the world. More importantly, if India does not allow free or critical thinking on social and political issues, how can it advance with new knowledge in different domains, not just science and technology? Where is knowledge production possible? How will it assimilate new knowledge generated elsewhere? How will it compete in the global realm of ideas where knowledge contestation takes place? The closing of the Indian mind is a danger if travel in and out of India is restricted for scholars and knowledge creators in every field, given that collaboration across national boundaries is a must for advancing one's status and sustaining it. India is slowly allowing foreign universities to establish campuses to stem the tide of Indians flocking to foreign universities, but the increasing curtailment of freedom is likely to deter ranking universities from coming to India to set up campuses.

Strategy and Diplomacy

Grand strategy is crucial for a state to achieve its global status and higher se-curity goals. Grand strategy has historically been associated with war, but in today's world, it is also connected with the translation of hard and soft power for achieving and enhancing power, security, and status. A grand strategy is defined as "a political-military means ends chain, a state's theory about how it can cause security for itself."[42] Grand strategy considers all the resources at the disposal of a state and arrays them effectively to achieve security in both war and peace. Grand strategy, often used in the context of increasing power and security, is equally relevant in status enhancement. For an aspirational rising power like India, grand strategy seeks to achieve higher status, pros-perity, and security in a competitive international system without war.

Some scholars have criticized India for not developing a proper grand strategy. George Tanham, in a critical analysis, contends that the dominant cultural view derived from the Hindu ethos prevents a grand strategic ap-proach from emerging, as it views "life more fatalistically and that a certain passiveness in life as a dominant characteristic, has become embedded in the state as the political and bureaucratic elite of India have imbibed its values in their outlook."[43] Others believe that over time India has shown many elements of a grand strategy, even when it doesn't publicize its core elements as frequently as others, such as the United States and China. Nehru's grand strategy was aimed at increasing India's status using the soft power of diplo-macy while building hard-power assets such as science and technology, in particular in nuclear and space areas and higher institutions of education, with the aim of enhanced status in the long run. Grand strategy, associated with military security, was neglected, and as a result, some serious failures in relations with China and Pakistan occurred. Strategic autonomy remained a core of India's grand strategy, even when some tilting toward the Soviet bloc took place in the 1970s during the Indira Gandhi period.

The absence of a grand strategy was evident in India's nuclear policies, the 1974 testing in particular, and the decision not to develop a nuclear deter-rent in the aftermath. While this has changed considerably since the 1990s, the greater challenge has come from China with its earlier "peaceful rise" strategy and the most recent Belt and Road Initiative (BRI), both of which can be characterized as evidence of a higher level of grand strategy planning than in India. This may very well be due to the authoritarian system which allows continuity and higher levels of bureaucratic attention in China versus the electoral democracy of India, which often produces short time horizons for strategic planning and implementation. Yet, India has come up with strategies such as the Bay of Bengal Initiative for Multi-Sectoral Technical and Economic Cooperation (BIMSTEC) and Asia-Africa Growth Corridor, but it has not been implementing these with the same vigor and speed with which China is pursuing its grand strategy goals. China's grand strategy also includes overtaking Western dominance in every technology domain, something India has no desire to emulate. India's current grand strategy of multi-alignment and strategic autonomy while maintaining close relations with the West, especially the United States and Japan, seemed to have been effective in some dimensions to enhance its status in the Indo-Pacific. The decision not to join the BRI and to exit from the Regional Comprehensive Economic Partnership (RCEP) in Asia-Pacific negotiations while strengthening the Quad have indeed been a part of Modi's grand strategy of gaining strategic autonomy. Scholars call this "zone balancing" to "evasive balancing" (i.e., avoiding military hard balancing) as it does not add much military punch to the balancing equation.[44] The Indian elite seems to think that the Chinese model will fail, and that India's economic size and market will attract others to India.

Diplomacy has two key dimensions that can be soft-power assets and status enhancers. The first is the actual diplomatic practices and policies shown by diplomatic representatives through their activism in global institutional forums and foreign capitals. The second dimension is *public diplomacy*, which relies on the distribution of information and cultural programs overseas, aimed at improving the prestige, image, and status of a country. They are also means to counter negative stereotypes and propaganda generated by opponents or others who do so out of lack of knowledge or specific prejudices they carry. In this sense, diplomacy is also a tool for status enhancement.

India's Strategy and Diplomacy: The Historical Legacy

Even before India became independent in August 1947, the Congress Party, under the leadership of Jawaharlal Nehru, was planning major international activism and was embracing the role of a peace-maker and an agent of change. The interim government he headed held a conference of Asian and African colonies in New Delhi in 1946, where he argued that if not resisted, the U.S.-USSR struggle for expansion would produce efforts by them at empire building.[45] From a purely material perspective, some have asked why India would pursue such an audaciously independent non-alignment policy when material help from the superpowers was viewed as an absolute necessity to meet the basic needs of the country and to protect itself from external threats. Along with non-alignment, India also engaged in a high-profile mediatory role, largely through UN General Assembly, which had mixed results in elevating India's diplomatic status. Two crises where Indian diplomacy was active were the Formosa or Offshore crises (1954) and Indochina (1954).[46] In the 1950 Korean War, India was also an interlocutor between China and the United States. In a brief decade and a half, Nehru accomplished much in enhancing India's status internationally and domestically, largely through soft power and diplomacy. Despite its non-alignment policy, India did receive much aid from the West, especially the United States, which feared that India's failure could help communism in Asia. Later, India received a significant amount of military aid from the Soviet Union. In the arena of foreign policy, India embarked upon a highly activist approach, often challenging the European colonial powers and the superpowers, especially the United States, to change the international order in favor of the suppressed nations and colonies.

The Policy of Non-Alignment as a Status-Builder

An argument can be made that Nehru followed a policy of non-alignment, largely motivated by the fear of India entangling in military alliances and thereby jeopardizing its security and freedom, won through decades of struggles. He feared that a third world war was likely and that the freedoms and security of the newly emerged countries would be the first casualty of such a war, as imperial powers would attempt to carve out their domains in the new order. Moreover, the war would involve nuclear weapons with potentially massive destruction of the planet. The Bandung Conference of 1955 assumed major significance in analyzing India's quest for status. In April 1955, 29 Asian and African states met at the Indonesian city of Bandung, under the leadership of Nehru, Sukarno, and Nasser, and adopted several resolutions, including the five principles of coexistence, equality of races and nations, rights of individual and collective self-defense, encouraging newly emerging states to refrain from joining the superpower-led military alliances, and demanding the freedom to rename French and Dutch colonies.[47] This event was significant for a number of reasons. It was the first time in history that previously subjugated countries gathered to press for reforms using institutional mechanisms. It also took shape under the leadership of post-colonial leaders like Nehru and Sukarno, who would emerge as champions of freedom and independence for the still subjugated peoples of Asia and Africa. The successor to Bandung, the Non-Aligned Movement (NAM) and its summit meetings, starting with Belgrade in 1961, and at the United Nations, would become arenas of global activism for decolonization and a new international economic order.

India pursued diplomacy quite successfully until the 1960s as a soft-power asset. Nehru had some successes and failures in attempting to mediate on Korea and Vietnam, and he made key proposals to the United Nations on nuclear testing and non-proliferation, as well as decolonization. By organizing the newly emerging Afro-Asian states and by leading their cause at the United Nations, supporting and promoting peacekeeping operations, and offering mediation during major power conflicts such as in Korea, Nehru's India received more influence and status in the global arena than its hard power warranted.[48] This changed dramatically as China, the other emergent power, viewed Indian activism as affecting its position in Asia and engaged in punitive military action, which exposed India's inability to withstand a powerful military challenge. Since the 1960s, India has lowered multilateral diplomacy as a tool of soft power, although activism continued in specific venues such as the UN forums.[49] Only in the 1990s, in the aftermath of the Cold War and its own economic liberalization, did India resume increased global activism.

Nehru left an indelible legacy in terms of India's status quest. Non-alignment would become an article of faith of the Indian elite, even when they whittled down its principles as expediency demanded them to seek support from the Soviet Union in particular. India could not resist the security pressures emanating from its neighborhood and the global reconfiguration of balance-of-power coalitions. Yet, Nehru's short-term achievements in status elevation, largely through soft power, were remarkable. However, in the long run, those soft-power assets could not be sustained without substantial improvements in economic and military capabilities.[50] The problem was that in facing hard security challenges, soft power was not effective in resisting a challenger that relied heavily on hard power and coercive strategy.

During the 1960s and 1970s, the United Nations and its associated organization, the UN Conference on Trade and Development (UNCTAD), took an active role in the formation of the G-77 of developing states from Africa, Asia, and Latin America, pushing for the demands of the developing countries for a new international economic order. The various governments led by both the Congress and Janata parties pursued non-alignment in a diluted fashion. The collapse of the Berlin Wall in 1989, followed by the Soviet Union's dismemberment, and the end of the Cold War in 1991 were watershed moments for India as it now pivoted to a new strategic terrain where the United States obtained near-unipolarity while the world order witnessed intense globalization, especially in the economic arena. In the post–Cold War world, India once again began using its diplomacy more effectively, be it at the United Nations, G-20, BRICS, the World Trade Organization (WTO), global climate talks, or engagement with the European Union and the ASEAN states. To some, there is increased confidence and pragmatism in India's global diplomacy and engagement.[51] It also comes out of a realization among the Indian elite that its hard-power resources are growing substantially and that if the present trends continue, within a few decades India may overtake many of the other lead countries in the world, except China and the United States, in gross economic terms. Today, India is also viewed in many Asian capitals "as a predictable, stabilizing, cooperative and attractive rising power," and there is a "lack of apprehension about India's rise," unlike that of China.[52] This general absence of worry about India's rise may have partially to do with India's soft-power assets, in particular the strategy of not challenging the international order in a frontally revisionist manner.

In international negotiations, India has adopted a "veto player" role, often stopping negotiations or preventing others from imposing their preferred options on India. This was most evident in the Doha rounds on world trade in which India, along with Brazil, successfully blocked a new global trade deal in 2011.[53] During the climate change negotiations in Paris (2015) and Glasgow (2021), India played a role in whittling down the final declarations, generating negative reactions toward India's diplomacy. The sheer size of India makes it most difficult for any power to ignore it in such negotiations, giving it a peculiar status in terms of global collective action problems.[54] Others have called on the "bridge-building" efforts by India and its role as a "link power."[55] India has also been called a "swing state," which gives it some amount of leverage in international bargaining. Despite these characterizations, some scholars like Brahma Chellaney contend that "India still punches below its weight in global affairs."[56] In many respects, seeking strategic autonomy has been a hallmark of India's foreign policy behavior, which is today reflected in multi-alignment or plurilateral strategies, with all their limitations.[57]

Status enhancement through soft power has been a major plank of Prime Minister Modi's policies since coming to power in May 2014, especially in the first term. During his early years in power, Modi made a major effort to promote soft power and to improve India's status through that marker. In the first year itself, Modi visited some 20 countries and many more afterward until Covid-19 hit in 2020. While touting India's soft power, Modi also made major pitches for economic and military interactions with key countries. Modi framed soft power abroad as a way to attract the support of the Indian diaspora, as well as improving his electoral position at home, which is increasingly based on the Hindutva nationalist agenda. Modi has promoted Buddhism with an aim to increase India's soft power among Buddhist Asian countries. The boosting of yoga and meditation internationally implies an aim of showing the world that India wants to rise peacefully.[58] The question arises whether the Modi efforts at soft-power enhancement are sufficient to elevate India's international status. According to one analyst, "unless India's development model succeeds in changing the lives of the majority of citizens for the better, its exercise of soft power will produce limited results."[59] Another analyst calls the soft power efforts as "rhetoric for image-polishing" more than "a genuine effort to exploit its huge soft power potential."[60]

Despite the early successes of Modi, by the second term, his policies were marked by increasing polarization and suppression of minority rights, affecting India's secular and democratic credentials. Modi has basically innovated and adapted the policies of his predecessors, Narasimha Rao and Manmohan Singh, of increasing involvement in regional institutions and mini-lateral groups such as Quad and the ASEAN Regional Forum (ARF). He has also concluded a variety of strategic and economic partnerships and has been successful in gaining economic and security benefits from all leading powers, including the United States, Russia, Japan, and the European Union.[61] With the help of the Indian diaspora, he has had more success in showcasing Indian foreign policy for electoral gains than his predecessors. In September 2023, India hosted the annual G-20 meeting of the heads of governments of 19 countries plus the leadership of the European Union and successfully steered the adoption of a final declaration. It contained many initiatives on climate financing, food security, sustainable development, digital infrastructure, medical emergencies, and women's participation in national economies.[62] Yet, in geopolitical terms, the omission of a direct reference to the Russian invasion of Ukraine made the communique a partial success. Deft diplomacy by India and others involved was evident in getting the consensus agreement, gaining the support of Russia and China. Prime Minister Modi turned the summit into a spectacle, with some 200 pre-summit meetings across India in 50 cities with "yoga, cultural performances and specially curated menus" with an aim at boosting his chances at the 2024 national elections. The capital was beautified for this occasion, with slums enclosed by temporary cloth walls and cutouts of monkeys installed to deter animals from encroaching on the meeting venues.[63] In obtaining a consensus document, India was helped by the United States, which now views it as a pivotal player to counter China's influence in the Global South. From the Bandung meeting of the Afro-Asian countries in 1955 to New Delhi in 2023, India has come a long way in gaining international status and acceptance by other leading powers, especially Washington, which had looked at India's earlier activism in organizing the Global South, particularly through NAM, with much suspicion and outright hostility.

Diaspora

Indian governments, especially since the time of Prime Minister Manmohan Singh in 2008, have been attempting to use India's diaspora for status improvement and economic investments, technology linkups, and above all as a source of soft-power dissemination. In 2020, India had the largest diaspora in the world, with some 18 million people spread around various countries, with the largest concentration in the United Arab Emirates, the United States, and Saudi Arabia.[64] Some 20–30 percent of graduates from India's prestigious IITs and engineering colleges end up overseas for work or higher studies, especially in the United States and other Western countries.[65] In the United States, as of October 2018, some 309,986 H-1B visa holders or three-fourths of the total 419,637, were from India, although this number has come down in subsequent years due to the pandemic and the Trump-era immigration restrictions.[66]

Indian immigrants and the second-generation expatriates have emerged as powerful economic and social groups in many host countries, as they hold wealth, technological skills, and political clout, especially in the United States, the United Kingdom, and Canada. In the United States, in 2020, the wealthiest ethnic group was the 4 million-strong Indian-origin population, with some US$123,700 per capita income, which is double the national average.[67] The Indian diaspora has increasingly been playing a significant role in the national politics of many Western countries, as shown by the election of Kamala Harris as U.S. vice president and several ministers and members of Parliament in countries such as Canada, the United Kingdom, Ireland, and New Zealand. In October 2022, Indian-origin Rishi Sunak became the first person of color to become the prime minister of Britain, although his routes are from the African Indian expatriate community. In 2022, several multinational corporations, including PepsiCo, Google, Twitter, Microsoft, FedEx, Chanel, Barclays, GAP, and Starbucks, were headed by Indian expatriates in 2022.[68]

In 2022, India became the country with the largest number of outbound international students, despite the pandemic and travel restrictions, and this number is expected to reach 1.8 million by 2024.[69] Despite earlier skepticism of the value of the diaspora, today Indian expatriates have emerged as a key factor behind India's emergence as a "knowledge power." Expatriates have also helped disseminate India's culture, values, and other soft-power assets in the global arena. Much of the Indian arts, music, and dances are kept alive in these diaspora communities, which also include sizable populations in many Caribbean states—the descendants of indentured laborers that the British colonial rulers brought in the nineteenth century to work in the plantations. Second- and third-generation Indians in migrant countries such as the United States, the United Kingdom, Australia, and Canada increasingly are yearning for knowledge of their roots.[70] In order to utilize the diaspora more effectively, in 2003, India started new policies under the *pravasi* (nonresident Indian) banner, including the formation of a ministry in the central government and declaring a day annually in honor of *pravasi*s. Yet, unlike China, India is yet to design a program like the "Thousand Talents Plan," which attracts hundreds of recent PhDs from Western universities to return to China by offering them internationally competitive salaries and startup research funds, which in turn boosts China's productivity and talent utilization.[71] Despite all its successes, the Indian diaspora also contains some ardent supporters of Hindutva and illiberal ideas, although they benefit immensely from the liberal order, especially in Western democratic countries where they have settled.

While there is much to be praised in India's soft-power attributes, how useful has it been in changing world perceptions of India in terms of its status? Rohan Mukherjee suggests that it has not been very effective, despite projections to the contrary by some scholars and politicians, as "significant sections of public opinion in the West and in Asia are still not favorable toward India. Moreover, one is hard pressed to identify a significant role played by soft power in India's diplomatic gains since the early 1990s."[72] To another scholar, "India still seems to follow a defensive soft power approach and is reluctant to transform her capacities into capabilities to increase the country's international clout."[73] However, a form of reverse causality maybe working here, as members of the Indian diaspora gain more status in their chosen societies, they are helping to boost India's international status as well.

Conclusions

The discussion so far has shown that India has many soft-power assets for status advancement in the contemporary world, and yet some are not utilized effectively, or are constrained by countervailing factors. Since the 1990s, India's soft-power assets have become recognized globally more than ever before. The two major reasons for this are India's rapid economic growth and the globalization of information through social media with the arrival of new information technologies. Knowledge, especially scientific knowledge, has both hard- and soft-power values. The biggest ambassadors of America's soft power have been the millions of foreign students who have studied in the United States since the 1940s and who carry American ideals of freedom and entrepreneurship back to their home countries and to the global arena. India has a number of teaching institutions, some of high quality, though others seem to lag behind. Status advancement would require more human interactions and cooperation between local and foreign academic and cultural institutions. Soft power for status enhancement is a delicate process, and there is an intimate relationship between hard-power markers and the appreciation of soft-power assets for status enhancement. One without the other need not produce durable status, and both are required for legitimizing one's global status ranking. It should also be noted that a country playing with too much soft-power promotion can attract hostility, as others may feel threatened. China's aggressive promotion of soft power through its Confucian institutes has been criticized by others, especially in the West, as propaganda institutes, and some of them have been forced to close down.

Hence soft-power assets for status enhancement can be a double-edged sword. While aggressive soft-power promotion might help mobilize the diaspora, it may promote negative outcomes for status enhancement, as receiver countries and populations could view them with suspicion. India's soft-power efforts and attribution for status enhancement have been a complicated process, largely due to the mutually reinforcing roles of hard and soft power, as weaknesses in the former have affected the latter. Ultimately, this has limited India's ability to accrue higher status in the international arena.

5

The Great Powers

In January 2020, I met former Prime Minister Manmohan Singh at his residence in New Delhi for an informal discussion. Singh was the primary architect, along with President George W. Bush, of the 2005 U.S.-India Nuclear Accord. I asked him what the key motives behind the deal were, and he answered that the main aim was to remove India from the "nuclear apartheid" to which it had been subjected for over four decades by the nuclear powers, especially the United States. The implication was that the material benefits from the deal (i.e., acquisition of nuclear power plants from the United States and other supplier states) was secondary, but the accommodation of India as a de facto nuclear power was the prime objective, showing its status value in both symbolic and substantive dimensions.

As rising powers wish to be accepted as coequals, or to surpass the established powers, it is incumbent upon the latter to accept the new state into their fold, so that peaceful power transitions are made possible. Like other social-status settings, peer group acceptance is pivotal to status acquisition by a new power. In the past, in the majority of cases of status contestation, great power war was the outcome, as the established powers refused to accept newcomers with material capabilities and status ambitions into their fold, generating much resentment and eventually violence. As Graham Allison states, 12 out of the 16 power transitions during the past 500 years have occurred through wars.[1] Although some cases, like the U.K.-U.S. transition in the late nineteenth and early twentieth centuries, stand out as examples of peaceful status accommodation, war has been the lingua franca of great power accommodation or decline. As John Vasquez puts it: "The price of world power is death."[2] New power configurations were often recognized as a result of wars and were accomplished in the immediate postwar settlement when new institutions were created in which the winners were given a leading role. The states whom the winners did not want to be included were denied their privileged position. The 1815 Vienna, 1919 Versailles, 1945 Yalta/Potsdam/San Francisco settlements, following the Napoleonic Wars, World War I, and World War II, respectively, often neglected the claims of the defeated, except in the first case, where vanquished France restored its status as a European great power through deft diplomacy. As the defeated powers of the last major war, Japan and Germany, for instance, were denied status as great powers by the victorious Allied powers in 1945. Although it started off as an inclusionary model, the U.S.-led post–World War II order soon became exclusionary vis-à-vis the Soviet bloc, and vice versa, which both were viewed as constituting a major mutual existential threat.[3]

There were two pivotal moments when India missed the boat when status hierarchy was institutionalized in the post–World War II international system. The first was in 1945 and the second in 1968, when established powers refused to accept India as a member of their core grouping. In the first instance, India was a British colony in 1945 when the great powers institutionalized the international order and the power hierarchy in international institutions. As recounted by leading Indian scholar M.S. Rajan, in April 1945, at a British commonwealth conference, an Indian spokesman staked a claim for India gaining a permanent seat on the Security Council, as opposed to China, for its "great contribution to the War effort in the Second World War." Subsequently, at the UN formation conference in San Francisco, Canada, Yugoslavia, and Australia "did openly raise the question of India being made a permanent member of the Security Council but nothing came out of it (perhaps because . . . India was yet to become . . . an independent country)."[4] It is still a puzzle as to why the Congress Party did not press for active participation and permanent membership in the Security Council at this conference, considering the immense contributions Indian soldiers had made in the war effort. Likely they were deflected by the intense freedom struggle they were engaged in and the British antipathy toward India in the wake of the Quit India Movement, launched by Mohandas Gandhi in 1942, right in the middle of World War II.

In 1968, the unequal Nuclear Non-Proliferation Treaty (NPT) was adopted in which only the countries which had tested nuclear arms by January 1, 1967, were given the right to maintain their weapons, and all others, including India, were classified as non-nuclear-weapon states. India emerged as the most powerful critic of the NPT and the associated non-proliferation regime because of the institutionalization of status discrepancy. However, partial status accommodation was accomplished in 2005 when the United States recognized India as a de facto non-NPT nuclear weapon state with some institutional privileges, which most other great powers subsequently accepted.

There are multiple reasons for varied responses of each of the present-day great powers toward India's status accommodation. This chapter addresses the policies of the United States, China, Russia, France, and the United Kingdom toward India's rise, in addition to brief references to the changing policies of Japan and Germany, the two countries that are global economic powers, whom India increasingly looks up to for both strategic and economic partnerships. What is noticeable is India's acceptance by almost all leading powers as a candidate great power and the recognition of such a role through their statements, increased diplomatic engagements, and visits by leaders, as well as accordance of membership in most international organizations. India's foreign policy elite also seem to see much wider opportunities offered by the changing power equation.[5]

The United States: Partial Accommodation

Analysts have coined the term "estranged democracies" to describe U.S.-India relations throughout the Cold War.[6] The status dimension in this relationship is rarely analyzed as a cause of this discord. The differing status ascriptions assigned to Washington and New Delhi need to be explored to understand the roots of this estrangement. The schism between the world's two largest democracies was not purely based on divergent strategic interests, but also on the socio-psychological reason arising from the status aspirations of a new state with major power potential to maintain its strategic autonomy and the determination of the most powerful state to resist those efforts as long as it could. During the early stages of the Cold War, Washington not only could not develop a strong strategic relationship with India, but also engaged in policies that depreciated India's status vis-à-vis the regional adversaries, Pakistan and China, especially between 1972 and 2005. This policy posture was largely the result of India's unwillingness to join the Cold War alliance against the Soviet Union and its allies. The non-alignment policy of Nehru was derided by the former U.S. secretary of State John Foster Dulles, who termed it an "immoral and short-sighted conception."[7] While a significant segment of liberal America viewed India as a beacon of hope for democracy among developing countries, even this group began to sense estrangement as India opposed many liberal causes, be it nuclear non-proliferation, international human rights, and more importantly, Cold War conflict with the Soviet bloc. In addition, the violations of democratic rights by the Indira

Gandhi government in the 1970s and, prior to that, restrictions on foreign scholars visiting and conducting research in India also generated much consternation in the West. India's tilting toward the Soviet Union for balance of power considerations to challenge the U.S.-China-Pakistan trilateral alliance was another major cause of this estrangement.

The socio-psychological roots of this status discord need to be further explored. One of India's perennial complaints against the United States has been the deliberate or inadvertent "status deprivation" and "status slights" that India has experienced at the hands of Washington, especially vis-à-vis Pakistan. From Washington's perspective, this was nothing but part of its strategic priorities and policies in the region and globally, in which India did not figure as importantly as others, especially India's chief rivals Pakistan and China, in particular during the Cold War era. The status insensitivity of the U.S. elite could largely be because India was not very materially consequential for American strategic or economic interests to consistently pay attention to Indian concerns. During the 1950s, a number of U.S. elite viewed India as a "basket case" and yet taking "independent positions," and that India "needed to be put in place."[8] As Selig Harrison states:

> Many Indians have what might be called a "post-dated self-image." They are confident that India is on the way to great power status and want others to treat them as if they had in fact arrived. By the same token, to many Americans, India's ambitions are pretentious nonsense, given its widespread poverty, and New Delhi should be prepared to deal with the United States on the basis of the actual power relationship now existing between the two countries.[9]

The end of the Cold War and India's economic liberalization changed the equation to some extent, only to be challenged by India's nuclear tests in 1998. However, the big thaw came in the early 2000s, when the United States made a series of efforts to develop a rapprochement with India, once again driven by its larger strategic and economic interests vis-à-vis rising China. Financial markets began to recognize India as an "emerging market economy" and an influential Goldman Sachs report in 2003 elevated the Brazil, Russia, India, and China as powerful economies of the future.[10] Substantial improvements in India's aggregate economic capabilities, as well as its possible part in balancing China's power, played a significant role in this reorientation and even the elevation of India's status in the U.S. hierarchy of relationships. During the late 1990s, India emerged as an aid giver and food exporter, shedding its aid-recipient role that was a feature of much of the Cold War.

The U.S.-India Ties during the Nehru Era

Washington made initial overtures to India, seeking support for Western efforts at challenging the Communist bloc. India, however, rejected the idea, wanting to create an independent foreign policy path.[11] This was reflected in the 1955 Bandung conference of Asian-African states, which Nehru took a lead role in organizing, and subsequently the Non-Aligned Movement (NAM), which became active in the 1960s. In Nehru's calculations, the U.S. hegemony was a continuation of the colonial and imperial order from the European colonial powers, and the superpower rivalry would lead to a third world war in which countries like India would suffer the most. He was against an international order supported by balance of power or great power condominium (i.e., sharing of power by a small group of states, excluding all others). The U.S. elite could not fathom an alternate world order that India was propounding as they were "convinced that their nation's strategic and material interests happily coincided with the universal aspirations of the human race for peace, prosperity and freedom."[12] The divergent historical experiences of the two states are part of the challenge here. As Strobe Talbott correctly points out, the American hegemony was viewed by many Indians as a continuation of the British Empire.[13] There were also status considerations that permeated Nehru's thinking. By accepting the role of a secondary ally, India would forever forfeit its status aspirations and would simply be treated as an appendage of the United States.[14] Even if it meant forgoing considerable material advantages that such a relationship would have brought to India, the concerns of autonomy and status won the day in India's calculations.

Pakistan jumped to the occasion and began to befriend the United States by offering military base facilities and political support. The intent of Pakistani leaders—Ayub Khan in particular—was to gain U.S. support for its conflict with India over Kashmir and to obtain weapons and economic support. The 1954 U.S.-Pakistan Mutual Defense Assistance Agreement was a significant event, as it allowed Pakistan a considerable amount of qualitatively superior weapon systems, such as M-47/48 Patton tanks, F-104A Starfighter and F-86 Sabre aircraft, and Sidewinder air-to-air missiles.[15] It also elevated Pakistan's status in the eyes of the United States and its Western allies, who provided considerable economic and military support. India also received major aid from Western countries, as the fear existed in the United States and the West of India failing as a nation-state and falling into the Communist orbit. The fact that India was receiving considerable foreign aid, including food supplies from the United States (under the program called PL-480), its allies, and U.S.-led multilateral funding agencies such as the Paris Club, did not help elevate India's status in the perceptions of U.S. decision-makers. India's criticism of American policies in Korea and later Vietnam also caused further rift.

During the 1962 war with China, which nearly saw India's military collapse, Washington, under President John F. Kennedy, rushed in much-needed military aid toward the end of the war and was even requested to join in the air war and supply fighter-bombers to India. As China pulled back, there were fears of the war repeating, and India–U.S. military relations began to strengthen, including the use of Indian bases for the Central Intelligence Agency's U2-spy aircraft for conducting clandestine operations in Tibet.[16] The subsequent lessening of tensions with China and Nehru's determination to continue the autonomous path pulled him away from forming a military alliance with the United States. If the Chinese had not withdrawn from Indian territories and had continued their military challenge, U.S.-India relations would have strengthened considerably. Surprisingly, during this period a status elevation move took place from the United States. The UN Security Council seat assigned to China was held by Taiwan, and the United States offered India that post. Nehru rejected this overture, concerned that an ostracized China would become a huge threat to international order in the nuclear age, and he proposed that the People's Republic of China be given the UN Security Council veto-holding seat.[17] This willingness on the part of India to recognize China's status did not produce any kudos from Beijing. China derided Nehru as a "lackey of U.S. imperialism" and a "pawn in the international anti-China campaign."[18] It was possible that Nehru was upset over the efforts by the United States and the United Kingdom to gain concessions from India on Kashmir in return for the UN seat. That Washington was using India's defeat in 1962 as a strategic opportunity to elicit concessions from it toward Pakistan might have been one of the reasons for Nehru's decision not to foster a better relationship with the United States. What is also noticeable in the Western effort was to equate the two South Asian foes and to create artificial strategic parity between the two. This would elevate the Pakistani elite's conceptions of their own status and power and determination to use military force to wrest Kashmir from India, as they did in 1965. Subsequently, India also bitterly complained that the U.S. weapons supply was a major reason for Pakistan to launch the 1965 "Operation Gibraltar" to seize Kashmir from India, as it sensed a window of opportunity.[19]

The U.S.-India relations deteriorated from the mid-1960s until the late 1990s due to a variety of structural and personality-related reasons. The 1965 India-Pakistan War further saw the United States treating India and Pakistan as coequals, as it imposed sanctions on both countries. The crucial differences arose over the NPT and the U.S. war in Vietnam. In 1965, President Lyndon Johnson's Gilpatric Committee Report recommended that the United States make every effort to bar the spread of nuclear weapons, arguing that "as additional nations obtained nuclear weapons, our diplomatic and military influence would wane," and "they would eventually constitute direct military threats to the United States."[20] Johnson made efforts at restraining India, especially blunting its critical position on U.S. bombings of Vietnam, through the policy of "short tether" treatment of personally releasing food supplies under the PL-480 program at the last minute.[21] This made the Indian leaders very bitter toward the United States, and the launching of the "Green Revolution" under Indira Gandhi was primarily driven by a need to obtain self-sufficiency and not remain dependent on the United States for food supplies.[22] Status humiliation played a significant role in Prime Minister Gandhi's determination to end food dependency by adopting new agricultural techniques, such as production and distribution of high-quality seeds, fertilizers, and other measures, making India self-sufficient in food production by the late 1960s. Moreover, the U.S. rapprochement toward China, beginning in 1969, would dramatically upset the balance of power relations in the subcontinent, forcing India to tilt toward the Soviet Union.

Victory in the 1971 War and Short-Term Status Elevation

The 1971 Bangladesh War saw the strategic interests of the United States and India diverge in a substantial manner. The United States, under President Richard Nixon and his national security advisor Henry Kissinger, took a clear tilt in Pakistan's favor during and prior to the war. The United States had elevated Pakistan as a closer strategic ally in view of its pivotal role against the Soviet Union and also its help in linking the United States with Communist China. Nixon and Kissinger developed a strong personal antipathy toward Prime Minister Indira Gandhi, and their communications (now available) show the contempt they exhibited toward the Indian leader during her unsuccessful visit in November 1971 to the White House before the Bangladesh War.[23] The influx of some 10 million refugees to India in response to the brutal crackdown of the East Pakistani nationalist movement and the pleading of India for international intervention fell on deaf ears. The daily telegrams from U.S. diplomats in Dhaka painted an extremely dismal picture of the brutality of the Pakistani army, yet President Richard Nixon and National Security Advisor Henry Kissinger rejected them, all under the guise of strategic necessity.[24] Nixon in particular had a strong antipathy toward India and Prime Minister Gandhi, whom he referred to as a "bitch" and an "old witch," while Kissinger condescendingly commented, "The Indians are bastards anyway."[25]

Washington took a strong position against India to the extent of sending an aircraft carrier, the *USS Enterprise*, to the Bay of Bengal in December 1971 in a threatening posture during the closing days of the war, ostensibly to prevent an Indian offensive on West Pakistan. Indira Gandhi had decided to declare a ceasefire after the liberation of Bangladesh, and the Shimla agreement in 1972 saw India returning some 90,000 Pakistani prisoners of war. There was a brief period of India's preeminence as the strategic power in South Asia, but this was short-lived. In fact, the United States was attempting to prevent Pakistan's total collapse and at the same time make sure that India's position did not become overwhelmingly superior, as it was perceived as a regional challenger to the United States' wider global interests, in particular the emerging rapprochement with China, which was viewed as a potential balancer against the Soviet Union.

The U.S.-China Rapprochement and India's Status Challenge

Perhaps the most significant status challenge to India came from the U.S. accommodation with China, through which U.S. relations with two of India's key enemies, China and Pakistan, were elevated simultaneously. The rapprochement was led by Nixon and Kissinger, who viewed China as a pivotal balancer to prevail over the Soviet Union, in view of the ongoing chasm between Moscow and Beijing. Both considered Pakistan's military ruler Yahya Khan as the best conduit to link up with China secretly. In fact, Kissinger's first secret trip to China and meeting with Premier Chou Enlai took place via

Pakistan in July 1971, where he discussed Nixon's upcoming visit in February 1972.[26] The rapprochement also opened up the U.S. market to Chinese products, and the subsequent Chinese economic liberalization and modernization undertaken by Deng Xiaoping substantially elevated China's status position in the world, especially in terms of the United States and its Western allies. India's reluctance to liberalize its economy and its continued economic weaknesses further lowered its status in the perceptions of the United States as well as its Western allies. India's ongoing strategic alliance with the Soviet Union was part of the cause of this perception. In Washington, the notion of "either you are with us or you are against us" often dominated the thinking.

As China-U.S. relations began to improve, Deng's reforms and export push to the United States made China's rapid economic progress possible. During the 1970s and 1980s, India also suffered status deprivations from the United States, partly due to New Delhi's opposition to the non-proliferation regime, as was starkly evident in the 1974 tests, its positions on the Soviet Union, including its occupation of Afghanistan, as well as the United States' adoption of Islamabad and the Taliban as its favorite partners in the struggle against the Soviets in Afghanistan. This situation offered a major opportunity for Zia ul Haque's military regime to build nuclear weapons clandestinely with the United States closing its eyes.[27] Subsequently, Pakistan supported the insurgency in Kashmir, including the training and dispatching of militants, affecting India's security and status quest.

U.S.-India Rapprochement after the End of the Cold War

The end of the Cold War, a major systemic change, altered Washington's relations with India. The Cold War came to an end in 1991, preceded by the fall of the Berlin wall and the collapse of the Soviet empire. India lost its chief security and economic benefactor as the Soviet Union began to unravel and to lose much of its economic and security capabilities, thus drastically reducing its support for countries like India. In July 1991, reeling under an intense foreign exchange crisis, India, under Prime Minister Narasimha Rao and his Finance Minister Manmohan Singh, ushered in a major reform program and liberalization of its closed economic system. This encouraged many U.S. multinational companies to look to India as a major investment opportunity. India's advantages in telecommunications and the internet encouraged American companies to recruit technical workers from India, and this was accelerated during the Y2K phase of the new millennium in 2000. However, the United States still attempted to contain India's nuclear and space programs and ambitions. The 1996 negotiations over the Comprehensive Test Ban Treaty (CTBT) also saw strident opposition from India.[28] In 1995, the NPT was extended in perpetuity, reinforcing the freezing of the unequal nuclear order. As Strobe Talbott points out, for Indians "the NPT embodied 'the three D's' of US nuclear policy—dominance, discrimination, and double standards."[29] India, although not a signatory to the NPT, saw this as an ominous sign of the perpetuation of an unequal regime, forever closing its entry into the great power club. The established nuclear powers and their allies indeed wanted to freeze the nuclear order and to keep all nuclear have-nots, including India, in the lower-status group.

In May 1998, the newly elected BJP government, led by Atal Behari Vajpayee, tested five nuclear devices in Pokhran in the Rajasthan desert, openly defying the non-proliferation regime and the great power club itself. The P-5 was furious at this status challenge from India, and they imposed major economic sanctions. The sanctions would not last more than two years, as the United States initiated a new serious diplomatic discourse with India with the Jaswant Singh–Strobe Talbott strategic dialogue.[30] During this interaction, Singh questioned the hyphenation of India and Pakistan. In his view, Pakistan was a "relatively small, incurably troubled, and incorrigibly troublesome country that dreamed of a parity with India it would never attain or deserve. China was a power and a threat worthy of India's strategic attention, not Pakistan."[31] He further asked: "Why do you Americans keep hyphenating us with Pakistan?" and asserted, "these linkages are unwarranted—they are deeply resented in my country. . . India-Pakistan is a false equation."[32] Bill Clinton's visit in March 2000, less than a year before the end of his term in office, was a major success in thawing the relations. The most significant status elevation was Clinton siding with India in July 1999 and forcing Pakistan to withdraw its army from their occupation of Kargil Hills.[33] His subsequent visit to India for five days and to Islamabad for five hours[34] helped to remove the status parity treatment toward India and Pakistan, and the United States continued its favorable treatment toward India, somewhat differentiating the two, especially on nuclear issues.

The arrival of the George W. Bush administration in 2000 saw a major fillip to U.S.-India relations. Bush and his Secretary of State Condoleezza Rice had high opinions of India, and both viewed India as a balancing force against China. However, the September 2001 terrorist attacks put a dent in

U.S. relations with India, as the United States now needed Pakistan's support for waging the war in Afghanistan. Despite this strategic predicament, in 2005, the Bush administration signed the U.S.-India Nuclear Accord with the Manmohan Singh government, thereby accepting India as a de facto nuclear-weapon state. In Rice's words, the deal was not just about building nuclear reactors in India, but a move that "would unlock a wide range of possible areas of cooperation with a country that was an emerging power in the knowledge-based revolution in economic affairs."[35] This was a major status-altering event, as now India was treated in a separate class by itself, as none of the other new nuclear states had such a recognition. It also elevated India's status among the other great powers, as they now deemed India a worthy candidate for engaging both economically and strategically. It was able to enter many of the clubs the nuclear regime had created, except the Nuclear Suppliers Group (NSG). The Bush administration abandoned incremental policies to accommodate India, convinced that the nuclear issue continued to impede a U.S.-India rapprochement, and claimed that by "establishing enduring strategic ties with India, it needed to cut this 'Gordian knot.'"[36] As Ashley Tellis, an official with the U.S. ambassador in India, Robert Blackwell (who himself was a strong proponent of the nuclear deal), and one of the behind-the-scene architects of the agreement, contends, the opportunities for forging a "critical geopolitical relationship do not come often in a lifetime."[37] The accord prompted Indian analysts to claim that India was now "on the verge of becoming a great power. . . . And a swing state in the global balance of power."[38] A more confident India, along with Germany, Japan, and Brazil, pushed for inclusion as a UN Security Council permanent member. This was opposed by China and smaller states such as Pakistan. India was, however, successful in creating and joining some key institutions following the 2008–2009 financial crisis. Membership in the BRICS and its associated New Development Bank (NDB), Asian Infrastructure Investment Bank (AIIB), East Asia Summit, G-20, and the Shanghai Cooperation Organization (SCO), all came one by one, elevating India's institutional status ranking, along with a few other pivotal states.

As of 2023, U.S. accommodation of India has been steadily increasing. The Obama administration continued the friendly policies of the Bush administration after some initial trepidation. Yet the promised deals involving U.S. corporations to set up several nuclear power plants in India never materialized. Some positive developments took place in the military area, where the United States viewed India as playing a role in the Pivot to Asia strategy. Military-to-military contacts improved, and in 2017 the United States and India signed a naval agreement on refueling, a major step in a strategic partnership, considering that in the past India showed opposition to offering any military links of this nature. Signs of increased cooperation included the annual "2 plus 2" meeting of the Indian defense and external affairs ministers and their U.S. counterparts, the secretaries of defense and state; the 2016 designation of India as a "major defense partner," allowing it to buy many restricted U.S. weapons; the Logistics Exchange Memorandum of Agreement (LEMOA); the Communications, Compatibility and Security Agreement (COMCASA); the Industrial Security Agreement (ISA); and a series of military exercises involving the three services of the two countries.[39] The arrival of the Trump administration in 2016 presented some challenges for continued rapprochement with India, except in the military realm. Following a transactional approach toward allies and adversaries, the Trump administration imposed trade sanctions on India, although the amount in contention was small compared to what it placed on China.

Some key initiatives at cooperation, many symbolic in terms of institutional recognition, have taken place. The significant steps are the Quad, the annual *Malabar* military exercises involving the United States, Japan, India, and Australia, and the agreement on using satellite imagery constituted the categories of limited hard-balancing and soft-balancing efforts, as no concrete alliance has yet come into effect. Trade relations increased significantly, and in 2021, the United States became India's leading trading partner, replacing China. The total trade figure of $159.1 billion (with India's exports at $102.3 billion and U.S. exports at $56.8 billion) was a big increase from the previous year's figure, $120.6 billion. Similarly, in 2020, FDI from India to the United States stood at $12.7 billion, and U.S. FDI to India at $41.9 billion.[40] A limited free trade agreement has also been at the negotiation stage. During the Ladakh border confrontation in 2020 involving Chinese and Indian forces, U.S. Secretary of State Mike Pompeo made some statements supporting India. The Xi Jinping regime's aggressive moves in the South China Sea, Hong Kong, Taiwan, and Xinjiang rattled Beijing's relationship with the United States, and a new Cold War has emerged. In this context, India as a swing state has gained higher status in the view of the United States and other Western allies, but even that is restrained by India's domestic constraints and the lingering desire to maintain strategic autonomy. Ultimately, the main link that connects the United States and India is in the strategic realm, the result of the rise of China and its acts of revisionism in the Indo-Pacific.

The Biden administration has continued the status recognition and has widened military and economic relationships, even though in private the administration officials have expressed reservations concerning the Modi government's illiberal policies, especially toward minorities. In May 2022, Biden and Modi signed a joint initiative on critical and emerging technologies in an effort to meet the challenge from China in this regard.[41] The steady use of the terms "Indo-Pacific" by the United States instead of "Asia-Pacific" has been a symbolic recognition of India's importance for the security and order in the larger region.[42] The renaming of the Hawaii-based "Pacific Command" as "Indo-Pacific Command" and the recognition by regional states such as Australia, Japan, and most Southeast Asian nations of the term "Indo-Pacific" also give it an added significance, which it had historically possessed, especially in the pre-colonial and European colonial eras. It also signifies that "the Pacific and Indian Oceans are connecting through trade, infrastructure and diplomacy, now that the world's two most populous states, China and India are rising together."[43]

Yet, in U.S. intellectual and journalistic circles, especially liberal-oriented ones, India's soft power has not been improving. India's neutral position, which President Biden characterized as "shaky," on the Russian invasion of Ukraine in February 2022 generated much unease in the administration.[44] They have since tacitly acknowledged the Indian position and constraints, a short-term victory of sorts for India's diplomatic position. In June 2023, Biden received Modi at a state dinner at the White House, and Modi later gave an address to the U.S. Congress. Subsequently, in September, Biden was among the world leaders attending the G-20 meeting in Delhi, which raised India's profile and image. India's signing of a side deal on creating the *India–Middle East–Europe Economic Corridor*, along with Saudi Arabia, the United Arab Emirates, France, Germany, Italy, and the European Union, aims at building a cost-effective road, rail, and shipping network for smooth trade and investment among countries in the regions, was a concrete achievement.[45] This constitutes a significant effort to compete with China's Belt and Road Initiative (BRI), although it is unclear how effective it will be vis-à-vis BRI's $1 trillion already invested, with many more trillions to come.[46] Today, the United States clearly considers India as a key interlocutor in its efforts to counter China's influence in the Global South, a far cry from the Cold War days.

The United States' status recognition of India through symbolic acts and speeches by presidents and secretaries of state were all crucial for India's improved relations with Washington. In fact, it was the United States that dropped many irksome demands on India, such as signing the NPT, CTBT, and tolerating a series of "noes from India" on U.S. interventions, Kashmir, climate change, trade agreements, and so on. It seems it became apparent to the Americans that "India continues to place great stock in its international relations, especially those gestures that indicate India is being taken seriously as an interlocutor. The Americans have been particularly astute on this point, having learnt that staying quiet on sensitive issues may bring greater dividend than public denunciations of Indian actions."[47] As Washington keeps a low profile on India's domestic illiberal turn, the geopolitical importance of New Delhi may shield the BJP government as it pursues anti-minority and illiberal policies. It was under the U.S. geopolitical shield that Zia ul Haq was able to turn Pakistan into a fully Islamic state and also was successful in pursuing nuclear weapons, as on both issues Washington closed its eyes due to the value Islamabad held for fighting the Soviets in Afghanistan. Yet another indicator of U.S. recognition of India as a higher-status state was the unwillingness to enforce many sanctions on India for buying Russian weapons or oil following the Ukrainian invasion in 2022. In earlier times, these would have led to automatic sanctions. But today, the tighter security relationship, especially through Quad, has emerged as a key part of the U.S. strategy in the Indo-Pacific, and it "would not survive the US sanctioning one of its members."[48]

While there is substantial improvement in India's status elevation by the United States, the opposite is the case with China, the key Asian great power which has emerged as India's key status challenger in the contemporary international order.

China: India's Primary Status Challenger

In 1973, in a conversation that has now been revealed, Henry Kissinger and Mao Tse-tung expressed their disdain for India and its civilizational claims. Kissinger stated: "There is a sentimental love affair between Western intellectuals and India based on a complete misreading of the Indian philosophy of life. Indian philosophy was never meant to have a practical application." Concurring with this assessment, Mao responded: "It's just a bunch of empty words."[49] Mao's understanding seems to be the commonly shared view of Chinese elite and many intellectuals, accentuated by their frustrations of India not accepting their geopolitical viewpoints. What Mao and Kissinger did not understand was that the Indian philosophy and culture they derided (Buddhism and strands of Hinduism), language (Sanskrit), and art forms (many based on the epic *Ramayana*), had a powerful impact on much of Southeast Asia and even China and Japan, with local adaptations. Although both are right that the Indian ethos seems more spiritualistic than practical, what they were questioning was India's geopolitical moves in East Pakistan and gaining closeness to the Soviet Union; both are great examples of practical realpolitik moves by the Indira Gandhi government for reasons of security and status. This episode also showed the status ascription that the Chinese and U.S. leaders had for India and the subaltern notions of the latter they carried with them.

The status conflict between China and India is partially driven by the beliefs of each state's elite about their relative material and civilizational strength, as well as their actual power position within the region. As Xiayou Pu contends: "While China often seeks to engage India as a regional South Asian country, India wants to engage China as an equal rising global power."[50] The status discrepancy is also a reflection of the differing conceptions of international and regional order they hold. China carries a modern-day Tianxia (tributary) model, a hierarchical notion of power relationship in which Beijing leads the order. Indian views range from Gandhian to Nehruvian to Hindutva, but all assume that India will remain an independent center of power in a multi-polar world order.[51] As one scholar puts it:

> The story of China and India is that of two post-colonial and imperial polities seeking to deepen their rule over Himalayan regions where they encounter people starkly different from their "core" citizenry. . . . On the one hand, India and China see themselves as victims of imperialism; on the other, they resort to claims and governance methods inherited from it.[52]

There is little chance of India acquiescing to the Chinese hegemony or accepting a new form of hierarchy, which is evident in its rejection of BRI in 2017 and the Regional Comprehensive Economic Partnership (RCEP) in 2019, which India feared would entrench China's economic and geopolitical dominance.

The People's Republic of China has emerged as the biggest status challenger for India globally since the 1960s, and in South Asia at large and the Indian Ocean area since 2014. The latter occurred partly as a result of China's increasing global ambitions and the developmental plans under BRI, as well as the massive leap China has made in developing cutting-edge technologies such as artificial intelligence (AI), cyber, internet, and 5G. Often India's status markers are judged relative to China by the larger world. When the two states were established in the late 1940s, they had several areas of equal comparative rankings—economy, population, and the level of development. Until the last decade of the 1900s, their GDPs were very close to each other; in 1990 it was $360 billion (China) and $320 billion (India), and the per capita incomes of India for the same year was $360 and of China $318, giving the former a slight advantage.[53] For that reason, Nehru thought and acted as if they were status equivalents and often portrayed India as a supporter of China in world forums, given the extreme hostility it faced from the Western countries. In the Korean War, China relayed some information to the United States through Indian ambassador K.M. Panikkar. At the Bandung Conference of Afro-Asian states in 1955, Nehru took the initiative to extend an invitation to Chou Enlai to attend it and break Peking's diplomatic isolation, but it proved to be a mistake for India's status aspirations, as other leaders of newly emerging states were eager to interact with Chou, stealing some of Nehru's thunder at the meeting. Some scholars attribute the event as the beginning of the rivalry between the two states.[54] Even though India acknowledged China's takeover of Tibet in 1950, the accordance of refugee status to the Dalai Lama in India was resented by Beijing and was viewed as a challenge to China's rise as a unified, powerful state under Communist rule.

After a short period of friendly relations, marked by the *panschila*, or five principles of peaceful coexistence, "Hindi-Chini Bahai Bhai" policies, the conflictual interests in the border and Tibetan issues began to enter the relations in a powerful way. Status challenge was a crucial calculation of China in launching war in 1962 to humiliate Nehru, who was emerging as a key leader of the developing world.[55] Despite the early efforts at friendship by Nehru and Chou, they held differing notions of each other's status in the world order. The divergent status conceptions predate the occasional bonhomie between Chinese and Indian nationalist leaders. As Rudolf Wagner argues: "For Chinese reformers prior to 1939, India became the model of a polity that had failed to secure its integrity and independence to the point that the Buddhist teachings originating in India were held responsible for weaknesses in China's modernization drive and effort to fight the Japanese occupation."[56] India's efforts at a border settlement along the British-era lines while maintaining Tibet's autonomy within China was viewed as a continuation of imperialism by India and a challenge to China's status and power.[57]

As discussed before, the U.S.-China rapprochement in the 1970s dealt a major blow to India's status ambitions in both security and economic domains. China opened up its economy and through a concerted economic program managed to raise its GDP growth rate, living standards, and infrastructure development. India took another decade to liberalize and then too tepidly, and despite strong economic growth for two decades, India still lags behind China in many indicators. The material markers of status have widened, and China's relative success in inclusive growth and tangible improvements in infrastructure development and living standards are more evident than India's, as visitors to the two countries can easily recognize. This material difference seems to have inflated China's aspirations and its treatment of India as a non-equal in status terms. China's changing diplomatic relations with India show the status dimension in various manifestations. Until the 2010s, whenever China needed an ally in bargaining with the West, such as on climate change or trade talks, Beijing found India as a partner. This was most evident immediately after the 2008–2009 financial crisis and the creation of the BRICS mechanism. Status sharing, albeit on a limited level, was evident during this period. However, China's reluctance to accept and accommodate India's status as a rising power is evident in its opposition to India becoming a full-fledged permanent member of the UN Security Council and the NSG. The BRI was conceived as a Chinese-led grand strategic scheme, which India rejected partially for status reasons. The larger challenge is status related:

India's view of China is defined by hostility and fear while China's view of India is marked by hostility and condescension. This is in part a product of China's confidence in its destiny as a global power that requires itself to be benchmarked against other global powers such as the United States, rather than be tied down by a country it has long seen as a regional irritant punching above its weight.[58]

Today, as Kanti Bajpai argues, the persisting negative perceptions of each other, differing views on territorial perimeters, and their strategic partnership with other powers, as well as the widening asymmetry, have caused the rivalry to intensify.[59]

The rejection of China's preeminence in Asia by India has increased China's status assertion toward India. The "PRC views India as an emerging power, dissatisfied with its current international status," and thinks it "might seek to achieve its great power ambition at the expense of China's interests."[60] The Xi Jinping regime has an ambitious grand strategy to replace the United States as the global leading power, in particular in the Indo-Pacific. To Rush Doshi, this strategy involves blunting the hegemon's capabilities, and "secur[ing] the deference of other states through coercive threats, consensual inducements, or rightful legitimacy,"[61] all of which India firmly opposes. India's standing in its way is more than an irritant, as China fears that India aligning with the United States, Japan, and Australia could form a powerful coalition which not only could balance China's expansion, but also reduce its status ranking in the region. There are not many other compelling explanations for the sudden increase in border clashes and intrusions since 2017, largely perpetrated by the PLA. Until Xi's active phase of self-assertion, China was considering India as a co-power to challenge the Western order. India working with BRICS served the Chinese interests, but New Delhi rejecting BRI and RCEP showed that the China-led order may not be acceptable to India. Limited incursions on the border could show that China is in charge and that it can dictate the relations in the years to come.

During the 2017 Doklam border crisis, Chinese media and spokesmen constantly reminded India of not learning lessons from the 1962 war, and that if challenged, India would face the same fate. Indian spokesmen replied that the status balance had changed between the two countries and that India would resist.[62] During the Ladakh crisis of 2020, these conversations on expectations were repeated. During this crisis, which saw some 20 Indian and an undisclosed number of Chinese soldiers killed, the Chinese media once again proclaimed the status discrepancy. Many articles warned of teaching India a lesson once again and advised it not to forget past defeats. India's cancellation of some 54 Chinese apps, including the popular Tik Tok; banning of Huawei and the 5G spectrum; and prohibiting Chinese investors from taking undue advantage of Indian companies and stock ownership, all were aimed as status challenge by New Delhi.[63]

The increasing frequency with which China now challenges India on the Line of Actual Control (LAC), separating the two countries' positions, and the quick buildup of roads and other infrastructure show that China considers the India border a key theater to challenge its Asian neighbor. However, surprisingly, India appears very minimally in China's national security documents or defense white papers.[64] The main focus is on the United States, showing that the Chinese elite, at least outwardly, do not view India as their status challenger or equivalent. The *Global Times* articles often show disdain and contempt for India and its status pretensions.[65] The relative material weaknesses of India are part of the reason for this derision, but the buried fear appears to be that India, in alliance with the United States and Japan, could pose disruption to China's march toward global status and its replacement of America as the lead power. The possibility of a U.S.-India alliance or the Quad becoming a military alliance, and not a mere soft balancing coalition as it was in 2020, concerns Chinese strategists, and Beijing's efforts have been to prevent this outcome. In any event, status sharing with India appears to have disappeared from China's strategic calculations under Xi, unlike his predecessors.

The status challenge from China was accentuated by the 2020 coronavirus (Covid-19) crisis which emanated from Wuhan, China. Initially, India had very few cases, but this changed dramatically by the late summer of 2020, when several Indian states emerged as hotspots and the number of cases spiked. The effect on the Indian economy was devastating, with the GDP taking a major beating, placing India's growth in negative territory. Initially, the Chinese economy appeared to have weathered the crisis better, enlarging the distance between the two large economies in terms of GDP and per capita income, but Chinese growth stalled in 2022 as a result of restrictive policies in major cities such as Shanghai. As the Chinese economy is projected to return, even at a lower level of growth, the differences between China and India in material capabilities will not easily be bridged in the medium term. China also has an ambitious leader and a grand strategy to replace the United States as the hegemonic power. China's aim is to create a new globalization (globalization 2), led by China with its state capitalism and vast networks of state-run corporations managing world trade and achieving technological superiority. In this status contestation, it also aims to show the weaknesses of the democratic models of the West and India in providing public goods and achieving rapid economic growth.[66] Added to this mix is the technological superiority of China in diverse areas such as "cyberspace, hypersonic weapons, antisatellite systems, drones, robotics, artificial intelligence, advance computing, and more—that within a decade or two, it may be able to win a war with the United States."[67] In the diplomatic realm, the increasing chill in relations was evident when Chinese President Xi Jinping decided not to attend the G-20 meeting in New Delhi in September 2023.[68] Instead, China was represented by Premier Li Qiang, which had all the markings of a status competition, as if Xi did not want to be present at an event which elevated India's and Modi's global standing.

The challenge is not just official relegation of India by China, but by a considerable number of Sinologists globally. A small but significant element of the status challenge is the large-scale ignorance or avoidance of India by China scholars in their accounts of India. As a reviewer of many academic manuscripts on international relations over the years, I notice that there is a near reluctance to give India any status equivalency in treatments by Sinologists. This is not just among native Chinese scholars, but by Western scholars who teach and research Chinese foreign policy or Sino-U.S. relations. Only in the context of rising powers, and projections of India's economic prospects since 2009 or so, did the mention of India along with other BRICS countries increase. There has also been a lack of appreciation for India's border claims vis-à-vis China among many Sinologists. For the outbreak of the 1962 War most blame India, especially Nehru's forward policy.[69] Similarly, during the Cold War era, India's non-alignment policy and visa restrictions on Western scholars widened the gap in terms of Sinologists' interest and understanding of India. Even with restrictions, once they traveled to India, it was like an open book: poverty and underdevelopment were visible everywhere. Malnourished and ill-clad Indians revealed more poverty than their Chinese counterparts, even though deep poverty existed in many parts of China. China's rapprochement with the United States radically changed the perceptions of Western scholars, as they tend to take cues from geopolitical alignments in their interests in a country or its subject of study. China's rapid progress compared to India's further accentuated this tendency. Barring some specialists in Indian history, there appears to be a different kind of orientalism among Sinologists when it comes to India, and an unwillingness to recognize the second-largest civilizational state that has produced what Asia is today.

The historical connections between the two countries and the role that Indian religious philosophy (which Mao despised in his conversations with Kissinger) has played are easily ignored by contemporary Sinologists. The Communist penchant to sideline the largely religion-based Indian civilization could be a reason for this. But in exhibiting the Buddha's influence in the Chinese civilizational world, the impression one is given is that China reinvented it, and that Indian civilization had little to do with the religion in its spread to other parts of East and Southeast Asia. The Chinese desire to decide who the next Dalai Lama will be, the claim over Tibetan Buddhism's important location in the Indian-controlled Tawang, and the efforts China has been making to include Buddhist tourist centers as part of its soft-power campaign, all suggest an effort at appropriation of this powerful influence that China received from India for over a millennium. As Amartya Sen laments, the "intellectual links between China and India, stretching over much of the first millennium and beyond, were important in the history of the two countries. And yet they are hardly remembered today. What little notice they do get tends to come from those interested in religious history, particularly Buddhism."[70] The Buddhist university of Nalanda, located in India's Bihar state, has attracted many Chinese visitors, such as Yi Jing, who studied Buddhist philosophy as well as Ayurveda, the traditional medicines of India, and collected Sanskrit documents to take back to China. Many "Indian scholars went to China and worked there between the first century and the eleventh. They were engaged in a variety of work, which included translating Sanskrit documents into Chinese (mostly Buddhist writings), but also other activities, such as the pursuit of mathematics and science."[71] It is no wonder Chinese history textbooks rarely mention India; the Communist education system and the regime's hostility toward religion contributed to the disdain. Further, China's lingering ideas of the Middle Kingdom and the Tianxia tributary model do not give India a status role.

China's embrace of Pakistan for balance of power reasons, especially the assistance in nuclear and conventional weapons and more recently the China-Pakistan Economic Corridor (CPEC), was viewed in India as not simply an act of balancing in the military sense, but balancing for status, with the hope of keeping India as a regional power, along with Pakistan.[72] The Chinese low valuation of India is reflected in the smaller number of India experts in China versus a larger number of China experts in India.[73] A Chinese official captures a prevailing view that the root cause of India's poorer economic performance is its "'immature democracy' with too many parties representing particular regions of languages, competing on the basis of not government policies, but of communal interests."[74] In recent years, this attitude began to change to some extent, as India, in combination with the United States and other Quad partners, started mounting a major challenge to China's hegemonic ambitions in the region. Divergent status aspirations are a source of conflict between the two large Asian states. In the future, this is likely to widen; India sees little chance of a status accommodation from China, as it would reduce China's pursuit of a hegemonic position in Asia and the larger world. This is also a challenge to Modi's notion of status elevation through civilizational means, and recognition from all the great powers on this account is unlikely to happen. Material markers have a better chance in the Sino-Indian status contest in making a dent in China's perceptions of India's international status. As Ashley Tellis contends:

> India's sheer size and location make it difficult for Beijing to forget New Delhi altogether, in part because India's strong and continuing grievance about "status incongruity" in international politics—that is, the discrepancy between India's standing as a "great civilization" and its lack of status as a "great power"—could result in strategic surprises by India that redound to China's disadvantage.[75]

In the years to come, this rivalry has major potential for escalation from the regional to the global level and in that sense could have a significant impact on global order in the twenty-first century.[76]

Russia and India's Status Elevation

While the United States and China have shown opposition and ambivalence in ascribing India any significant status elevation, the Soviet Union during the Cold War treated India as the predominant power in South Asia. The material and diplomatic support at the United Nations by way of vetoing hostile resolutions allowed India to withstand pressures to end the war in Bangladesh before full victory in 1971. The diplomatic help was also essential to keep the United States away from militarily intervening on the side of Pakistan, despite sending in the Seventh Fleet to the Bay of Bengal. In view of the deteriorating security situation with Pakistan and the U.S.-China alignment with Islamabad's military regime, India, under Indira Gandhi, signed a Treaty of Friendship which saw Moscow offering substantial military and economic aid to India, as well as political support at the United Nations through its veto power. Thus in 1971, it was the Soviet Union that saved India from a UN Security Council censure, and it was Soviet weapons that gave it an edge over Pakistan in the Bangladesh liberation war. It was also the Soviet support that partially prevented U.S. military intervention against India, even before status considerations permeated this relationship. In April 1969, Soviet Premier Alexei Kosygin visited India in the background of a reported Soviet deal to sell arms to Pakistan when Prime Minister Gandhi told Kosygin, "Nothing should be done from which it could be inferred that the Soviet Union treated India at par with Pakistan . . . an equidistance between India and Pakistan tended to cause irritation in India."[77] After that, the Soviets heeded this advice. The changing policies of Leonid Brezhnev in terms of Russia's approach toward the developing world, and an expectation of the correlation of global forces turning in Moscow's favor, gave India higher status in Moscow's strategic approach.

An important dimension here is that the Soviets, for ideological reasons, sensed India's status significance in the developing world and elevated it to a higher pedestal than most Western countries ever did during the Cold War era. The visits of Indian leaders to Moscow were major events, with streets decorated with Indian flags as well as significant media coverage. India reciprocated, offering similar recognition to Soviet leaders during their visits. Even when the Soviets disagreed with India, there was less overt pressure to accept Soviet positions, although on many issues, including the mixed-economy model that India adopted and the urban housing, Moscow's influence was apparent. Further, Soviet and Indian positions converged on many areas, including decolonization and the new international economic order that the non-aligned countries championed. Russia also paid outward attention to nuclear arms control positions of the non-aligned countries, even when Moscow was building some of the most lethal nuclear weapons. The colonial powers being all Western, did help the Soviet standing among the non-aligned countries.

While the Soviet Union was willing to accord the "managerial position" that India sought in the South Asia region and to offer the most sophisticated weapons in their arsenal to New Delhi, the United States showed much reluctance to do either.[78] Moreover, it was Moscow that substantially helped India's heavy industry as well as weapons-manufacturing capabilities. Russia's support was pivotal for India winning the 1971 Bangladesh War.[79] For America, an ally is someone who obeys Washington's commands, and there is not much of a gray area. Whereas for Moscow, even if one was not a close partner, one could be treated respectably, for goals such as its position in the larger Global South. Reciprocity in equal measure was what India demanded from the Soviets, and it often got what it sought.

Stephen Cohen also contends that unlike the United States, the Soviets in negotiations gave the Indian officials a sense of equality and status. He cites an incident when an Indian defense official refused to negotiate with a lower-ranking U.S. official even though "the official was the decisionmaker responsible for the particular issue to be discussed. The Soviet Union had considerable success in negotiating with New Delhi, partly because it was willing to treat India as a 'major power,' whatever its private views [were]."[80] However, one event that affected India-Soviet relations to a great extent was the Soviet invasion of Afghanistan in 1979. This ill-conceived invasion by the Brezhnev regime negatively affected not only India's security, but also its status aspirations vis-à-vis Pakistan. The United States and many of its Western allies, as well as Islamic states, adopted Pakistan as the frontline state fighting the Soviets and provided substantial military and economic assistance to the military regime of Zia ul Haq. Pakistan, in turn, with the help of the United States, created the Mujahideen forces, which engaged in a brutal guerrilla warfare against occupying Soviet forces. More importantly, Pakistan under Zia ul Haq developed nuclear weapons during this period— all the while the United States closed its eyes and China supported Pakistan materially and politically. The 10-year-long war in Afghanistan brought considerable stress to India and a decline in its security and regional status. The advantage it had built over Pakistan in the 1971 war all but vanished. It took the end of the Soviet occupation and the collapse of the Soviet Union in early 1991 to allow India to re-emerge as a significant player, now free of this relationship and the economic model that it had partially adopted.

The successor state, Russia, maintained its strong weapons sale program to India, but beyond that, not much was happening in this relationship. The co-development of some cutting-edge weapons like Brahmos short-range supersonic cruise missiles and the sale to India of one of its aircraft carriers also perhaps gave India minor status gains in the hardware domain, as this missile now is in high demand among Southeast Asian and Gulf states, making the Indian defense industry a somewhat credible weapons exporter. While Moscow has supported India's admission to key forums, India's rapprochement with Washington and Russia's lowered status in New Delhi's dealings have not yet diminished Russia's support for India's permanent membership on the UN Security Council as well as in the Nuclear Suppliers Group (NSG).

During the 2022 Ukraine crisis, India adopted a position of neutrality, which was partly derived from material reasons, such as Russia's supply of weapons and spare parts and gas and oil on favorable terms to India.

Additionally, India has been wary of a tight Russia-China and potentially Pakistan alliance. But there is an underlying status reason which the Western media often has failed to recognize while criticizing India's continued friendship with Moscow. Indian commentators have reminded the media of the six or seven instances when the Soviet Union exercised the veto at the UN Security Council that prevented a UN reprimand on controversial Indian actions in Kashmir, Goa, and the 1971 Bangladesh War. The general tone of the Indian argument has been that at crunch time it was Moscow, not Washington, that came to India's rescue, and that Russia's recognition of India's status ambitions is more deep-rooted than that of the United States, which is a much more recent vintage.[81] This argument may be getting kudos from Moscow, but it is not necessarily helping relations with the United States and the West. The large-scale popular apathy, or even sympathy, in India toward Moscow in the aftermath of Vladimir Putin's aggression in Ukraine in February 2022 is due to the memory of Russia's historical efforts in status enhancement of India—not status humiliation, as from past U.S. policies.[82]

Second-Ranking Powers

The United Kingdom

As India's former colonial ruler, and the closest ally of the United States, the United Kingdom exhibited somewhat similar status consternation toward India during the Cold War era. The first evidence of this was the objection to include India as a permanent member of the UN Security Council in the 1945 San Francisco conference which formed the United Nations. The hastily organized retreat of the British colonial power from India contributed to immense human suffering in the partition of the subcontinent and the creation of two states which were differential in size and capabilities, though Britain attempted to give them status equivalence. Since then, the United Kingdom has tried to maintain an even balance between India and Pakistan, at times tilting in favor of Pakistan on the Kashmir issue. India's membership in the British Commonwealth, the presence of a massive diaspora that now has become a major part of British society and the UK economy, and the personal ties between various Indian and British leaders from Nehru's period have helped to maintain decent relations, without necessarily producing much by way of India's status elevation.[83] Although Britain supported India militarily in the 1962 war with China, while attempting to pressure it into negotiating on Kashmir, it also showed a greater affinity toward Pakistan, as was evident during the 1965 war and beyond. Britain's effort to keep India as a lower-ranking state in the nuclear non-proliferation regime was evident throughout the Cold War, as it was a major sponsor of the unequal NPT.

At the end of the Cold War, the United Kingdom changed its strategy toward India, although the main policy planks have still been somewhat similar to those of the United States. In 1998, Britain opposed India's nuclear testing and at times continued its tilt toward Pakistan, especially on Kashmir. However, it seems that a realization occurred by 2010 or so that the United Kingdom needed to develop its historic relationship and make use of India's economic rise for its own good. Prime Ministers Tony Blair, David Cameron, Theresa May, and Boris Johnson all visited Delhi many times to increase trade and investment volume in particular. Britain's exit from the European Union (Brexit) in 2016 and the subsequent weakening of its economy further put pressure on British leaders to look to India as a source of trade and investment. It is argued that "the UK's Brexit vote was underpinned by the idea that the UK would be freed to re-establish links with its former empire. It was backed by numerous explicitly Anglospherist thinkers, and the subsequent foreign policy narrative of 'Global Britain' is itself deeply reminiscent of Anglosphere narratives."[84] Britain was attempting to revive the Commonwealth advantage and thereby compensate for the loss of revenue from Brexit, and in that context India emerged as the largest Commonwealth market for UK leaders.[85] These efforts have not borne much fruit, as there is a tendency in India to seek the United States, not Britain, as its main trading and strategic partner. However, traditional links are still a major pull factor on both sides. As David Scott argues, "Britain's relationship with India is now primarily driven by economic considerations rather than political/normative considerations." However, "the relationship is an asymmetric one in which India is more important to the UK than the UK is to India, and in which the UK is pursuing India more than India is pursuing the UK."[86]

The status dimensions of this relationship are important in terms of role transformation. The tables on status have turned upside down as India slowly liberalized and became a major economy. In October 2022, an Indian-origin Conservative politician, Rishi Sunak, became British prime minister, succeeding Johnson after his immediate predecessor Liz Truss's government imploded almost immediately after taking office. Today the corporation East India Company, bearing the trademark and coat of arms whose forefathers colonized India, is owned by an Indian businessman, Sanjiv Mehta, who acquired it in 2005.[87] However, the lingering colonial ascriptions and hierarchical notions still haunt this relationship—a Britain unwilling to completely unshackle the past, and an India not so sure it wants to be too close, for status hierarchy reasons among others. Revisionist colonial historians continue to unravel the story of the harm the East India Company and colonial Britain had done to India, its economy, and society, even when some calls for reparations have been voiced.[88] Despite all these, India is still a major source of immigration, especially students in cash-starved British universities and increasingly in corporate investments. Additionally, in recent years, Indian cuisine has emerged as the national cuisine of Britain, with tikka masala as the favorite dish in pubs and restaurants, a status improvement of sorts in soft-power terms. In 2022, India emerged as the fifth-largest economy, replacing the United Kingdom in that position. However, the relationship with Britain is likely to have less impact on India's status pursuit than in previous eras due to the United Kingdom's ongoing relative economic decline. This case shows that India's status ascension in official Britain is largely due to the economic advancement of India—a material factor, more than anything else.

France, Germany, and the European Union

Unlike Britain, France showed much appreciation for India's non-aligned position, as it had a somewhat autonomous streak under Charles De Gaulle. It was France that helped India diplomatically and materially immediately after the nuclear tests in 1998 to weather the sanction regime imposed by the United States and other Western allies. As the first Western country to conduct a strategic dialogue with India in 1998, France was motivated by "an opportunity to address much broader issues, which define the present debate on what the global order should be, and which illustrate as well, the Indian quest for a higher status in the community of nations."[89] France obviously eyed the Indian market, especially for the sale of advanced French weapons. However, the French desire for strategic autonomy resonated with India's own policy inclinations. France had also been a steadfast supporter of India's inclusion in the UN Security Council as a permanent member. Various French leaders regularly visited India, showing the high regard they carried, even though at the societal level, attitude toward India had waxed and waned. Various

Indian cultural activities were organized in France. On the sensitive subject of civil nuclear energy, France had been willing early on to grant India special status and was the first to sign an agreement with New Delhi weeks after this status was granted by the NSG.[90]

By 2022, Indian-French relations had widened to a variety of areas, including an annual joint military exercise in the Indian Ocean, a supply of advanced weapon systems such as the Rafale aircraft and Scorpion submarines, and cooperation in joint explorations such as the space program. During an April 2022 meeting, French President Emmanuel Macron and Modi termed their partnership as "premium," based on a common desire for the creation of a "multipolar world order" and "shared vision of a free, open and rules-based order in the Indo-Pacific."[91] France's policies show that the French view India as a close strategic partner, and they also welcome India's rise as an independent center of power.

As a long-standing trading partner, Germany has been supportive of India's economic rise. During the Cold War, German policy had been similar to that of its Western allies. After initial enthusiasm, the relationship stagnated until the late 1980s, and then became more robust after India's economic liberalization in 1991.[92] The end of the Cold War raised hopes for UN reform, and Germany joined hands with Japan, India, and Brazil to work toward permanent membership in the UN Security Council. However, the relationship is heavily focused on economic ties, and as a leading investor and trading partner, Germany is playing a role in India's economic development. Indian technical workers have also migrated to Germany in increasing numbers. Yet, favorable perceptions in both countries have not matched the improvements in official and business-community perceptions.[93] Both France and Germany helped to set up the annual EU-India summit in September 2002, and the creation of this forum suggests status elevation since India liberalized its economy and became a vigorous actor in the global economy. They have cooperated in areas such as climate change, data protection, maritime security, 5G technology, and human rights.[94] In 2021, the European Union emerged as India's third-largest trading partner with 88 billion euros, constituting 10.8 percent of India's trade, while for the European Union, India is the tenth-largest trading partner, constituting 2.1 percent of its foreign trade, way behind China's 16.2 percent.[95] The relationship is still marred by the European Union's questioning of India's human rights record and lingering skepticism in terms of India's protectionist policies. Yet, France's desire to balance China strategically and Germany's hope to balance

China economically have been motivating factors for EU's improving relations with India.[96]

Japan

Japan's relations with India showed early promise at the end of World War II, as India was one of the first countries to normalize relations with Japan and forgo claims of any war reparations. This bonhomie did not last, as during much of the Cold War era, Japanese policies toward India mirrored those of the United States and other dominant Western countries. Japan adamantly opposed India's nuclear ambitions and imposed hard sanctions after India's 1998 nuclear tests. These were lifted, however, as the United States began improving relations with India. India's "Look East Policy," launched by former Prime Minister P.V. Narasimha Rao (renamed as "Act East Policy" by the Modi government), played a significant role in improving relations with Japan and South Korea, as well as Southeast Asian countries. According to Rao, Japan was "at the heart of India's Look East Policy."[97]

Japan began to elevate India's status in the 2010s, partly due to the opening of the Indian economy and, more importantly, converging security interests vis-à-vis rising China. It was facilitated immensely by the burgeoning U.S.-India relationship and the easing of nuclear sanctions on India by the United States, earlier imposed in response to its nuclear weapons acquisition. Japan joined India, Germany, and Brazil in the effort to elevate themselves to the UN Security Council permanent membership. Both Prime Minister Manmohan Singh and Prime Minister Modi developed geniality with former Japanese Prime Minister Shinto Abe. The membership in Quad has helped to elevate Japan's strategic relationship with India to heightened levels. A series of high-level meetings at the prime ministerial level have occurred since then. In addition, Japan has emerged as a key investor in India, and in March 2022—despite differences over the Ukraine war—Japanese Prime Minister Fumio Kishida announced the investment of some $53 billion in India, demonstrating the higher level of status that Japan accords India in the new geopolitical environment.[98] Prior to that, in September 2017, Japan invested in India's first bullet train project between Mumbai and Ahmedabad. The 508-kilometer-long route was based on the high-speed Shinkansen train system of Japan, and it has been making progress despite some delays in land acquisition, construction, and financing.[99] Japan and India have steadily

increased their defense cooperation, which has advanced from regular strategic dialogue to joint military and naval exercises, in particular the annual
Malabar naval exercise, joint research, and development of new technologies,
including weapon systems.[100]

The transformation of Japan's relations with India is driven by economic
and security interests, but a recognition of the latter has increased India's
status partly due to its material advancements. India's joining of the East
Asia summit and regular meetings between prime ministers, and defense
and foreign ministers of both countries, show the increasing importance that
Japan accords to India.[101] It appears there is a form of domestic consensus,
along various political spectrums, of the value of India as "a partner that can
help Japan back to being a normal nation."[102] Accordingly, an "implicit bargain" has been struck between the two countries, by which "Japan invests
in bolstering India's long-term capabilities and in policy coordination with
India while India offers diplomatic support and weight to Japan's increasingly precarious position in East Asia."[103]

The Global South Countries

While India in recent years has pivoted its attention to obtaining status recognition from existing great powers, much of its independent history was done
via the Global South and India's leadership role in international institutions.
The NAM was the key arena, and helped to form the G-77 in the United
Nations, which was instrumental in negotiating with the West in areas such
as decolonization, the structure of the international order, peacekeeping, and
climate change.[104] Trade negotiations was an arena where India played a significant role, first in the General Agreements on Tariffs and Trade (GATT)
and then in the World Trade Organization (WTO), where it often acted as
a veto player. Its leadership in those organizations offered India a certain
status ranking, as did its role as an interlocutor for Global South countries.
The Doha rounds of trade negotiations collapsed in November 2011 after
10 years of negotiations, partially due to the opposition from India, China,
and Brazil to the U.S. unwillingness to protect poor farmers from its ambit.[105]
As India's economy grew after the Cold War's end, it abandoned the NAM
and its Global South leadership role to a large extent. Increasingly, though,
the Modi government has recognized the value of the Global South in
elevating India's status in the world order. In 2022, India assumed leadership

of the G-20 grouping, but a key platform of India was to engage the rest of the Global South and facilitate their concerns, including environment, global pandemics, and other issues. In January 2023, India held a virtual meeting called Voice of Global South Summit, with some 120 countries in attendance, and promised the G-20 meeting it was hosting in September 2023 would help conclude a sustainable green development pact and bridge the digital divide among countries.[106] Yet, reticence can still haunt India's grand strategy, as the elite, preoccupied with internal matters, ignore the hard work necessary for gaining status recognition from both great powers and Global South countries. In India's case, its dual identity as a Global South country with leadership aspirations and a rising power with global ambitions has increased, as its improving material capabilities are encouraging India to seek more explicit great power goals.[107] The moves by Modi vis-à-vis Global South countries are indeed intended to enhance India's status globally and not just among great powers. The inclusion of the 55-member African Union (AU) as the 21st member of G-20 and the incorporation of many themes for reforms proposed by Global South countries in the deliberations of the grouping have the potential to elevate India's status in the years to come if it can work together with the West and the rest to bridge the gap between the North and South. India's membership in BRICS and the support it has garnered from leading states like Brazil and South Africa can be assets in this regard.

Conclusions

The great powers have come a long way in their attitudes toward India's status elevation in the international system. During the Cold War, India was often bracketed with Pakistan by the United States and the Western powers, and its role was viewed as a regional power confined to South Asia. The alliance relationship of Pakistan with the United States and China, India's non-alignment policy, and its limited role in the world economy were largely the cause of this non-recognition. The non-aligned policy that India sponsored called for equidistance between the superpowers, which sometimes meant taking sides with the Soviet bloc, which was viewed adversely by the West. The Soviet Union was the most sympathetic to India's status aspirations and provided support with crucial economic and military aid when the United States and China formed an alliance and included Pakistan as part of that coalition. The 1971 war saw India's status challenged by the United States and China, although winning the war temporarily increased India's status aspirations. India's unwillingness to sign the NPT generated opposition from both the superpowers and Western countries.

The end of the Cold War and India's economic liberalization altered the perceptions of India as a rising power. Indeed, sustained economic growth for over two decades resulted in considerable improvements to India in terms of its status in the perceptions of the world. The rise of China initially challenged India's status aspirations, but China's increasing hostilities with the West resulted in India receiving enhanced status from the United States and other powers, such as Japan. Balance-of-power considerations play a big role in the partial status accommodation of India by these states. The U.S.-India nuclear accord elevated India to a de facto nuclear weapons state. The importance of India as a strategic partner is evident in the creation and further evolution of the Quad as a soft balancing forum to a more substantive economic and security arena. Despite all the capability improvements vis-à-vis other states in the international system, India's ranking still remains murky. In today's world, it is difficult to see the old status ranking used by European great powers re-emerging, such as victory in wars against other major powers. The capacity to influence events significantly beyond one's region and the ability to project power globally can be achieved by a state differently than how the colonial powers did it in the past. A dominant global economic presence and the ability to project military power in the Indo-Pacific region will be critical to India's further status elevation within the great power system.

India has some ground to cover to be accepted as a major power by the leading powers of the day, especially the United States and China. Beijing opposes India emerging as a peer competitor in Asia. As the U.S.-China rivalry widens, India has an opportunity to elevate itself as a key ally of the Western powers and a swing state that can help the balancing and containment of China. In this endeavor, India's internal hard-power strengths—economic, military, technological, and demographic—will be crucial, as will its soft power attributes: in particular, its image as a secular, liberal democracy. This may cause China to step up its challenge on the border and in the Indian Ocean. Conflicts over status matter the most in this dynamic relationship. The key dilemma for India is how to become such a swing state, being an important ally to the West, while keeping its identity as leader of the developing world, and its autonomy as a post-colonial, independent country with its own destiny to achieve.

6

The Neighbors

In an interesting episode in 1949, Pakistan's first prime minister, Liaquat Ali Khan, threatened to go to Moscow first instead of Washington, D.C., if he was not accorded the same reception that India's prime minister, Jawaharlal Nehru, was given by the United States under the Truman administration. At a subsequent meeting, Pakistan's finance minister, Ghulam Muhammad, told George McGhee, visiting assistant secretary of state for Near East Asia, "It was of the utmost importance that [the Pakistani prime minister] should be accorded a reception equal to that received by Nehru."[1] This incident shows that a regionally dominant state need not obtain automatic status in the perceptions of its neighbors. Historically, a state needed to become status-dominant in its immediate region before it gained global power status. Although India commands considerably higher status and material capabilities than other South Asian states, as it constitutes over two-thirds of the subcontinent's territory, population, and economy, contrary to general expectations, India's status ranking in its own region has been at times ambivalent and at other times has evoked hostility among a number of smaller states, not just Pakistan. In the twenty-first century, this pattern appears to be changing, as a rising power can emerge dominant in other regions even when its position in the immediate region is contested. In this respect, both China and India have regionally contested status positions, although they are increasing their status in other regions, China disproportionately.

The scholarly literature on status tends to privilege the global dimensions of the phenomenon.[2] This is largely because competition, conflict, and accommodation in the status arena among great powers matter the most for international order and stability. Less appreciated is the status competition that goes on in regional theaters. More importantly, for an aspiring rising power, its graduation from regional to global power status can be facilitated or hampered by regional dynamics; in particular, its conflict interactions with regional states that have strong links with great powers. Smaller rivals can use their geostrategic proximity to great powers to slow the march of a rising power. Both China and India face this hurdle in the Indo-Pacific and

South Asia subregions. India's case is an interesting one in this sense, as its rise is somewhat constrained by its intense rivalry with Pakistan and the role that two great powers, the United States in the past, and China since the 1960s, have been playing in keeping Pakistan as a status equivalent and challenger to India. This status challenge is also the biproduct of security relations among the great powers and Pakistan's utility in their rivalries with each other, partially due to its pivotal geostrategic location. This chapter focuses on the smaller states in the South Asia region to explore the opportunities and challenges India has faced in the areas of acquisition, maintenance, and enhancement or diminution of status in the regional context.

It was William Thompson who brought to our attention the need to study global and regional hierarchies separately, even though they may overlap, as well as the necessity to understand big status (S) contests from small status (s) competitions among great powers. The regional contexts could vary as far as which markers or capabilities matter most for status hierarchies at the global and regional levels.[3] For powerful middle-ranking regional states, the immediate concern is protecting against security threats in the neighborhood while also maintaining a higher status as well as preventing their status denial and depreciation by their neighbors and by those great powers active in their regional spheres. Status is one of the key hierarchical equations that connect the bigger regional states and the smaller ones surrounding them. There is indeed status interdependence between the stronger and weaker regional powers, although for the latter, it could be highly asymmetric. The bigger regional states can use multiple strategies to acquire and maintain higher status. The extent of the material gap and the level of dependency determine the amount of status advantage a state can obtain through outright dominance or hegemony. Thus, if the power-capability discrepancy and dependency levels are not overwhelming, the secondary rival may view that continuous status challenge is feasible. If the power-capability discrepancy is very wide and if the smaller state is in a dependency relationship with the larger neighbor, a status challenge is unlikely. Those second-ranking states, highly sensitive to status hierarchy, could make attempts to ward themselves off from more powerful regional rivals by pursuing isolationist policies and by closing their borders for trade and other economic interactions. It is often in the DNA of the smaller states with a high sense of autonomy to seek to break out of this structural dependency by engaging in multiple asymmetric strategies. In that process, often their strategies can collide with the status aspirations of the larger power in the region.

Larger regional powers have also used tributary model strategies to elicit cooperation or subservience, as in the case of historic China in East Asia. The Chinese-led *Tianxia order* is defined as a "Sino-centric hierarchical relationship among unequals, governed according to Confucian principles of benevolence."[4] Under this "all under heaven" order, secondary states accepted Chinese (Central Kingdom's) suzerainty, paying tributes to the Chinese emperor, who acted as the "son of heaven," and reciprocated them with lavish gifts.[5] Today, some scholars argue that this is a feasible alternative to the U.S.-led Westphalian order that China can pursue, which appears more likely to bring a peaceful order in East Asia in particular.[6] The ideal tributary model is less coercive than outright hegemony, and it relies partly on cultural affinity to evoke allegiance. The vassal states in a tributary system are expected to accept the overall suzerainty of the dominant actor and to offer it periodic tributes, in return for protection as well as freedom to exist as political units.

The United States also has enunciated the Monroe Doctrine, which is somewhat akin to a tributary model, for the Americas. According to Yuen Foong Khong, the United States, with its hub-and-spoke system, is the "epicentre of the most extensive network of formal and informal alliances ever built," as it offers its "allies and partners—or tributaries—military protection as well as economic access to its markets," in return for acceptance of its hegemony and emulation of its political ideas.[7] The United States has shown a benign attitude toward Canada due to their deep-rooted security and economic relations and Canada's acceptance of American dominance, but toward Mexico in North America and the states of South America and the Caribbean, the threat of coercive intervention has often been part of the American approach. India has also been following a lighter version of the Monroe Doctrine with respect to the South Asia region for some time and has attempted to prevent external intervention in the affairs of the smaller states of the region. This is most clearly articulated in the 1983 "Indira doctrine" by Prime Minister Indira Gandhi, who stated: "India will neither intervene in the domestic affairs of any states in the region, unless requested to do so, nor tolerate such intervention by an outside power; if external assistance is needed to meet an internal crisis, states should first look within the region for help."[8]

The South Asia region comprises eight states, from tiny Bhutan and Maldives to middle-sized states Bangladesh, Afghanistan, Nepal, Sri Lanka, and the second largest of all, Pakistan. India holds nearly 65 percent of the land area, 80 percent of GDP, and 75 percent of the population of the

South Asia region. In terms of culture and civilization, India commands a very pivotal role in these states as the key source of most of their language, music, cinema, and other cultural attributes, especially religion. The very size differential, as well as its civilizational outreach, should give India higher status among its smaller neighbors by default. Where India is lacking is in providing adequate economic support to most of the regional states that could substantially boost their sustainable development. India's failure in this area has diluted its leadership role to an extent. Today, with China as an active player in the economic development of regional states, this source of status for India has faced more challenges. Just like India itself, the economic development of these states has been tardy and uneven and their socioeconomic integration more prolonged and cumbersome. Global warming and other ecological catastrophes plague the region all the more. They also have many ethnic conflicts, with majority-minority relations highly conflictual in some cases. All of them are inherently nationalistic, and the bogeyman of outside intervention is often the rod that unites them internally.

As Mohammed Ayoob describes it, the Indian strategy of regional managerial leadership arose from the British Raj conceptions of a strategic unity of the subcontinent. The assumption of the Indian elite was that India's material superiority and overwhelming size would help achieve "a form of regional predominance whose legitimacy would be accepted by all states in the region."[9] The desire for a preeminent position in South Asia also arises "from the Indian elite's perception that it inherited the Raj's strategic and political legacy, including the strategic unity that Britain had imposed on the subcontinent."[10] However, India's efforts to create a strategic consensus in the region, built around its managerial leadership role, has been challenged most visibly by Pakistan, but also periodically by other smaller states that want to maintain their freedom to maneuver.

In India's case, over time regional hegemony became difficult, and as a result, India attempted intermittent coercive strategies and positive non-reciprocal concessions toward its smaller neighbors. The smaller states of South Asia in general are weak or very weak, with multiple internal schisms, uneven economic development, and state coercion. Often the weaknesses of these states have provoked India's direct or indirect interventions, generating challenges to India's own security and status among them. The challenge is that in countries like Sri Lanka, Nepal, and Bangladesh there are sizable minority populations with ethnic kinship affinities to India, and they expect

India's support when the majority-community-dominated governments engage in suppression of their demands for autonomy or more fundamental rights. The large Indian states with the closest kinship to these minority populations—Tamil Nadu and West Bengal—generate pressures on the central government in Delhi, as well as other state governments, to support the minority cause in the neighborhood. This irredentist challenge often has pitted India against the security and autonomy of these neighboring states. The smaller South Asian states, knowingly or unknowingly, have caused major challenges to India's security and integrity, as well as status aspirations, partly due to the irredentist challenge they face from India. The smaller states at times have shown insensitivity to India's security interests and status concerns.

The extended regions for assessing India's status aspirations comprise Southeast Asia, Central Asia, the Middle East, Persian Gulf, and Africa, with which India has had powerful historical and contemporary links. Southeast Asian states such as Myanmar, Thailand, Singapore, Malaysia, and Indonesia also increasingly matter for India's regional influence and status aspirations. The Arab and Persian Gulf states such as Saudi Arabia, the United Arab Emirates, and Iran have traditionally been linked to India—demographically, economically, and culturally—through the millennia. India's status aspirations and achievements among these near abroad countries have waxed and waned, partially due to Cold War–era alliances and the somewhat effective exploitation of Islamic politics by Pakistan. Increasingly, China's outreach has affected India's status aspirations among these states, despite the fact that this factor may offer India more geopolitical opportunities than in the past, in particular if Beijing becomes more aggressive in its power ambitions in the Indo-Pacific. Most states in these subregions have begun to view India as a balancing power vis-à-vis China, some more strongly than others.

Although India commands considerably higher status among South Asian states, contrary to general expectations, India's status search in its own region has been at times ambivalent and at other times has evoked hostility among a number of smaller states. The exception is Bhutan, which depends on India for major economic and political support and has a treaty relationship which gives India an overwhelming say in its foreign policy. For that reason, India's behavior toward Bhutan has been markedly different from the others on the list—it is a benign hegemony at its best. India's military interventions or coercive diplomacy vis-à-vis the others—Sri Lanka, Nepal, Bangladesh, and

Maldives—as well as the ethnic irredentist challenges arising from the first three, are major challenges to obtaining the friendly hegemonic status India has been coveting in the region. More importantly, all the South Asian states are highly sensitive to their sovereignty, and within their domestic politics, pro- and anti-India positions have been used as mechanisms for garnering electoral support by political parties. They are quintessential Westphalian states, wanting to retain their national identity and sovereign independence as much as they can. Yet, India looms large in their strategic horizons due to its elephantine size and potential ability to deny or improve their security and economic prosperity to a considerable extent.

During the early Cold War years, many of the smaller South Asian states looked up to New Delhi through the Non-Aligned Movement (NAM) despite the testy relationships over its involvement in their domestic affairs. Since the end of the Cold War, most of them, except Bhutan, have attempted to prevent India from becoming hegemonic, often courting outside powers, increasingly China, to foil this outcome. If regional dominance is a necessary condition for global power status, India may have much more work at its hand in the years to come. This is partly the reason why India has been transcending the region and moving toward East Asia, with policies such as "Look East" and "Act East," as it seems to realize much greater potential for status acquisition as well as material benefits when engaging with Southeast Asian and East Asian states. During much of the Cold War era, India pursued a sort of Monroe Doctrine to prevent outside powers from interfering in the region's security affairs. Today, as China has entered the subcontinent in both economic and military arenas, with larger pocketbooks and infrastructure projects, India has experienced some status depreciation and competition among its smaller neighbors. Part of the challenge has been India's relatively weak economic relationships with smaller states, especially in the areas of trade and infrastructure investment, where China is making considerable headway. Intra-regional trade in South Asia constitutes 5 percent of the region's total trade, and India's share ranged between 1.7 and 3.8 percent of its overall trade with the world. In contrast, "China has consistently increased its exports to the region from US$8 billion in 2005 to US$52 billion in 2018, a growth of 546%."[11] As a result, for the smaller states of the region, their main trading partner today is China.

The next section discusses Pakistan's status competition with India and its implications for regional peace, followed by the approaches of smaller South Asian states toward India.

Pakistan's Status Challenge

No other regional state challenges India's status aspirations more consistently and intensely than does Pakistan. While the other smaller states of South Asia have been willing to accept some form of Indian preponderance, Pakistan has steadfastly refused to accord India higher status, and this has been one of the major reasons for the persistence of the rivalry between the two states. Though China has been frequently attempting to deprive India of status, both globally and regionally, by treating it as a secondary power in Asia, India has a deeper antipathy toward Pakistan's claim for equal status. The roles are reversed in this case, as the larger power, India, is in no mood to give any impression of status equivalency to Pakistan and makes every effort to deny the weaker party's claims for equal status. At times, China has made limited status accommodation of India, but for Pakistan, even a nominal recognition of India's dominant regional status has not happened. Even as the material power differential between the two states has widened, Pakistan has shown no willingness to compromise on territorial conflict as well as status competition. In response, India has been redoubling its efforts under the Modi government to treat Pakistan as a status-deficient nation by exposing its use of terrorist groups to weaken India's control over Kashmir. Indian leaders' refusal to meet with Pakistani counterparts and their highlighting of terrorism in speeches and global forums have been part of this status competition strategy.

Status contestation is a big part of the India-Pakistan rivalry that is yet to be properly understood or analyzed by scholars.[12] This competition is one of the root causes of the lack of economic integration between the two countries and thus has produced many negative outcomes in terms of peace and cooperation. The onset of the India-Pakistan status rivalry goes back to the partition of the subcontinent in 1947, which originated from the fear of both power loss and status depreciation felt by the Muslim minority elite. The Muslim League Party, the chief proponent of Pakistan, viewed itself as the representative of the nearly 24 percent strong Muslim population (92 million) of undivided India's total population of 390 million and sought parity with the Congress Party by demanding an electoral role on the basis of communal representation and eventually partition. The secular Congress Party refused to accept those claims of sole representation of Muslims by the Muslim League. The Muslim elite feared that in a united India, the status and power positions of Muslims would always be inferior to those of the Hindus, despite assurances by the Congress of a secular India they planned to create, where Muslims would enjoy their civil and religious rights.

These claims were based on historical and religious grounds and were rooted in the considerable anxieties that had been brewing since the late 1930s among the Muslim elites, which they were able to transfer to the Muslim masses over time. After the two states were formed, status competition continued to play a part as a key source of conflict between the two states. The markers for status that the Pakistani elite uses to differentiate themselves from India tend to vary from Western indicators, especially material capability and size differentials. The Pakistani elite's version of history has been based on a peculiar reading of the bygone era when India was under Muslim rule. Since approximately AD 1000, the Indian subcontinent had been invaded and ruled by Muslim kingdoms in several phases and in diverse areas of the vast region. The most prominent ones were the Delhi Sultanates (1206–1526) and the Mughal Empire (1526–1858). In addition, powerful kingdoms such as Mysore and Hyderabad in the South, Junagadh in the West, and Oudh in the North were under Muslim rulers. The Mughals were the largest of those kingdoms, and during their zenith under Aurangzeb and before subsequent decline, the Empire stretched from Afghanistan in the West to Bengal in the East and Karnataka in the South. In fact, after the Mauryan Empire (322–187 BC), it was the first time a larger part of pre-partition India was under one rubric. At the time of partition in 1947, of the 584 princely states, several were under Muslim rule.

The decline of the Mughal Empire in the nineteenth century helped the British deepen and widen their rule in the subcontinent. After initial hostility due to the participation of Muslim kingdoms such as Oudh and the Mughals in the 1857 revolt, Muslims were treated by British rulers as a separate political community as part of their divide-and-rule strategy. The awareness as the erstwhile ruling elite of India gave Muslim leaders a sense of status superiority, as well as status anxiety over the Congress Party, which they viewed as being led by Hindu ethos, even though the Congress had many Muslims in prominent positions—for instance, Maulana Azad, who would emerge as a leading figure in Nehru's cabinet. The Congress leaders' pronounced advocacy of secularism and inclusiveness was not sufficient to mollify those concerns. The unwillingness of Congress to accept the Muslim League as a coalition partner in the 1937 elections to 11 directly ruled British Indian provinces under the partial autonomy scheme of the 1935 British India Act also encouraged Muslim leaders to think of Congress as unwilling to recognize their political aspirations.[13]

Mohammed Ali Jinnah, the founding father of Pakistan, demanded as much status equivalency in the territorial and asset divisions of the subcontinent as was feasible. He argued for the entire Punjab and Bengal to be part of Pakistan. The British decision not to grant such a large area of undivided India to Pakistan generated immense discontent among the Muslim leaders. Jinnah, for instance, complained of the "moth-eaten Pakistan" that would emerge after partition. The deeper roots of this demand came from the expectation that Pakistan represented the successor state to the Mughal Empire which had ruled much of the Indian subcontinent and that Islam could be protected only through the creation of a state somewhat equal to India. The partition allocation of 30 percent of the army, 40 percent of the navy, 20 percent of the air force, and 17 percent share of revenue of British India to Pakistan and the delay in the disbursement of the latter generated considerable bitterness in Pakistan.[14] The funds were disbursed after a "fast unto death" by Mohandas Gandhi, who through this act embittered the Hindu nationalists in India. One of them, Nathuram Godse, would later assassinate him in January 1948.

After partition, a sense of martial superiority entered the Pakistani leaders' psyche, ignoring the fact that the Punjab, from where the majority of Pakistani soldiers and officer corps came, also had produced similar martial tendencies on the Indian side, especially among the Sikhs as well as Punjabi Hindu soldiers. The illusion of superiority was evident in 1965, when many Pakistani generals thought five Hindu soldiers were equal to one Pakistani Muslim soldier.[15] Similarly, prior to the outbreak of the 1971 war, military ruler Yahya Khan, in response to Henry Kissinger's suggestions for allowing the United Nations to engage in relief efforts of refugees and the early appointment of a civilian governor in East Pakistan, revealed this deep-rooted expectation. Kissinger recounts: Yahya responded that "he and his colleagues did not believe that India was planning war; if so, they were convinced they would win. When I asked as tactfully as I could about the Indian advantage in numbers and equipment, Yahya and his colleagues answered with bravado about the historic superiority of Moslem fighters."[16] This attitude of the Pakistani elite may very well be the manifestations of an "honor culture" which tends to carry "both superior sense as well as a sense of humiliation and resentment," and an "elevated sense of self-worth" vis-à-vis the chief opponent.[17] After scores of military defeats and political setbacks, Pakistan has been struggling to keep up with India as a strategic and political equal. Nevertheless, Islamabad insists on status parity and does not relent in its pursuit of revanchist goals. Honor cultures also tend to produce much status anxiety, the buildup of which could generate resentment and conflict behavior.[18] It seems the BJP also is following an honor culture attitude toward Pakistan and other minority religious groups in India.

Pakistan made every effort from the beginning of statehood to equalize status and power with India. For a time, it was somewhat successful in this endeavor. The Kashmir conflict has been partially driven by status and identity concerns. The Pakistani elite was convinced that the size differential with India could be overcome by pursuing smart strategies, alignment with great powers, and acquisition of qualitatively superior weaponry. Pakistan's strategic location was crucial to this calculation. Jinnah had recognized this advantage even at the early days of independence. In his interview with the U.S. journalist Margret Bourke-White in September 1947, barely a month after independence, he contended: "America needs Pakistan more than Pakistan needs America." In Jinnah's view, "Pakistan was the pivot of the world, as we are placed . . . [at] the frontier on which the future position of the world revolves." Further, if the United States was willing to defend Turkey and Greece against Russia, it would be "much more interested in pouring money and arms into Pakistan," because if Russia walks in here, . . . the whole world is menaced."[19] As mentioned previously, when the Truman administration invited Nehru ahead of the Pakistani leader to visit Washington in mid-1949, then Pakistani Prime Minister Liaqat Ali Khan felt slighted and made every effort to encourage Washington to invite him and accord him the same reception,[20] which the United States bestowed on the Pakistani leader when he visited in May 1950. This tendency continued into the twenty-first century, even after the United States upgraded its relationship with India and removed the parity in treatment following Bill Clinton's visit to India in March 2000. In March 2010, Pakistan's Army Chief General Ashfaq Parvez Kayani, while visiting Washington for a strategic dialogue on Afghanistan, insisted that "Obama should visit Pakistan and that it should equal the length of time he spends visiting India . . . Obama went to India in November, skipping Pakistan."[21]

The first strategic opportunity for obtaining status parity with India came to Pakistan in 1954, when the United States, in its intense Cold War conflict with the Soviet Union, adopted Pakistan as a frontline state. Washington was given the right to fly spy planes from the city of Lahore, and in one famous incident, the Soviets shot down a U-2 plane which had flown from Pakistani territory. This cooperation elevated Pakistan's status in the Western world, and Western media began to treat India and Pakistan as geopolitical coequals. India's inability to win the 1947–1948 and 1965 wars with Pakistan reinforced this perception of status parity. In 1969, Pakistan acted as a conduit in developing the U.S.-China relations, facilitating Henry Kissinger's and later Richard Nixon's groundbreaking visits to Beijing. Nixon visited Pakistan a few months after his election in 1969. In August 1969, Air Marshall Nur Khan, governor of West Pakistan, told the visiting Kissinger of Pakistan's unwillingness to settle the Kashmir dispute, as a settlement "would require appeasement of India, . . . which in turn would formally declare Pakistan's second class status in the subcontinent."[22] A former Pakistani ambassador to the United States, Husain Haqqani, states: Khan "effectively told Kissinger that Pakistan was in a permanent state of war with India over Kashmir and had no interest in resolving the conflict through talks. Pakistan did not want to be seen as less important or less powerful than India; equal status with India took priority over specific issues such as Kashmir."[23]

India's victory in the 1971 War helped to change the status equation somewhat, but this was only temporary, as the Soviet invasion of Afghanistan once again gave Pakistan a frontline role, while marginalizing India in Western strategy in the subcontinent and beyond. The Indian victory affected the Pakistani elite's status competition with India. The Indian act was considered as perfidy, and it needed to be avenged in different ways. Even if the material gap could not be bridged, different asymmetrical strategies and weapons acquisition could maintain a semblance of parity. Nuclear weapons fit the bill very well, as they are powerful tools in obtaining strategic parity, especially if Pakistan could obtain deterrence and eventually a mutual assured destruction (MAD) capability. The 1971 defeat profoundly affected Pakistan's status aspirations. In some respects it increased the resolve of Pakistani leaders to regain lost status by waging an asymmetric battle, especially in Kashmir.[24] Russia's military aggression toward Ukraine in 2022 is another powerful example of what status loss can do to countries and their leaders.

Status competition appears very prominently in Pakistan's nuclear acquisition efforts from the beginning. The attempt was clearly to equalize status relations with India, as evident in Zulfikar Ali Bhutto's many statements on this subject. The most poignant statement by Bhutto was in January 1972, at a meeting with Pakistani nuclear scientists in Multan when a nuclear weapons program was launched: "We are fighting a thousand year war with India, and we will make an atomic bomb even if we have to eat grass."[25] Pakistani Prime Minister Nawaz Sharif's statement after the nuclear tests in May 1998 was: "Today we have settled a score and have carried out five successful nuclear tests," implying that Pakistan had equalized its status competition with India in the nuclear realm.[26] Pakistan views nuclear weapons as a "great equalizer" not only in strategic terms, but also in status terms. As Haqqani states, the 1974 Indian nuclear test was considered:

> A near catastrophe. Since independence they had sought parity with India, only to learn over the course of three wars that they could not militarily defeat their larger neighbor. After each defeat Pakistan's leaders had generated an explanation for failure, thereby keeping the rivalry at least at a psychological level. In the eyes of Pakistanis, theirs was a special country destined to compete with India's Hindu imperialism. Pakistan's military was even more special, being the inheritor of proud Muslim warrior traditions.[27]

The India-Pakistan conflict cannot be reduced to Kashmir, but rather should be ascribed to a lingering desire in Islamabad to equalize status with India and to undercut India's status aspirations in South Asia and beyond. India has steadfastly resisted this by making countermoves to undercut Pakistan's status claims. The status objective has become one of the core elements of Pakistan's strategic culture, especially for its dominant societal and political actor, the military.[28]

The Cold War in general and the Soviet invasion of Afghanistan in December 1979 offered Pakistan extraordinary opportunities in its quest for status parity with India. It was the Soviet invasion of Afghanistan that allowed Pakistan to pursue an active nuclear program. The Carter and Reagan administrations attempted to strengthen Pakistan as a frontline state, backing the Mujahideen resistance in Afghanistan.[29] This U.S. policy indirectly facilitated both Zia's nuclear program as well as his active offensive strategy toward India. The strategy of a "thousand cuts" adopted by Pakistani leader Zia ul Haq assumed that India was vulnerable to asymmetric warfare.[30] India's highhanded tactics in suppressing Kashmiri separatists, as well as playing dirty politics in the state's elections, generated opportunities for recruiting insurgents. The end of the Afghan war following the Soviet retreat made available thousands of Mujahideen from different parts of the world, many of whom were happy to join the struggle against India.[31] With the help of these Islamic warriors, Pakistan launched its most active insurgency in Kashmir in 1989.

Pakistan's status claims with India became weaker following the United States' adoption of India as a strategic partner and the de-hyphenation of the two South Asian states, especially after the 2005 U.S.-India nuclear accord. This has generated much status anxiety in Pakistan. China helped to restore some sense of importance when it initiated the China-Pakistan Economic Corridor (CPEC), the largest component of the Belt and Road Initiative (BRI). The problem, however, is that economically, once the CPEC projects are established, Pakistan will become even more dependent on China, although its strategic value for China could increase. As of June 2022, Pakistan's national debt had ballooned to an unsustainable $129 billion while it held less than $9 billion in foreign currency reserves. Pakistan's economy has been in deep trouble partially due to its debt servicing to China. In June 2022, the economic crisis prompted Pakistan's planning minister, Ahsan Iqbal, to advise people to drink one to two cups of tea a day to cut down on foreign imports.[32] Pakistan is no longer considered a viable status challenger to India, as evident in India's membership in exclusive international institutions like G-20 and Quad, and the United States and the West are increasingly courting New Delhi as their preferred balancing power vis-à-vis China.

India has made every effort to deny Pakistan the equal status it has been craving. Various forums, especially the United Nations, were used by India to show Pakistan's initiatives in fomenting terrorism and nuclear proliferation. Pakistan's nuclear proliferation activities, especially the transfer of nuclear materials to states such as North Korea under the A.Q. Khan network, offered New Delhi a major opportunity to portray that India was different from Pakistan as a responsible nuclear weapon state. Similarly, Pakistan's support for terrorism in Afghanistan and Kashmir was used by India as a status differentiator. In the Modi era, the refusal to hold any meetings or initiate any peace overtures until Pakistan abjures terrorism also shows that India views Pakistan differently on status markers. India's unwillingness to offer a favorable modus vivendi to Pakistan on Kashmir is partly driven by status concerns. India fears that Kashmir, whether independent or under Pakistani control, will deprive India of a major security and status asset, showing that the Muslim League's logic of partition won. Similarly, Indira Gandhi's decision to support Bangladesh liberation was driven by status denial to Pakistan. India believed that cutting Pakistan down to size was a way to permanently make Islamabad abandon its parity search and security challenge. However, it probably increased the determination of the West Pakistani elite to pursue nuclear weapons and other asymmetrical strategies to regain status parity with its larger neighbor.

Smaller Neighbors

Beyond Pakistan, India's status relationships with its smaller neighbors have been less belligerent. However, the smaller states often are wedded to sovereign equality of the Westphalian orientation and take their independence very seriously. This is in contrast with the hierarchical vision of India, the aspiring great power. Projected or feared Indian influence and interventions are also a big domestic issue for the competing political parties in these countries, which often are divided among pro- and anti-India, or in the current era, India versus China. In the past decade, China has entered the domains of South Asia's smaller states much more actively than before and today invests heavily by way of infrastructure development as well as trade links with them. The BRI connects all of them with China, and although India has attempted to reduce the footprint of Beijing in the region, it has had limited success on that front. The status sharing of China with India has increased, and that despite regional states' displeasure with the debt-trap diplomacy of China, many of them have joined hands at best on the economic bandwagon of China. One source of solace for India is their reluctance to offer military bases to China. There is indeed a strange attachment and detachment (love-hate relationship) that the smaller neighbors show toward India. A popular but controversial Bangladeshi writer, Tahmima Anam, stated in 2007 that India was "aggressively self-interested," suffered from "the peculiar paranoia of the strong towards the weak," and that "[w]e cannot love India. The relationship is too unequal for romance."[33]

India's Historical Legacy with Smaller Neighbors

India's first prime minister, Jawaharlal Nehru, had a benign yet at times hegemonic attitude toward smaller South Asian neighbors, partly due to an inherited understanding of India's regional primacy from the British Raj. India's special relationship with the Himalayan kingdoms of Bhutan and Sikkim, before the latter joined India in May 1975, and to some extent, Nepal, were the most dominant cases of hegemony. The Indian leadership perceived the necessity of offering protectorate status to the Himalayan kingdoms neighboring China. These were buffer states that the British had kept against potential expansion by Chinese empires. During Indira Gandhi's period, a key event took place: the accession of tiny Sikkim to the Indian union in 1975. Although this was the result of an overwhelmingly favorable majority vote in a referendum in the kingdom, it did generate doubts among other states that India's intentions were benign. Prior to that, the liberation of Bangladesh by Indian military intervention in 1971 also was received with mixed response by the regional states. It was only Bhutan and Nepal that supported India in the UN General Assembly, showing the ambivalence among other South Asian states on the Indian intervention.[34]

The interlude of coalition governments in the 1990s in India saw a kind of non-reciprocal approach on India's part toward South Asian states. The so-called Gujral Doctrine, enunciated by Foreign Minister Inder Kumar Gujral in September 1996, offered some of the smaller South Asian states—Maldives, Bangladesh, Nepal, and Bhutan—Indian economic and trade concessions without reciprocal obligations on their part. The only expectation was that the smaller states would not act contrary to India's security interests or intervene in each other's internal affairs or bring in extra-regional powers to settle intra-regional disputes. This approach was very popular among some South Asian states, and India's status and goodwill did seem to go up among them for a period of time.[35] The Rajiv Gandhi era saw major activism in the neighborhood. The separatist movement in Sri Lanka, spearheaded by the Tamil Eelam, generated intense pressures on India to intervene. Gandhi's decision to send in Indian peacekeeping forces to quell the Tamil rebels in July 1987 produced a disastrous outcome. With several casualties among the Indian peacekeeping forces, India was forced to withdraw before quelling the violent Tamil secessionists, and not pleasing the Sri Lankans either. Prior to that, Gandhi had sent in the Indian military to save the beleaguered government in Maldives in 1988 from a coup attempt, which might have temporarily boosted India's status as a security provider of the small states.

The BJP era (of both Vajpayee and Modi) showed relations changing from good to bad in some cases and improving in others. While Vajpayee had some success in regional relations, the Modi era has witnessed the partial erosion of Indian status and influence among many of the regional states, partly because of China's increasing presence in the region. Modi has made some conscious attempts to reverse this trend by frequently visiting some of these countries and offering them economic and political support. Smaller states have attempted to use regional institutions to constrain India and its status as the preponderant power in the region. The creation of the South Asian Association of Regional Cooperation (SAARC) was the result of a proposal made by Bangladesh Prime Minister Ziaur Rahman in 1977. India had resisted this institutional mechanism to discuss any controversial issues like security, partly because of its lingering conflict with Pakistan and because the smaller states have limited benefits to offer India in material terms. India feared that the diplomatic forum will whittle down India's dominant status, as the smaller powers could gang up and also demand juridical equality while using normative and legal principles to obtain status equivalency. The intense conflict with Pakistan discouraged India from engaging in any serious discussion of regional security issues under SAARC. Economic cooperation with regional states increased during the 1990s, but still constituted only 1.7 to 3.8 percent of India's total global trade.[36] The failure of India and the smaller states to create meaningful economic cooperation opportunities has offered China an important opening to enter the region and to challenge India's status dominance and aspirations. One positive note for India has been the increasing convergence between India and the United States on relations with most South Asian countries, something that was missing during the Cold War era.[37]

The Sino-Indian Status Competition in South Asia

Since 2010, China has arrived in the Indian Ocean region as a serious contender to the power and status of the United States and India. This has offered the smaller states a major opportunity to increase their leverage vis-à-vis India, and they have managed to gain substantial benefits from China. That has forced India to come up with economic assistance which is considerably higher than it had given in previous eras. Despite their huge power asymmetry with their neighbors, both China and India have not been able to fully translate their superiority into drawing smaller states in the region into hegemonic subordinate relationships, although China has had more success than India in recent years due to its deeper pockets. More importantly, security rivals, such as Japan and China, and China and India, have been expanding their economic relationships, a paradoxical behavior from the point of view of balance-of-power theory and practice. The absence of a zero-sum security and economic rivalry among them enables smaller powers to not join either side in a military alliance, but at the same time to extract resources and infrastructure development funds through asymmetrical bargaining strategies. Both China and India have also made some efforts to rope in regional states as partners, but not to the extent of seeking military alliances. The managed and limited rivalry between China and India has allowed smaller states to play one against the other and to gain maximum economic benefits. Domestic opposition to giving excessive concessions plays a role in the ability of the ruling elites of smaller states to balance the two powers. Ultimately, the smaller states of South Asia are constrained by India's geographical proximity and historic ties, but increasingly have been able to balance that with China's higher levels of economic assistance to them.

While intensifying its trade relationship with India, China has engaged in the infrastructure development of countries such as Pakistan, Sri Lanka, Nepal, Maldives, and Bangladesh that has both economic and security implications. The construction and development of deep-sea ports in places like Gwadar (Pakistan) and Hambantota (Sri Lanka) and border area roads (Nepal and Myanmar) are part of the BRI projects. The maritime element has been dubbed as part of what some call the "string of pearls strategy"— a long thread of ports and bases that allows China access throughout the Indo-Pacific region.[38] China has also established Confucian institutes in smaller states such as Nepal, Sri Lanka, Maldives, Pakistan, and Bangladesh to increase its soft power and thereby status, although their value is yet to be seen. India has also attempted soft power approaches and offered economic incentives to the smaller neighbors based on "non-reciprocity," "connectivity," and "asymmetrical responsibilities."[39]

Nepal

The history of India-Nepal relations is characterized by conflict and cooperation, and India's attempt at dominance has been a major challenge for the Nepali political elite. India has not been able to establish hegemonic stability over Nepal, despite the latter being very weak and unstable.[40] The 1950 treaty between the two countries has kept the border open, and Nepali citizens were given "non-discriminatory treatment" in "economic and commercial affairs."[41] The 1951 trade treaty allowed transit rights through Indian territory for Nepal's trade with third countries. A large number of Nepalese have been able to work in India, mostly in lower-paying jobs as security guards or household workers. India's involvement in Nepal's elections and support for or against different political parties have generated much anger among the Nepalese, even when some of the same parties vie for Indian support. The ill-treatment of an Indian-origin minority ethnic group, the Madhesis, by the Nepali governments prompted a violent rebellion by them. India supported the Madhesis, which generated additional problems. The assassination of Nepal's monarch, King Birenda, and 10 members of his family, including the queen, in a massacre in June 2001 by the crown prince, Dipendra, also generated tensions with India. The Maoist rebellion in Nepal that began in 1996 caused a great deal of bloodshed. The Indian opposition to this rebellion did not stop the subsequent victory of the Maoists. That said, India did assist in the eventual transformation of Nepal into a democratic state. Maoists joined the Nepali government in 2008, and India supported the government reluctantly.[42] India attempted on a few occasions to squeeze Nepal with economic sanctions and border closings when it did not pursue Indian policy preferences. These Indian sanctions have generated more antipathy toward India's attempted hegemony. Amid these ups and downs in relations, India and Nepal have signed many treaties for water sharing and hydroelectric projects.

However, the arrival of China in Nepal has transformed India's influence and status in the country. Since 2015, China has assisted Nepal's economic development in a massive way by increasing its economic and infrastructure support, especially in hydro-power and road-construction sectors. This support has forced India to modify some of its earlier strategies. There is a clear status diminution here for India, as landlocked Nepal finally managed to break out of India's trade route monopoly. The 2015 earthquake in Nepal also garnered much Chinese assistance.[43] But the most significant development has been Nepal joining China's BRI and, as part of that, gaining considerable investment for the development of infrastructure, especially road, rail, and air links, and possible trade routes via China that parallel the existing trade route with India. China has promised some $8.3 billion for infrastructure development, including the Kathmandu-Lhasa rail link, while India's formal support remains much less ($317 million). That said, Nepal depends on India in a variety of areas, including fuel supply and remittances. But increasing Chinese support has meant that India will no longer have the ability to successfully place highly punitive sanctions on Nepal, as it did on some previous occasions.

In response to China's increased activism in Nepal, India has ratcheted up its support for Kathmandu by pledging more economic assistance, along with frequent visits to each other's capital by Indian leaders and Nepali politicians. In recent years, Nepal has been somewhat successful in not giving in to either China or India in the area of military cooperation, while reaping considerable economic benefits from both. India imposed an economic embargo on Nepal in December 2015 after the latter issued a new constitution that did not take into account Madhesi minority interests. India also was upset over the main Nepali parties cozying up to China. Some weeks later, the Nepali prime minister visited India, and New Delhi lifted the embargo in February 2016. This incident increased China's interest in Nepal, and currently eight railroads linking Nepal with Tibet are under construction. Nepal's hope of breaking the landlocked country's dependence on India may soon become a reality.[44]

In the summer of 2017, Nepal attempted to remain neutral during the Doklam crisis that saw skirmishes between Chinese and Indian troops. In November–December 2017, a coalition of Communist parties won the Nepal elections, defeating the pro-Indian Nepali Congress. The new government has successfully strengthened economic relations with China. Some predict that this might bring the Indo-Nepal relations to more of an even keel, allowing more maneuvering space for Kathmandu.[45] The election of Maoist leader Pushpa Kamal Dahal as prime minister of Nepal in December 2022 has placed further strains on the relationship, as the previous government heightened some of its border disputes with India. However, Dahal has since then engaged India diplomatically to maintain an even keel with China.[46] India's earlier status dominance in the triadic relationship has been changing as China ratchets up its ties with Nepal. In this case, status sharing may be the result, which is a far cry from India's near dominance of Nepali affairs for nearly 70 years.

Sri Lanka

In Sri Lanka, India has had considerable influence and status dominance since 1947. This situation has changed with the arrival of China in the island nation as a major source of investment, especially in the infrastructure area. After being the number one trading partner of Sri Lanka for decades, India lost that position to China in 2016. In 2020, bilateral trade amounted to $3.6 billion, with the balance of trade in favor of Colombo.[47] The opening of reduced-tariff trade with Sri Lanka, a large number of Indian tourist visits, and cooperation in a number of areas have helped maintain the relationship, and India's help in Sri Lanka's economic development is now viewed by a majority of Sri Lankans as a positive development. This attitude is a change from the turbulent days of the violent secessionist struggle headed by the Tamil Eelam, which ended in 2009. India's own unwillingness to assist the Tamils when the Sri Lankan army brutally suppressed and defeated them in May 2009 also helped in changing the relationship.

However, in Sri Lanka, China has made major forays through its infrastructure development programs, especially by acquiring the Hambantota port on the southern side of the island state in a 99-year lease. This has generated both security and status concerns for India. The port was built with Chinese assistance, and in July 2017, Sri Lanka signed a $1.12 billion agreement allowing a Chinese company to run the port due to huge operational costs and lack of profit. Following Indian protestations, Sri Lanka declared that the port would be used exclusively for civilian purposes and that China could not bring naval vessels to the port. In May 2017, Sri Lanka had rejected a Chinese request to dock its submarine on this port because of concerns raised by India, as well as protests by Sri Lankan opposition groups. In December 2017, Sri Lanka and China signed a 99-year lease for Beijing to develop and use the port for civilian-only purposes.[48] The latter part of the agreement was a clear signal to India to consider the deal as not threatening India's security interests in the Indian Ocean. Moreover, Sri Lanka has been encouraging India to invest in the now closed airport at Hambantota.

China has acquired other infrastructure projects in Sri Lanka, especially the huge Colombo port city, and many highway developments. India has also been actively developing projects in Sri Lanka and provides a large part of the Island nation's railway, truck, and other transportation vehicles, and it has offered over $2.4 billion in investment in recent years.[49] Colombo witnessed a massive economic downturn in 2022, partially due to the inability to pay interest on heavy debts it owed to foreign lenders—some $51 billion (of which to China some $6.5 billion)—and to the mismanagement of the economy by President Gotabaya Rajapaksa and his brothers, who ran an ineffective government. The political establishment collapsed as a result of major protests and food riots, following which Colombo approached India and the World Bank for support, and India responded with some $1.9 billion and supplies of essential goods such as oil.[50] It is yet to be seen if Indian magnanimity and the hostility among the Sri Lankan public toward China will generate a status enhancement for India in its contestation with China. The most likely outcome is shared status for India with China, as Sri Lanka cannot afford to lose either.

Bangladesh

Over the years, India's relations with Bangladesh also have witnessed ups and downs. Large-scale migration from former East Pakistan to India began with the suppression of Bengali nationalism by Pakistan prior to the 1971 war. India has had many reversals in its status and influence in Bangladesh, despite the liberation of the state by India's military intervention. Since 2014, Bangladesh has played a delicate balancing game between China and India. China has promised considerable economic assistance to Dhaka, which has been eager to join the BRI as well as the India-Japan initiative linking Northeast India and Southeast Asia. In October 2016, Bangladesh signed a memorandum of understanding with China for a $24.45 billion bilateral assistance for some 34 projects in addition to a preexisting $13.6 billion of Chinese investment for joint ventures, thereby receiving a total of $38.05 billion in Chinese assistance. This materialized following a much smaller Indian contribution of $2 billion for socioeconomic projects in Bangladesh. Although the Chinese funding is much larger, Bangladesh declared that it has no desire to be part of any geopolitical alliances and that it wants to "maintain good relations with everyone."[51]

Under pressure from a possible China-Bangladesh active relationship, India had already softened its stance toward Bangladesh on territorial disputes and signed a border settlement agreement in November 2011. This agreement was ratified by both countries in June 2015, under which India transferred 111 enclaves and in return received from Bangladesh 51 enclaves where their respective populations lived.[52] Border connectivity and hydro-electric power generation were also part of the Indian commitment to Bangladesh. In addition, India is spearheading the Bay of Bengal Initiative for Multi-Sectoral Technical and Economic Cooperation (BIMSTEC) group of nations as a parallel to SAARC, which has been somewhat inactive due to the continued India-Pakistan rivalry. The new grouping consists of India, Nepal, Bhutan, Bangladesh, Sri Lanka, Myanmar, and Thailand.[53] The Modi government attached considerable importance to this grouping, as evident in the invitation of all BIMSTEC leaders to his inauguration in 2019. India appears to be looking to this forum to enhance its links with Southeast Asia, improve its status in the region, and counter Pakistan and Afghanistan. Similar to Sri Lanka and Nepal, Bangladesh has managed to obtain considerable economic investments from both China and India, showing that status competition among rising powers can be a source of increased leverage for smaller states. As of 2023, India has managed to maintain a reasonably strong position in Bangladesh, partially due to the continuing rule of the Awami League Party, led by Sheikh Hasina, which is somewhat pro-India.[54]

Maldives and Seychelles

India has maintained for some time a benign hegemony over the island states of Maldives and Seychelles. The Indian Navy helped to restore Maldives's beleaguered regime after a coup attempt in November 1988 by rebellious forces along with Tamil separatists from Sri Lanka. Indian economic aid was crucial for the island state to survive. However, in recent years, Maldives has become a focal point of China in its efforts to gain access to the Indian Ocean area, especially for its BRI links. China has offered key infrastructure projects, including expansion of the international airport under a 50-year lease by a Chinese firm signed in December 2016, a bridge connecting the capital and the island where the airport is located, and several other projects, including the construction of a new port. India also offers Maldives naval presence for its protection and is keen that the island nation does not allow China military facilities.

A December 2017 free trade deal gave China a major economic edge over India in Maldives. But immediately afterward, Maldives's politicians flew to Delhi to reassure India of no security concessions to China and expressed the island state's "India-first policy."[55] The elections in 2018 saw the defeat of the pro-China candidate, Abdulla Yameen, who ran an "India Out campaign," and the victory of the pro-India candidate, Ibrahim Mohamed Solih, who was able to build a better relationship with India. India quickly followed suit with $1 billion in aid and political moves to consolidate the relationship. Subsequently, India offered much help during the Covid crisis by providing free vaccines and medicines. India thus has been able to put a temporary dent in China's status advancement in this island nation. This may not last, though; a future election could see the pro-China, Maldivian Democratic Party (MDV) return to power. The visit of President Xi Jinping in August 2022 has produced more favorable deals for Maldives and it has emerged as a critical link in China's maritime component of the BRI.[56] The domestic divisions among Maldives's political parties on China versus India is a major challenge to India with regard to retaining its dominant status and influence in the island republic. Status sharing is again the possible outcome.[57]

In Seychelles also, India has increasingly been facing challenges from China to its preexisting defense cooperation and economic dominance. In 1986, India helped to quash an attempted coup against Seychelles leader

France-Albert Rene. India also leased Seychelles's Assumption Islands in March 2015 for joint naval activities. Facing China's increasing presence in the Indian Ocean, India has attempted to establish a full-fledged naval base there that was not agreed by Seychelles.[58] The fear of the small nation getting into a tussle between China and India places it in a stronger bargaining position vis-à-vis India. India has been attempting to promote relations with the island republic under the 2015 SAGAR (Security and Growth for All in the Region) agreement for enhancing maritime cooperation in the Indian Ocean region. Under this program, the two countries have signed a number of trade, anti-piracy, and medical tourism agreements.[59] India has been able to develop a base in the Mauritian island of Agalega, giving it some military presence in the area.[60] Since Seychelles joined BRI in 2016, several Chinese leaders have visited the islands, and it is once again proving to be a challenge for India's regional status, as it may have to share its position with China.

Bhutan

Bhutan remains close to India, which has acquired quite a bit of status and influence in the Himalayan kingdom since the early days of Indian independence. During the colonial period, Bhutan was a British-India vassal state. The 1910 treaty between British-India and Bhutan allowed internal sovereignty to Bhutanese, but the latter agreed to be "guided by the advice" of the British on matters of foreign policy. In practical terms, the kingdom was allowed to retain a semi-dependency status but with isolationism as its state policy.[61] The August 1949 treaty with India saw Bhutan retain its sovereignty but with "Indian guidance on foreign policy."[62] Since then, Bhutan has been almost like a protectorate of India, heavily influenced by Indian policy preferences, especially toward China and on border issues. India has offered much economic assistance to Bhutan, in particular through the setting up of many hydroelectric projects, with India buying the electricity. Bhutan's economy has emerged as the most successful one in South Asia in terms of per capita income. Hydro exports to India now constitute some 60 percent of Bhutan's export income.[63]

Bhutan has also been going through political transformation, with periodic elections since King Jigme Khesar Namgyel Wangchuck has allowed increased political freedom to the population. India's tense standoff with China in the summer of 2017 occurred on the India-China-Bhutan trijunction in Doklam and in defense of the Bhutanese claims over the area where the Chinese were building roads. During the crisis, India was most concerned that the Chinese were testing India's status vis-à-vis Bhutan and how far New Delhi would go to protect its relationship with Thimbu. For China, this was an effort at showing its ability to develop independent links with the states that are under Indian dominance, as in the case of Nepal, Maldives, and Sri Lanka. Thus, the last remaining area of Indian hegemony in South Asia is now actively challenged by China, which is tempting the Bhutanese with overtures of economic and infrastructure support—just as China did with Nepal. The difference is a Bhutanese fear of their Buddhist culture being adversely affected by the Chinese presence given the considerable challenges the Dalai Lama and his Tibetan Buddhists have faced from China. However, in July 2022, it was reported that China had built some villages on the disputed Doklam region and inside Bhutanese-claimed territories, raising questions about India's ability to withstand Chinese pressures in this strategic corner. There are also concerns that Bhutan may opt for Chinese largesse and settle its territorial disputes in ways that may adversely affect India's status and relationship with the Himalayan kingdom.[64]

Afghanistan

Afghanistan poses considerable status and security challenges for India. India's status quest and strategic footprint in Afghanistan have been heavily affected by the competition with Pakistan, which has long supported the Taliban in order to diminish Indian influence there. The geopolitical conflicts involving the Soviet Union and later the United States and the Taliban regime have helped to shape these relations. Afghanistan, from the beginning of Indian independence, was pro-India because of its conflict with Pakistan over territorial divisions of the Durand Line and the issue of Pashtun minority rights in Pakistan. The champion of these rights was Abdul Ghaffar Khan, affectionately called the "frontier Gandhi" for his nonviolent approach. Many members of the Afghani elite were educated in Indian universities, and this connection gave India a high level of status in Afghanistan for a period of time. The Soviet invasion in 1979 changed all that, and the Indira Gandhi government, despite much strategic discomfort, maintained silence over the intervention. The United States' adoption of Pakistan and the Mujahideen to fight the Soviets further marginalized India's role in Kabul. After the Soviet withdrawal, the Taliban waged a brutal civil war with the Tajik groups that made up the Northern Alliance, which was supported by India. However, the Taliban's military victory in 1996 consolidated the anti-India forces in Afghanistan, and until 2002, the Taliban regime supported anti-India activities, including the hijacking of an Indian Airlines plane, which was released only after India freed three jailed terrorists and carried them on a plane to Kandahar, accompanied by Foreign Minister Jaswant Singh.

The U.S. military intervention in 2001 changed the dynamics, and India became a strong supporter of Afghan governments led by Hamid Karzai and Ashraf Ghani and supported the U.S. military presence. India had invested some $3 billion in development projects in Afghanistan during the two decades between the Taliban's collapse in 2001 and subsequent victory in 2021. It also built Afghanistan's Parliament building and the Salma Dam on the Hari River. India has provided much assistance by way of humanitarian aid and educational support by building schools and training both civilian students and military officials in India.[65] To assist landlocked Afghanistan's trade, India helped them circumvent Pakistani territory for trade. India worked with Iran in constructing the port at Chabahar and a road system that allowed Afghanistan to move goods through Iran and around Pakistan. These efforts were slowed down by new U.S. sanctions on Iran in 2019 imposed by the Trump administration and the Taliban's victory in 2021.

India's challenge has been how to convince Pakistan that it has no malign intentions in Afghanistan. Regional status competition between the two states is a big part of this story. Pakistan's military and ISI have been driven by the archaic geopolitical idea of keeping "strategic depth" in Afghanistan, which is based on the premise that if the Indian military is able to cut through Pakistani forces, in Afghanistan they have a place to hide and fight back. The chances of India succeeding in a pincer-like blitzkrieg operation against well-armed Pakistani forces through the mountainous terrain is virtually nil in the current context of nuclear deterrence. Pakistan has also been deploying short-range tactical weapons on the border to prevent any possible Indian assault. So, Afghanistan becomes a pawn in the chess game for regional status, even though it has little to offer by way of economic benefits to both sides. Pakistan's larger goal is status denial for India in Afghanistan and beyond, and its links with the Taliban makes this feasible.

India was not a member of the negotiations involving the Taliban, Pakistan, the United States, and China over the U.S. withdrawal in 2021. The U.S. efforts to form a coalition government that included the Taliban did not succeed. The eventual victory of the Taliban and its formation of a repressive government after a hurried U.S. exit has basically destroyed all of India's investments in Afghanistan. The lack of much international support for the Taliban by any major state has dented their ability to change the status quo in South Asia. Even though Pakistan has made some temporary gains in the status competition over Afghanistan with India, the Taliban itself is no longer playing according to Pakistani ISI dictates. The Taliban since its victory has made overtures to India in an effort to balance its relations with Pakistan and gain much needed economic assistance and infrastructure projects, but without much success.[66]

In its geopolitical and status competitions with India in South Asia during the past decade, China has had a great deal of success in creating a wedge between India and the smaller states that were traditionally closer to New Delhi, due to geography and preexisting cultural factors. However, even here the relationships have not matured to alignments, as South Asian states have benefited in the short term from the managed India-China rivalry. One of the key reasons for the smaller states' ability to maneuver strategically is the absence of an intense balance of power competition between China and India until now, which has enabled the smaller states to play off Beijing and New Delhi and gain economic assistance from both, without offering military commitments in return, such as naval bases.

The Near Abroad

India has been making efforts to transcend the immediate neighborhood of South Asia and spread its wings to Central Asia, the Persian Gulf, Southeast Asia, and Africa. There is clearly a status dimension to these efforts; becoming a significant player in different nearby regions is a hallmark of a great power. India's external affairs minister Yashwant Sinha in 2004 stated that its extended neighborhood "stretches from the Suez Canal to the South China Sea and includes within it West Asia [the Middle East], the Gulf, Central Asia, South East Asia, East Asia, the Asia Pacific and the Indian Ocean Region."[67] This has been driven by a desire to move out of South Asia, which has been a constraining region for India's status and power ambitions.[68]

Southeast Asia
In Southeast Asia, despite the deep civilizational connections, geopolitics and economics often curtailed India's status elevation in the region. The "Look East" and "Act East" policies have helped to widen its influence and status from where it was during the Cold War era. The ten ASEAN member states give considerable importance to India, as was evident in their

inviting India in 1995 as a full dialogue partner in the ASEAN Regional Forum (ARF). The free trade agreement with ASEAN also has helped improve India's relations and status aspirations in the region. Key states such as Singapore, Malaysia, Indonesia, and Vietnam have increased their ties with India. This is part of their hedging strategy toward China, partially due to apprehensions over China's South China Sea incursions. Yet, when it comes to trade, in 2021 China's total was $685 billion versus India's $78 billion and the United States' $362 billion.[69] India's unwillingness to join Asian regional free trade agreements like the Comprehensive and Progressive Agreement for Transpacific Partnership (CPTPP) and the Regional Comprehensive Economic Partnership (RCEP) also reduced its footprint in the region. Bilateral trade agreements have been India's preferred pathway, which are probably beneficial for India in the short run given its relative economic weaknesses vis-à-vis China. Even then, regional trepidations about China's rise offer India opportunities in its status aspirations in Southeast Asia. India became a dialogue partner of ASEAN in 1996, a strategic partner in 2012, and a comprehensive strategic partner in 2022, showing the status elevation for India within the regional grouping.[70] The need for balancing China, especially in the Indo-Pacific and the South China Sea, is a motivating factor for many ASEAN countries, such as Vietnam and Singapore, in developing stronger ties with India.

Africa

Africa is another traditional theater in which India has had much interest. India has a fairly high level of status recognition there, dating back to the decolonization era of the 1960s, when India played a key role in liberating the African colonies from European rule. India has been a major donor for development schemes in some African countries. India's political elite views Africa as an extended neighborhood. The India-Africa Forum Summit is held every three years and is often attended by top leaders of all African countries. India offers crucial aid and infrastructure projects, and these are considered as more benign than China's increasingly aggressive strategy in Africa. According to a report, unlike China's heavy investment in infrastructure development, which resulted in hefty debt levels for many African countries, India's $11 billion investment in Africa until 2021 focused on "human resources development, information technology, maritime security, education and health care." Moreover, Indian companies also employ mostly African workers, whereas China has been bringing in Chinese workers—a

source of resentment for many Africans.[71] The 3-million-strong Indian diaspora and the historical cultural and political links have given India many
advantages in Africa. India supplies some 60 percent of Africa's drugs and
vaccines, which also has benefited it. Even then, China's $254 billion trade
(2020) with Africa dwarfs India's $89.5 billion (2021).[72] This shows the un-
even playing field India faces in Africa, similar to other extended neighborhood regions where India is competing with China for status and influence.

The Persian Gulf and the Middle East

In the Persian Gulf and the Middle East regions, India has made remarkable strides in status enhancement since the 2010s. There is a greater recognition among the six Gulf Arab countries—Bahrain, Kuwait, Oman,
Qatar, Saudi Arabia, and the United Arab Emirates—of India's significance
as an economic partner and large importer of oil and gas. Indian workers
and expatriates constitute the largest concentrations of populations in these
countries. In addition, there has been major increase in trade numbers.
The United Arab Emirates, for instance, which is home to some 3.5 million
Indians, has emerged in 2022 as the third-largest trading partner of India
with $88 billion in two-way trade. The two countries also signed a compre-
hensive economic partnership agreement in February 2022 to consolidate
their relationship.[73] The Gulf monarchies have in fact changed their earlier
policy of equating Pakistan and India, and in some cases have downgraded
their relations with Pakistan. During the Cold War era, these countries had a
close relationship with the United States and simultaneously with Pakistan,
the latter partially for religious considerations. The end of the Cold War
allowed India to view these Gulf states as more reliable partners for trade, investment, and oil imports. As Islamabad became entrenched in radical Islam
during the 1990s, providing a haven to terrorist groups, the Gulf countries
de-hyphenated India and Pakistan as coequal states for their relationships.
During the Kargil conflict in 1999, the Gulf monarchies took a neutral position. Since the 9/11 attacks, they have been adjusting to U.S. preferences,
which has also been beneficial to India' interests.[74]

India's trade figures with the six Gulf Cooperation Council countries
showed a rapid increase in exports from $27.8 billion for 2020–2021 to $44
billion for 2021–2022. Imports have increased from $59 billion to $110.73
billion over the same period.[75] India's much improved relations with Israel
and Israel's opening to the Gulf region have helped in this process, as the
Palestine issue no longer constrains India's engagement in the region. Under

Modi, India has made some progress toward befriending Muslim countries. However, the policies of his government toward the Muslim minority within India have hurt India's position among these nations. Although a temporary coalition emerged among Turkey, Malaysia, and Pakistan questioning India's policies in Kashmir, the Gulf monarchies have strengthened their ties with India due to their changing geopolitical and economic interests and India's emergence as a leading oil importer. These monarchies are eager to expand ties with India and other Asian countries in a range of areas, including food security, energy technology, and defense and security. They have been following a "Look East" policy, which coincides with India's "Think West" policy.[76]

India has made some crucial agreements with Iran for the development of the Chabahar port and the highway connecting Chabahar with Afghanistan though Iran, thereby removing the Pakistani territory in trading with Afghanistan. India has also developed a crucial oil supply relationship with Iran, emerging as the second-largest importer of Iranian crude as well as a major investor in Iranian oil projects. New Delhi's opposition to Iran's nuclear program and the frequent imposition of U.S. economic sanctions on Iran have created major challenges to India's continued relationship with Iran, although Washington has been more accommodating of India's concerns than often depicted.[77] The relationship became more challenging after U.S. President Donald Trump decided to reimpose sanctions on Iran and break the Iran Nuclear Agreement in 2019. India's 2019 budget severely reduced the amount it spent on Chabahar, and oil imports from Iran were also curtailed. The slowness of the Indian investment in Chabahar and building of the rail link to Afghanistan caused Iran to step up its own investment in the project. China's $400 billion investment plan for Iran also challenges India's relationship with Teheran.[78] Despite these challenges, India still continues to be a key trading partner of Iran, especially in the oil and gas area, and this is likely to continue for years to come.

Future Prospects

India has realized that its great power ambitions lie with the regions beyond South Asia, and that it has to obtain higher status through peaceful strategies. Historically, most previous rising powers had resorted to aggressive warfare to develop their exclusive spheres of influence in their respective regions. In the contemporary world, such aggressive behavior will have a negative impact on a rising power's prospects. Both China and India have increased their footprints in the near abroad regions of Southeast Asia, the Persian Gulf, and Africa without military conquests and excessive unilateral gains in terms of spheres of influence. India has received greater status recognition from the states in these regions than before partly because of their desire to militarily and economically balance China, and this is bound to increase as the Indian economy becomes a central part of their trading and investor relations. India's improved relations with the West, especially the United States and Japan, have helped in these efforts.

There is also a realization in India that a major increase in South Asian regional status is not easy, partly due to China's increasing presence, and hence it has attempted to transcend the region by looking for relationships with East Asian and Southeast Asian countries. The "Look East" policy, pursued by Prime Ministers Narasimha Rao and Manmohan Singh, and its successor "Act East" policy of Prime Minister Modi were driven by this desire to go beyond the region to increase India's status and economic prosperity with the help of states in East and Southeast Asia. The Modi government in 2019 decided to elevate the BIMSTEC grouping, consisting of Bangladesh, Bhutan, India, Myanmar, Nepal, Sri Lanka, and Thailand, over the SAARC grouping of Afghanistan, Bangladesh, Bhutan, India, Maldives, Nepal, Pakistan, and Sri Lanka in an effort to prevent Pakistan from challenging India's dominant status in regional institutions.

In the years ahead, India is likely to increase its global status even without gaining much new leverage in the South Asia region. That is because the increasing presence of a deep-pocketed China is chipping away at India's previously dominant regional status. There is a reasonable chance, however, that some of the debt-trap situations that Chinese involvement has created may turn these states against Beijing, offering India more opportunities for status enhancement. In all likelihood, though, India will have to consider shared status in South Asia. India is also likely to focus more attention on global status markers in order to transcend South Asia. In fact, it has already made many strides in this regard. A lot depends on how many states will fall fully in China's orbit. As many are unwilling, India's efforts at a shared status position in Southeast Asia, East Asia, the Persian Gulf, and Africa look feasible. If China becomes a more threatening power, or attempts direct imperial ventures, India will have a higher potential of gaining additional status and leverage in South Asia and beyond, as long as it can offer a powerful military and economic counterweight. However, India may have to re-strategize its approach and become more open to the concerns of these states, as well as generate benign attitudes among their elite and public, if it wants to sustain and enhance its status position regionally. Having improved regional status can also help globally. For instance, in the wider Indo-Pacific region, states in Southeast Asia and East Asia such as Japan and South Korea already view India as their conduit for higher regional connectivity. In the twenty-first century, as the international system evolves into multiple centers of powers, the goal of a shared status posture is more feasible for India, unlike most other rising powers such as Brazil.[79] In the future, China's share of influence in the South Asia regional space is likely to grow, but India's share in the larger Indo-Pacific region is likely to increase relative to China's as well. In order to achieve these goals, India may need to become an actor of greater consequence, especially in the economic arena. It must also pursue deft diplomatic and military strategies, short of waging wars.

7

State Capacity

The Human Development Index (HDI) of the United Nations Development Program (UNDP) in 2022 ranked India as 132 out of 191 states, a marginal decline from the previous year's rank of 131.[1] Although there are many problems with indices of this nature, inclusive development has been a major challenge for India in achieving its desired global status and influence. India's status quest has been hampered by the continued prevalence of a weak state with a highly uneven socioeconomic development of the population, even though it has achieved many milestones of progress in its 76-year history since it began in 1947 as a free state. The second resurgence of Covid-19 in April 2021 showed the weaknesses and fragility of the state in India when it comes to providing basic healthcare and other public services that are taken for granted in a modern state. According to the World Health Organization (WHO) report, some 4.7 million people—nearly 10 times higher than Indian government's estimates—might have died from the pandemic through December 2021.[2]

For a period of time, the state, both in New Delhi and in the constituent states, was helpless before the extraordinary onslaught of the pandemic. There were few preparations, and as a result, scores of thousands of Indians in cities like Delhi died without hospital beds and essential oxygen, creating a heart-wrenching scene that played out for several weeks. International media showed the burning of corpses on pyres and makeshift arrangements for the sick and the dead and some bodies even washed up on riverbanks such as the Ganges. The Modi government attempted to deflect criticism by projecting a positive image on social media, but international media and some daring Indian outlets covered the tragedy that was profoundly afflicting India's population as well as its status aspirations. Part of the problem was that the Modi government had prematurely declared conquest of the virus and offered vaccines and medicines to the rest of the world. The crisis showed that whatever economic growth had occurred in India since the liberalization started in 1991, it could easily be upset, as millions who had entered the lower middle class had fallen below the poverty level once again.[3]

The consolation for India was that it was not alone in this difficult phase of a truly global pandemic crisis. In fact, Donald Trump's America, with one of the most advanced economies and medical care systems, held the second known cumulative casualty figure, followed by Brazil, another country often compared to India as an aspirational rising power.[4] The crisis indeed dented the status and reputation of all these states, including established and rising powers. Even Western countries such as the United Kingdom, France, Germany, and Italy faced immense challenges in dealing with the pandemic crisis. Interestingly, countries that have already achieved higher international status tend not to lose their status ranking that easily. It is much harder for an aspiring power if it is afflicted by weak state syndrome not to be affected disproportionately in terms of international perceptions and reputation. The Indian state has a reputation of being a reactive state, and it did fairly well in the third wave of the pandemic in January–March 2022. To the state's credit, more preparations were made to avert the catastrophe as witnessed in the second upsurge in 2021. Since then, economic recovery has been slowly happening, although it is not clear how rapidly employment rates for India's youth and rural populations can be increased.

Despite the fact that India has achieved many milestones in development since independence, there is great unevenness in this process. For instance, in February 2019, *The Economist* carried a satellite photo of India in terms of electrification of the entire country. Most revealing was the inequality in the availability of electricity, a crude but significant indicator of the uneven development of India.[5] Although in June 2018 Prime Minister Modi announced that India had electrified 100 percent of its villages, anyone living in India confronts power cutoff in many cities in the sweltering heat. Indian's electric transmission lines are often the most archaic, and power loss and theft are very common. Similarly, continuous supply of clean water to India's large urban population is still a dream. In several rural areas, women and children walk miles to collect drinking water for daily use. For three months during the monsoon season, India is often flooded due to incessant rains, and the swollen rivers eject water to the Arabian Sea and Bay of Bengal, with little water conservation efforts made other than through some big dams spread around the country's main river systems. In the urban areas, water supply has improved, but in rural areas, India has far to go. In this regard, China has achieved much more success in offering continuous water supply, while most Indian cities have limited hours of service.[6]

Although India's public highways have made improvement over the years, inadequately built and maintained Indian roads—and a considerable dearth of them in rural areas—are representative of a country with poor infrastructure development despite huge investments in recent times. The challenges are more noticeable in some parts of the vast country than in others. The Southern Indian states, such as Kerala, Karnataka, Andhra Pradesh, and Tamil Nadu, and the Western states, Maharashtra and Gujarat, have made much progress in improving their infrastructures and social safety nets, while others in the Northern Hindi belt lag behind on many parameters of development. For instance, in terms of GDP, per capita income, basic health, infrastructure, and life expectancy, many parts of the Northern and Eastern belts are akin to Sub-Saharan Africa. A 2015 study by Oxford researchers found that of the 1.6 billion people afflicted by multidimensional poverty globally, 440 million were in eight of the large Indian states—Bihar, Jharkhand, Madhya Pradesh, Uttar Pradesh, Chhattisgarh, Odisha, Rajasthan, and West Bengal—with a "similar number of poor as in 25 Sub-Saharan African states."[7] In 2021, this has not improved markedly, despite India pulling millions out of extreme poverty. Journalist Shekhar Gupta, quoting World Bank statistics, argued that much of Africa is richer than India in many indicators of development.[8] The regional variations in per capita GDP are huge: top-ranked Goa's GDP stood at $7,029, while Bihar's was $659 and Uttar Pradesh's was $1,043.[9] Similarly, the average life expectancy in India was 71 for the 2015–2019 period, and yet it varied from top-ranking Delhi's 75.9 and number two Kerala's 75.2, to Uttar Pradesh's 65.6 and Madhya Pradesh's 67.[10] Even then, this is a remarkable achievement, as several Indian states have higher life expectancy than Russia's 71.3 years for 2020. In fact, the male life expectancy of India in 2020 was 69 versus Russia's 66.[11]

At the national level, a vast network of railways, telecommunications, national highways, and postal services comprise some semblance of a rapidly developing economy, in addition to the urban centers with high-tech and outsourcing sectors. As discussed in Chapter 3, large-scale macro economic growth has happened since the liberalization in 1991, and the economic sectors that have made the highest progress are the most globalized—IT, telecommunications, and pharmaceuticals. These economic engines are also what gives India a much elevated status in hard-power domains, but this is a skewed view of India's progress. To Indians who lived during the pre- and post-liberalization eras, the progress is palpable. However, for those who travel abroad, especially to East Asia, Southeast Asia, and the Persian Gulf, the changes are at best limited, and the quality of life is often not equivalent to what one would expect for a country aspiring to reach middle income level by the 2030s. With increasing prosperity in many parts of the country came overcrowded roads and highly polluted urban centers, challenging the developmental model of India in many parameters. In short, the rapid growth of the Indian economy is not adequately reflected in its infrastructure or quality of life markers. In contrast, at every stage in the economic growth of the East Asian states, the infrastructure and living conditions showed marked improvements. What explains this discrepancy between aspiration and achievement in the developmental arena for India?

While India has achieved many milestone markers of status in an aggregate sense, it is still one of the world's most unequal rising powers, with a widening disparity in per capita income, and discrepancies in rural versus urban living standards, as well as between different communities/castes and gender. Poverty and malnutrition appear to be higher than in other developing countries at a similar stage of aggregate economic growth. The Global Hunger Index (GHI) that annually tracks the level of hunger globally placed India 107 out of 121 countries in its 2022 report.[12] Even noted in the Indian government's own report, 35.15 percent of Indian children suffer from child-stunting despite the many programs created to alleviate the scourge.[13]

India started off as an independent state with huge discrepancies, and these disparities have been difficult to bridge, even after years of economic progress. This inequality was glaringly present in March 2020 when millions of migrant laborers had to walk miles and miles in the scorching heat to reach their villages and towns when the Modi government enforced a national lockdown in the face of the coronavirus crisis, without much warning or adequate preparations. The workers from poorer parts of India are in fact the heart of the construction and service industry in most of India's urban centers and are the least protected due to the absence of a proper social safety net or labor laws. Governmental decisions and inadequate policies can affect them in the most negative way. Another example was the November 2016 "shock and awe" decision by the Modi government to suddenly withdraw the 1,000- and 500-rupee currency notes from circulation and clamp down on banking restrictions, with the aim of wiping out illegal cash holdings. The suffering of the population was immense, especially in the rural areas, as people had to stand in lines for many hours and days in front of banks or ATMs, unable to collect their meager savings for daily subsistence. This demonetization initiative hurt India's economic growth for some time and produced very little impact on corruption or black market activities.[14] Such drastic top-down whimsical measures hurt the ordinary citizens the most. Individuals with political and bureaucratic connections managed to convert their stack of banned currencies to good ones during the short window allowed for conversion, while the poor and tourists suffered the most.

India exhibits extreme richness in the middle of slums and shanti towns. An example is the newly built airport in Mumbai, India's commercial capital and named after Maharashtra's medieval hero Chatrapati Shivaji, who stood against the Mughal expansion in that region for a period. This airport can compete with any top-ranking airport in the world, and it has won many global awards, but it is surrounded by the world's largest slum, Dharavi. Some one million people live in this most crowded place on earth, of 2.1 square kilometers, which is depicted well in the movie *Slumdog Millionaire*. In contrast, Mumbai also has houses as expensive as those in New York or in Paris. The billionaire Mukesh Ambani built a lavish 36-story house in the heart of Mumbai with facilities such as swimming pools and helipads. The figures on inequality in India are staggering. For example, according to the 2022 World Inequality Report, in India "the top 10% and top 1% hold respectively 57% and 22% of total national income, the bottom 50% share has gone down to 13%. India stands out as a poor and very unequal country, with an affluent elite."[15] In 2022, India had some 221 billionaires, with about 70 additional ones created every year.[16] Even though the quality of life in India has shown significant improvements over the years, on various parameters, such as air quality, its cities are some of the worst in the world. For instance, New Delhi often is the most polluted capital city globally, and in a 2021 report some 63 Indian cites appeared in the top 100 most polluted cities worldwide.[17]

Many factors inhibit inclusive and equitable economic growth in India. Among them are the lopsided education and human development sectors. As a result, endemic poverty remains a major challenge, although India has come up with several programs to support the poor, such as the National Rural Employment Guarantee (NREG) scheme, which was launched in 2005 to offer some 100 days of guaranteed work to the poor. Annually, some $60 billion worth of subsidy is given by way of distribution of food, cooking gas, kerosene, fertilizer, petroleum, and other basics, mainly through ration shops. India also offers farmers base prices for their crops, the removal of which in 2020 led to mass protests. Yet, the enormity of the challenge is reflected in the fact that some 22 percent of the population live below the official poverty line of $2 a day. However, this number may be closer to 40 percent of the population and perhaps was even higher during the Covid era. The UNDP reported that by 2018, some 271 million had been lifted out of multidimensional poverty, measured in terms of monetary poverty, educational levels, and availability of basic infrastructure. However, high levels of associated maladies, such as calorie deficiency, stunted growth of children, and infant mortality rates have kept India in the developing country, and pockets of India in the least developing categories. Four Indian states, Bihar, Jharkhand, Uttar Pradesh, and Madhya Pradesh, have a total of 196 million multidimensional poor, revealing the concentration of extreme poverty in India.[18]

The question often arises, despite the high economic growth for nearly three decades, why has India not achieved the significant status markers of a semi-developed country, with clean water, decent healthcare, less polluted cities, and reliable infrastructure? Why do its shantytowns and slums keep growing? In fact, many Southeast Asian countries, and some with lower economic growth rates, have done better in building proper infrastructure, although shantytowns do exist in the poorer ones. In HDI, India's neighbors Bangladesh and Sri Lanka have performed better.[19] Can India achieve its full potential as a major power of the twenty-first century without adequate human development, even if it becomes a leading military and economic power in aggregate numbers? Regardless if India obtains global institutional accommodation, it will still remain a "truncated" or a "subaltern major power" with many pitfalls associated with skewed development until its elite understands and appreciates this reality by adopting a war-foot approach to tackle these issues.

Three critical factors are behind the developmental challenge to India's higher international status. The first is weak *state capacity*; the second is the often ineffective policies of *inclusive economic growth*; and the third is the increasing *intolerance in the polity*, especially toward minority Muslims and lower castes. The intolerance toward minorities, if it persists, will make the economic and social inequality even worse in the years to come. The efforts at making a coercive state that privileges the majority will not make India appear strong and legitimate in the eyes of other states, and internal polarization could sap the residual strengths built through democracy and secularism. These related umbrella factors capture a considerable amount of domestic-level reasons for India's fraught efforts to build its status today. At the global level, India will gain desired status rankings only if it is a state of consequence and if the Indian model of political and economic development has something novel to offer to the world.

A pivotal reason for India's developmental challenges is the ideational notions of Indian elite classes, both political and bureaucratic, and increasingly the middle class, about endemic poverty, its causes, and its solutions. Political parties in general make proclamations, but do not do much to alleviate endemic poverty. Sometimes this may be due to the fact that sloganeering gains votes and the Indian electorate often does not punish non-performance. Despite obtaining much progress, India has not achieved what it could have in 76 years if the Indian political and bureaucratic class were dedicated to strengthening India's human development and infrastructure on a war-footing and accomplishing higher status as one of the key goals of development. As a class, they have not become agents of rapid development like their counterparts in East Asia, in particular Korea, Taiwan, Singapore, and China, or even some of the Persian Gulf states such as the United Arab Emirates and Qatar. India's political and bureaucratic classes have yet to understand that they need to become strong developmental agents, capable of transforming their country on an urgent basis. As Indian scholar Aparna Pande puts it aptly: there is a great desire for the Indian elite for their country to be treated as a great power, but there is great "reluctance to implement policies and take actions that would help us achieve that goal."[20] Many of them seem more interested in the acquisition of private wealth at the cost of the state and its agencies. Even if they are supporters of development, and often work more effectively under crisis situations, their slow pace in approving and implementing developmental schemes is in effect hurting India's larger goal of emerging as a global power that can withstand the challenges coming from China and others.

There is considerable corruption at every level of the bureaucratic and political worlds of India. In the 2021 Transparency International's survey-based annual Corruption Perception Index, India was 85th among 180 countries based on perceived corruption in the public sector.[21] While this is not the absolute bottom level of corrupt countries, the score paints a negative picture of India's public employees. It is often stated that while the Indian bureaucracy is corrupt, the problem is that they do not deliver even after accepting bribes. The Chinese bureaucracy is also corrupt, but they often deliver. Corruption is evident in the everyday lives of the people handling police cases, traffic violations, court systems, small licenses, ration cards, and food supplies through the fair shops, railway tickets, and school admissions. Sadly, every layer of bureaucracy thrives on corruption. The district collectors belonging to the prestigious Indian Administrative Service (IAS) are supposed to be the agents of development, and many do work toward this goal. As Edward Luce states:

> many IAS officers, especially since the 1970s, when corruption appears to have become widely accepted as normal in India, have themselves become corrupt. Many even accept cheating as a legitimate part of the job. Since these bureaucrats are un-sackable there is almost nothing local people can do about a corrupt IAS officer, assuming they believe the official is not doing anything wrong in the first place.[22]

As the salaries of government officials are much less than their private-sector equivalents, there is a desire to acquire as much wealth as possible before they retire at the prime age of 60. A friend of mine in the IAS central cadre told me once that within the license raj system there were at least 50 areas where an officer could obtain bribes if he or she chose to do so.

Despite the persistent corruption and lack of dynamism as agents of social change, the Indian bureaucracy has at times responded to crises quite well. India is a reactive state in many ways (as opposed to a proactive one) and its bureaucracy is hamstrung from playing an active developmental role, except during periods of acute crisis. India's private sector as an agent of development has limitations, even though the service sector today employs the largest segment of the workforce.[23] More poignantly, the Indian state is susceptible to voluntary and involuntary "policy drifts" on crucial security and strategic issues, and these heavily constrain India's aspirations of becoming a major power in the short order.[24] Yet the state is so crucial for a country, especially one with extreme inequalities and uneven development, to achieve its developmental and international status goals.

India's Weak State Syndrome

In a previous work, I defined *state capacity* as "the ability of a state to develop and implement policies in order to provide collective goods such as security, order, and welfare to its citizens in a legitimate and effective manner, untrammeled by internal or external actors." Most previous understandings of state capacity were focused on the coercive power of the state, but today welfare and legitimacy are considered as crucial factors in determining capacity.[25] Strong states possess capabilities

> to achieve the kinds of changes in society that their leaders have sought through state planning, policies, and actions. Capabilities include the capacities to penetrate society, regulate social relationships, extract resources, and appropriate or use resources in determined ways. Strong states are those with high capabilities to complete these tasks, while weak states are on the low end of a spectrum of capabilities.[26]

According to Robert Rothberg, a weak state suffers from three key deficiencies in a perennial fashion: (1) security, by which state security forces are unable to provide basic security to all citizens in a legitimate and effective manner; (2) participation deficiency, whereby popular participation is weak and elections, if they take place, need not be impartial and fair; and (3) infrastructure deficiency, where the physical infrastructure is in a poor condition, with health and education accorded low priority.[27] In India's case, it is not an extremely weak state on any of these measures, as it shows some level of capacity, and hence, it can be termed a "truncated weak state."[28] While India is not a failed state, it certainly has many attributes of a weak state. One manifestation of the weak state is the inability of the state to collect taxes sufficiently for development and other requirements of the state. It is estimated that in 2022 only 5 percent of the population paid direct income taxes, producing a tax/GDP ratio of 10–12 percent for India. This is largely because of a reasonably high income threshold for beginner taxes, a smaller number of total people who are productively employed, and the fact that agriculture laborers comprise some 45 percent of the population—and they are largely exempted from paying any income taxes. However, the state collects goods and services tax (GST) from all, compensating direct tax deficiency to some extent.[29] The political system is also constrained by a slow-moving justice system in India. While the Indian judiciary occasionally has made strong decisions, the slow process makes the delivery of justice one of the most cumbersome in the world. The volume of cases that Indian courts has to handle is staggering. In May 2022, some 47 million cases were pending in Indian courts, with many languishing for 30 years or more. Despite a sanctioned strength of 25,628 judges, the actual number at work is lower, often due to the slowness of confirmation by the government.[30]

Education and Human Resource Development

One of the major signs of a weak state is that it has major difficulty in delivering its responsibilities adequately in education and human resource development. In 2020, the literacy rate in India was claimed to have grown to 70 percent for men and 62 percent for women. Outwardly, this is a remarkable achievement when taking into consideration how huge the population size is and from where it began this in January 1947. But it ignores the fact that much of this growth is in urban areas and in the Southern and Western states, while many Northern states still lag behind. Moreover, the level and quality of public education are generally poor, and as a result India's growing middle class prefers private schools and increasingly education aboard, draining a large amount of money in that process. In 2022 some 1.3 million Indian students, largely from middle classes, flocked to universities in 79 countries, with the United States, Canada, Australia, and the United Kingdom leading the list of host institutions.[31] This number is expected to grow to 1.8 million by 2024.[32] Although many return to India, the lack of an adequate number of internal educational institutions inhibits the progress of millions who cannot afford such opportunities. New plans were announced in January 2023 for attracting foreign universities to establish campuses in India, but given the challenges in regulations and infrastructure facilities, few top schools, if any, will follow through.[33] Inadequate teacher training and poor basic infrastructure plague many public schools, especially in rural areas. The lower social strata are not developing economically, partly due to the absence of quality education for their children. It must be recognized that over the years, primary, secondary, and tertiary education sectors have made some progress, and the midday meals program has reached some 90 percent of India's public schools, helping to keep children in school.

A key culprit for weak educational performance is the low level of investment in India in this sector. For a long time, the country spent 2 percent of the GDP, out of which 1 percent was for higher education and 1 percent for all other education. In 2022, the combined central and state government spending on education was 4.07 percent of the GDP, and it may take several years to reach the 6 percent target previously announced.[34] This is indeed low spending and the main reason why the demographic dividend is yet to be manifest in India's development.[35]

With respect to higher education, India produces large numbers of graduates in engineering and sciences, but barring the top tier, their employability and soft skills remain major challenges. One must appreciate that the basics in mathematics and sciences are taught in India's school and college curricula widely, and the top achievers in these subjects often end up in key Western universities and sometimes become important players in technology development in the West. Some of the large multinational corporations, including Google, Pepsi, and Citibank, have been led by luminaries who came out of India's top engineering schools like the Indian Institute of Technology (IIT). Despite the fact that admission into an IIT often requires more efforts than getting into top U.S. schools as the national examination is daunting to pass,[36] these institutions are mostly teaching schools and do not promote R&D adequately. In fact, some of the best research institutions in India were established and functioned on the merit principle during Nehru's period, when India was much poorer.

Most Western and increasingly Chinese universities partner with private industries (in the Chinese case, state-led industries) and develop research as part of their missions. This idea is missing in India. Unlike other nations, the increased wealth of the country has not been reflected in the establishment of higher-quality education, although some private universities have sprung up in recent years. Research and development are largely undertaken in state-led research institutions, as well as private companies that have their own facilities for R&D. The wealthy class (unlike in the West) also refrain from building world-class universities, although this has been slowly changing. Some campuses, such as Shiv Nadar, Amity, and OP Jindal, all near Delhi, and others such as BITS Pilani, encompass many facilities and building structures on par with Western universities. In 2022, some 430 private universities were operational all over India, along with more than 600 public universities and thousands of affiliated colleges.[37] Barring a few, such as the Indian Institute of Science and some IITs, only a handful reach the ranking lists of the top 200 global institutions. For instance, in the QS ranking for 2023, only three institutions—Indian Institute of Science, Bangalore, IIT Bombay and Delhi—were in the top, with rankings of 155, 172, 174, respectively. IIT Madras, Kanpur, and Kharagpur were in the top 200s.[38] The challenge is often confounded by a lack of strict commitment to merit-based evaluations for hiring, promotion, and career advancement. Increasingly, ideological commitment to the ruling party is a criterion for hiring in central and many state universities. In November 2020, the elite Jawaharlal Nehru University was alleged to have hired seven professors without proper qualifications by its BJP government-appointed vice- chancellor.[39]

In fact, education is an arena where almost all great powers and rising powers of the past devoted their core attention. They realized the crucial importance of this sector for power capabilities, both hard and soft, and their global status enhancement. The universities in these states also helped develop the crucial technologies and weapons of the day that elevated their material status vis-à-vis their peers. The most important universities were established in the United Kingdom (Oxford and Cambridge), France (Sorbonne), Germany (Berlin, Heidelberg), Austria-Hungary (Vienna), Japan (Tokyo), and Russia (Moscow State), along with their imperial expansions. America's international status and soft and hard power were substantially increased thanks to its university system, which has been a great incubator of industrial and technology developments. It is not just the Ivy Leagues, but also state-level institutions, such as the University of California and Ohio State, and second-tier private schools that have made a big impact. The university-industry nexus is pivotal to America's technology prowess. As an example, there would be no Silicon Valley without Stanford University's active presence in the U.S. technology hub.[40] In the soft-power arena, by attracting, training, and retaining millions of overseas students, the United States has benefited immensely, giving it elevated international status. In fact, India is a beneficiary of this system, as thousands of Indians students, educated in the United States have been a major source of technology collaboration between the two countries, as well as contributors to U.S. and Indian technological and intellectual advancements.

Both the United States and the former Soviet Union elevated R&D, especially in crucial technologies, and touted their achievements to maintain their higher status. Although the Soviets emphasized weapons technologies while ignoring more important civilian areas, they possessed some of the best technical training in geopolitically competitive areas such as space and nuclear technology. The low attention to civilian technologies has also been attributed to the Soviet Union's relative decline in both economic and status ranking and eventually the collapse of the empire itself.[41] Beijing has realized how crucial the higher education sector is for development and status acquisition and has placed enormous importance in developing links with foreign universities and bringing back trained graduates to work in its university system. As a result, from a very low base, China now has achieved top rankings for several of its universities. For instance, in the 2023 QS ranking, Peking University was number 12, Tsinghua number 14, and a total of 8 Chinese institutions were in the top 200 ranking list.[42] India, on the other hand, has placed inadequate attention on education, and there is a mismatch between the aspirations and the quality of education, in particular the infrastructure and the competence of the faculty, while students are yearning for better educational opportunities. There is a neglect of global-level research, scholarship, and competition in almost all fields in India. An increasing number of private schools display better infrastructures, but many have difficulties recruiting high-quality faculty. None of this is to say there are no exceptions. The 2020 new education policy aims to rectify many challenges, but the proof is in the pudding. The plans include early childhood care and education, dropout curtailment, holistic learning, equitable education for all, adoption of sound teaching and learning practices, as well as technology improvements for both teaching and assessments.[43]

Infrastructure, Urban Planning, and Waste Management

India has made some modest progress in infrastructure development since the liberalization in the 1990s. By November 2021, India had built over 200 national highways, totaling 140,937 kilometers, crisscrossing the vast land. It also improved its railway connectivity, telecommunications networks, and internet systems while building a number of world-class airports, largely through private ventures.[44] The posh airport terminals at Mumbai, Hyderabad, New Delhi, Bangalore, and many smaller cities, like Kochi and Tiruvanthapuram, show that Indians can produce high-quality infrastructure. The increasing number of decent metro lines in urban centers also shows that quality infrastructure building is possible in India, even though completion dates are often excessively delayed. Yet, India's infrastructure is still not at the level of a quasi-developed country, and although it spends nearly 8 percent of GDP on infrastructure, this is considered inadequate given the low starting point.

Money spent doesn't guarantee high-quality infrastructure. India's road construction has serious flaws, as its urban centers have very few side roads or pedestrian walk paths. Crossing Indian streets sometimes is done without traffic lights. In urban centers of India, it is not uncommon to see people running for their lives when crossing streets, especially women and children. Hardly any state has built-in bicycle paths, as the overwhelming interest has been to accommodate automobiles and not pedestrians or bicyclists. The increasing number of vehicles on crowded roads, often without emission control, means that one can get stuck for hours in Mumbai or Bangalore traveling even a short distance. Similarly, the drainage systems are some of the worst in the world, with raw sewage filling the waterways and canals, often flowing to rivers and lakes. Hardly any public parks are built for children's recreation, even in the newly built townships. Planned development of the urban space is at best sparse. Tree planting in urban centers is minimal; though this kind of green space planning was done in Chandigarh, the city developed in the 1950s, it has hardly taken hold elsewhere. Modern Indians have forgotten the ancient Banyan tree, once plentiful across India, and that Lord Buddha attained his *bodhi* (enlightenment) under one of them!

The weaknesses in urban planning are visible in almost every Indian city, as many of these cities do not have a single urban planner. It is simply not considered an important activity. The village panchayats (elected councils) in general ignore this dimension of development. According to one report: "Nearly 65 per cent of Indian cities are devoid of Local Area Plans, Zonal Plans and Master Plans." The same report pointed out that India needs some 300,000 urban planners by 2023 but is producing only 1,800 urban planning graduates from some 49 schools.[45] Huge migrations of job-seeking rural populations, who end up in shantytowns and slums, add to the woes of Indian cities. In 2021, some 493 million, or 35.39 percent of the population, lived in crowded urban centers, and urbanization is increasing at a rapid pace.[46] However, urban development and planning are not up to twenty-first-century or even nineteenth-century standards.

Variations in cleanliness are another challenge. For example, the southern city of Hyderabad has a fairly large lake called Hussain Sagar in the middle of the city, somewhat similar to Lake Geneva. Yet, this 450-year-old lake is one of the dirtiest water bodies one can visit, as people throw all kinds of garbage into it. It is not possible to touch the water or even walk nearby, as it is heavily polluted and there are no fish to catch. Surprisingly, Hyderabad was one of the first Indian cities that built advanced urban infrastructure under Chandrababu Naidu as chief minister in the 1990s, yet in 2022 the decline was palpable. The common argument against Naidu was that all the money was brought to the city while ignoring the rural populations. Yet, Gangtok, the capital of tiny Sikkim state, shows the opposite. The city is kept relatively neat, similar to small East Asian cities. The question is why and how it is possible that Gangtok can be kept clean, but not virtually any city in adjacent West Bengal, including Darjeeling, the tea plantation city where the British had their summer cottages?

In fact, the lopsided nature of infrastructure development shows the widely prevalent corruption among the bureaucracy, especially the Public Works Departments (PWD) and the contractors who build them, especially the roads. There are many Indian companies and entrepreneurs that build decent roads and other infrastructure in Gulf countries, winning contracts through competitive bidding. Some companies, such as Larson & Toubro, Punj Loyd, NNC Limited, Sobha group, and Tata Projects, have won many prestigious projects, such as the Dubai metro, international airport terminals in Saudi Arabia, Dubai, and Qatar, and the Dubai World Trade Center.[47] Yet, when some of them build the same roads at home, they tend to lag behind. Why is it so?

While Indian engineering schools produce large number of graduates every year, it is not clear that they develop adequate skill sets, such as innovation, new product design, and creative ideas to solve the myriad of technical and political challenges in their work. They also seem to lack training in ethics at professional schools; in particular, engineering and medical curricula do not seem to include guidance on ethics. Soft-skill development remains a challenge. Civil engineers in general seem to want to join the state PWD bureaucracy to amass money before their retirement, which is usually before they turn 60! Inculcating a high level of patriotism and equating that with corruption-free service ethos could help. State public works departments are notorious for corruption, inefficiency, and sloppy work practices. Yet, a certain percentage develop the skills and take opportunities to join the burgeoning multinational corporations looking for low-cost labor. The global IT boom since the 1990s helped Indian technical graduates tremendously.

Infrastructure is the area where China beats India significantly. The Chinese have developed superior quality infrastructure rather rapidly, as the Communist elite realized it was useful for speedy economic growth as well as status acquisition.[48] Every stage of economic growth showed improvements in China's urban and rural infrastructure and quality of life, something that is hard to say in the Indian case. Waste collection and disposal are a challenge for most Indian urban centers. In many places one can see heaps of trash scattered around roadsides. Stray dogs are a common sight in Indian cities and villages alike, and many carry deadly rabies. Stray cows and bulls also add to the milieu of animal-human coexistence in a chaotic way, resulting in traffic jams on crowded streets. Defenders of animal protection justify that these acts of kindness toward animals are part of India's civilizational ethos, but they don't make humans feel safe or improve the quality of urban life. Manholes and potholes, the latter often caused by the incessant rains of the monsoon season, add to the misery of road traffic in India, partly because of shoddy construction practices. Yet, compared to rural development, urban conditions are still at a much higher level, especially services for water supply and electricity, as well as education and healthcare. For this reason, millions migrate to the cities, even when they have to live in the appalling slum conditions. Maintaining the built infrastructure adequately is another challenge. New Delhi, for instance, developed somewhat decent infrastructure right before the 2010 Commonwealth games, but today it is back to square one, as many of the facilities are not properly maintained or cleaned regularly.

There are considerable weaknesses in rural infrastructure.[49] As a democracy, India has developed some innovative local governance institutions like the village *panchayat*. They have assumed importance over the years. In fact, some of the rural infrastructure and service providers remain at these village levels. What is often missing here are technical expertise and adequate record-keeping in these local bodies to provide services efficiently and equitably. In most local city administrations in the West, professionals are actively present in developing infrastructure and urban planning. In India, this is often left to poorly trained politicians and bureaucrats who possess neither the art nor the science of infrastructure development.

Healthcare

Similar to education, India has neglected healthcare, even though it is available in the private sector for the middle class. Even some hospitals cater to health tourism (e.g., the Apollo hospital in Chennai). India spends a paltry 1.04 percent of its GDP (2020) on healthcare, which is one of the lowest in the entire world. Yet, public-sector doctors are not often committed to providing effective services as they often hold their own private practices to supplement their incomes. India's success in eradicating some major infectious diseases such as polio, partly through international assistance, has received global attention. In March 2004, India was declared polio-free, after previously accounting for 60 percent of the world cases. According to the WHO: "A high commitment at every level led to policy makers, health workers, frontline workers, partners and community volunteers, working in tandem to deliver life-saving polio drops to every child wherever they were, be it at home, in school, or in transit."[50] Yet, despite some efforts, other diseases like tuberculosis (TB) are yet to be eradicated in India. The WHO's 2022 report notes an increase in TB cases, with a case load of 2.5 million, which is one of the highest in the world.[51]

One must appreciate that India's medical schools are still producing some top-class doctors who can work in very difficult conditions. Some of these medical schools are world class in their training, such as the Indian Institute of Medical Sciences (IIMS), Delhi, and Christian Medical Colleges of Vellore and Ludhiana. Despite limitations, healthcare improvements from where India started in 1947 are noticeable. If only the good aspects of healthcare practices in Southern Indian states like Kerala are adopted all over India, much relief could be provided to the poor in particular. The work of medical professionals is hampered by poor hygiene and other traits that Indian society as such still practices. There is hardly any hygiene training for children from their pre-school years onward, nor does mainstream religious ethos teach hygiene as a value or virtue. The newest educational reform in 2020 mentions children's extracurricular activities for healthy development, yet pays little attention to hygiene training.[52]

To his credit, Narendra Modi launched the *Swachh Bharat Abhiyan* (Clean India Mission) scheme in 2014 with much fanfare. According to a UNICEF Report, "through approaches such as people's participation, by 2019, the campaign realized over 100 million household toilets constructed, benefitting 500 million people across 630,000 villages. The Mission's model is now being mimicked by other national campaigns and has influenced equivalent policies in countries such as Nigeria, Indonesia and Ethiopia."[53] Yet the challenge of achieving all the set goals appears to be very high, even though the momentum is commendable. Due to the lack of adequate water supply and poor toilet training, Indians still have a difficult time keeping their newly acquired toilets and the surroundings hygienic.

Climate Change and Environment

Environmental issues have not received adequate attention in Indian policy planning, despite some key steps to get closer to the Kyoto and Paris climate accord targets. Coal is still used to produce some 70 percent of Indian electricity, while methane derived from cow dung is a key component of village cooking needs. The widespread development of solar energy was touted as an ambitious plan with much potential. India imports 70 percent of oil from abroad, and automobiles in urban centers have added to intolerable levels of pollution in Indian cities. As a result, in 2019, some 22 Indian cities were in the top 50 polluting cities worldwide. In the IQ Air Report, India ranked fifth with the worst air quality globally, while the Air Quality Life index from the University of Chicago placed India as the second most-polluted country in the world.[54] During the winter months, urban centers of Northern India in particular register highly unhealthy levels of pollution. In the future, climate change, especially from global warming, will generate many challenges to India. Mounting floods, followed by long dry seasons, and increasing number of hurricanes all portend substantial possibility for pulling down India's progress. Higher status ambitions can help a country to tackle some of these challenges. Yet, India, despite high ambitions for international status, shows a lethargic attitude on urban pollution and the ill-effects of climate change.

In public policy discourses and international meetings, India claims environmental achievements, especially aligning with the Kyoto and Paris accord targets on carbon emission. Some achievements indeed have taken place, especially in developing alternate energy sources such as solar, on which India has set an ambitious target of 100 GW by 2022. In addition, India has made progress in wind energy, bioenergy, and small-scale hydropower.[55] Often it is argued that India emits much less carbon dioxide, on a per capita basis than developed countries such as the United States, but this is no consolation, as India is one of the countries most afflicted by pollution and global warming. In fact, taking a leadership position in developing green technology and in designing global agreements on climate change could only aid India's long-term sustainable development, despite some short-term challenges it may cause. This could well be an alternate route of status advancement in the twenty-first century.

A Weak Developmental State

India never adopted a developmental state approach, unlike East Asian success stories in Japan, Korea, and Taiwan, and the partial successes of Southeast Asian countries such as Thailand, Malaysia, and Indonesia. The concept of a developmental state is often associated with Chalmers Johnson's work, *MITI and the Japanese Miracle*, in which Johnson contended that the success of the Japanese state was ascribed not to state control of the economy, but to state management, allowing private capital to develop and export-driven industrialization to flourish. The bureaucracy helped in this process, but did not impose a highly restrictive-interventionist approach.[56] India's approach was a mixed economy which privileged the public sector and bureaucratic intervention. Difficulties arose in private capital mobilization, as a domestic capitalist class was missing at the time of independence, and Nehru's socialist approach contributed to this policy framework, which pulled down India's growth for more than four decades. Excessive bureaucratic control, often dubbed as "license raj," was perhaps the most debilitating aspect for India's rapid development. Export pessimism ruled the elite's attitudes until the economic liberalization of the 1990s. The low growth rate meant the state coffers were weak and the taxation rates were abysmally low. Direct taxes, especially those paid by individuals, constituted a very low percentage, whereas indirect taxes, such as sales taxes, affected all, including the poor, and high tariffs impacted outside investments.

The question is: Why has India failed to become a strong developmental state, unlike many East Asian and some Southeast Asian counterparts?[57] Geopolitical and ideological commitments of the ruling elite were two critical factors preventing the emergence in India of a developmental state akin to the East Asian tigers. Inward-looking industrial policy was viewed as essential for maintaining autonomy from both global capitalism and political interference by powerful actors. This was directly related to status concerns and fears of the elite in charge. India's non-alignment policy precluded U.S. and Western help for rapid development of Indian industries. The Soviet support was critical for many heavy industries, which eventually became drags on the economy as they needed subsidies to survive. Is it possible the elite thought that obtaining certain self-ascribed markers would be sufficient for India to obtain a higher status in the international system in the twenty-first century?

The type of democratic contestation in India often allowed ruling parties to get away with showing limited achievements. Politicians are rarely punished for their lack of genuine efforts at development. Indian electoral politics generates many tendencies of a chaotic democracy, with communal and caste forces increasingly shaping the agenda. There has to be something admirable that others can imitate or value in the governance and politico-economic structures of a global power. Electoral politics in many other states have been sources of strength for the population as political parties often get elected and re-elected for their performance. Even dysfunctional democracies like Japan tend to progress largely because of its bureaucratic class's devotion to the developmental state model.

In India, caste plays a more pivotal role in the electoral politics than performance of a candidate. Even lower-caste Dalits in Northern Indian states such as Uttar Pradesh and Bihar vote on the basis of caste credentials rather than on developmental successes. Caste hierarchy is a persisting characteristic of India, despite the fact that the economic fortunes of different groups, especially the Brahmanical caste, have changed over time. Over the years, particularly since the economic reforms of 1991, significant changes have taken place in India in the economic fortunes of different castes, especially the lower castes. But caste still remains a major impediment to the lower strata's upward mobility.[58]

At every level—village, municipal, city, state, and central—of governance, weakness is manifested. The effort by the BJP has been to create a strong muscular state based on religious ethos and Hindu nationalism. The problem is: Can a twenty-first century great power be built on nineteenth-century European illiberal ideas and gain status and recognition by others? A multicultural, multiethnic society compressed into a quasi-authoritarian model built around majoritarian communal ethos is unlikely to be a power that others seek to emulate. The degradation of freedoms and secular values will hurt India's prospects, even when it achieves more progress on many parameters and material markers of status and coercive power. Achieving increased global status is a major goal of the Hindu right. They expect global acceptance of India based on its mythical past, even when current practices may be at odds with what a progressive state or society is supposed to look like. Luce summarizes a paradoxical behavior among their members: "they convey disdain for foreign ideas and culture and yet have a desire to win the recognition and goodwill of foreigners."[59]

Some believe an authoritarian top-down model may be well-suited for India, without realizing that the same bureaucratic class will be running India and there is no guarantee that an autocratic model will make them less corrupt or lethargic when it comes to rapid and equitable development. The semi-authoritarian eras under Indira Gandhi in the 1970s and Narendra Modi since 2014 have not proven that less democracy somehow will make India a better model of development or a nicer place to live, even though during Indira Gandhi's emergency period (1975–1976) some marginal improvements took place (which, however, were not sustainable). She lost the national elections in 1977 in the wake of a ruthless campaign on family planning, including forced sterilization, spearheaded by her younger son, Sanjay Gandhi, showing that without checks and balances, India could slide very rapidly into a personalist, authoritarian state.

Scholarship on the relationship between the type of political system and its impact on economic development is at best inconclusive. However, as Larry Diamond rightly observes, "there is nothing benevolent about suppressing an individual's right to speak, publish, think, pray, rally, satirize, criticize, read and search the internet. Apologists for authoritarianism insist that people have a right to order—but without the rule of law, only the ruled are constrained, not the rulers."[60] India's neighbors, especially Pakistan, played with authoritarian models and produced very little economic growth or human development, except for a brief period of Ayub Khan's rule (1958–1969). In fact, the extreme polarization of Pakistani society and the alienation of East Pakistan's Bengali population led to its violent bifurcation. Although there are some East Asian economies such as Korea and Taiwan that prospered under their authoritarian phase, thanks to their alliance with the United States, their democratic transitions in the 1980s helped them become even more prosperous and inclusive. The coronavirus crisis of 2020 showed that authoritarian or messy democratic systems with weak state capacity may not be the best suited to face crises of this magnitude. China confronted an immense pandemic crisis during 2022–2023 (after much of the world seemed to have managed to contain it), partially due to the policies of the authoritarian Xi Jinping regime.[61] In fact, according to the *US News and World Report*, all top 20 countries for quality of life are democracies, mostly social democracies, with Singapore, a quasi-democracy, as number 23. As the report states: "Beyond the essential ideas of broad access to food, housing, quality education, health care and employment, quality of life may also include intangibles such as job security, political stability, individual freedom and environmental quality. Through all phases of life, these countries treat their citizens well."[62]

Some members of the Indian elite class often look to China as a model to show that such systems in India can produce more unity and development. The reality is that India is not comparable to China, with its near singular ethnic identity, Confucian work ethic, and a historically ingrained attitude of meritocracy. Its elite since the time of Deng Xiaoping also devised clever strategies that benefited from changing balance of power and increased

economic globalization and received much help from the West, starting in
the 1970s, for some five decades. The Chinese Communist Party also forces
its local units to perform, unlike India, which does not place much emphasis on performance parameters for local bureaucracy or political power
holders. Before the opening of the economy by Deng, India and China were
quite similar in per capita income and India had much more freedom. This
shows that authoritarianism is not the answer, but smarter policies by the political and bureaucratic classes are. As one observer states, "India's economy
posted anemic growth rates in the three decades after independence because policy makers in those years embraced the same import substitution
and commanding heights, statist economic policies that depressed growth
in other developing economies, most notably in the military regimes of Latin
America."[63]

Conclusions

India's progress in all the developmental sectors discussed in this chapter
has been an ongoing process. India has indeed made many advancements
since independence in 1947 in all the dimensions of development discussed.
But the goalpost of India and its own status markers have changed since
the early days of independence. Today the Indian elite and many in the
general public believe that India could rise to the ranks of an advanced
state and a major power fairly soon. But the question is whether the developmental achievements of India are sufficient for a major power of the
twenty-first century. Can India gain special global status without further
substantial improvements in its domestic developmental attributes? Even
if it obtains international institutional recognition due to changing geopolitical relations among great powers and some level of successful diplomacy at the top elite level, will status remain skewed and shallow for India
for a long time to come? Those who believe it can and it must move up the
status chain would argue that if India develops in these areas, it could in
fact become a challenger to China and probably a world-class state, given
the size of its population and economy. For this to occur, the demographic
dividend has to be utilized and India's elite at every level has a role to play
to make this happen. They have a choice to make—whether what they are
seeking is the status of a subaltern major power, or the status of a modern-
day major power that develops comprehensive national power as a humane

society which treats its people fairly, irrespective of their religion, caste, class, and gender.

As discussed in this chapter, two associated domestic-level factors hamper India's rapid status achievement. The first is the weak state syndrome, and the second is an economic strategy that does not pay adequate attention to inclusive growth, and these have created a state with skewed capabilities, both hard and soft. A large part of the status elevation India has achieved is the result of favorable structural factors at the international level and some forays it has made in raw aggregate economic growth, but the developmental model remains highly lopsided. Major domestic structural and societal reforms will be required for India to emerge as a world-class developmental state, in particular with adequate welfare and democratic credentials. The elite, especially in the Hindu right, have many notions about respect and glory based on India's civilizational and religious past. But how that civilization takes care of its people, irrespective of their religion, caste, gender, and class, is crucial for a twenty-first-century major power to be considered worthy of global emulation. India's status will be enhanced greatly if its quality of life, education, healthcare, and general human development improve drastically. Infrastructure development, including climate-friendly power generation, water conservation, and equitable rural and urban development, would alter perceptions of it globally. Equating patriotism with measurable achievements in development and wealth distribution is essential for this to occur.

Blindly imitating other great powers of the day or the past may not be the most appropriate strategy for India to follow. Although one can see noticeable improvements in China's human development, infrastructure, and global economic presence, it is not a model for multicultural India to imitate when it comes to democracy and freedom. Beijing's handling of the coronavirus crisis in 2020 showed the damage that authoritarian systems can cause to humanity. The United States is impressive for its higher education, but is a poor model for lower-level education and mass healthcare. The deep racial divisions in the United States, especially the treatment of the Black minority, show that India's social fabric—if it adopts such discriminatory policies toward minorities—may even get worse due to its deep-rooted caste and religious structures. In fact, India could achieve much by identifying the source of higher status of Scandinavian countries, Canada, New Zealand, or its own states like Kerala and Sikkim. India needs to exemplify an efficient social democratic, yet developmental state to uplift its masses, not a kleptocratic, majoritarian state. Substantial enhancements in developmental parameters would improve India's GDP, per capita income, and living standards, resulting in the majority of the population living a productive life. This condition is denied to them now, due to various policy failures and adverse historical-cultural circumstances. The bottom line is that inclusive development will increase India's hard and soft power and, consequently, its international status. As the economy grows, people will join the middle classes, increasing consumption and demand for goods and services, which will propel the economy to higher levels. India's success as an inclusive democracy could result in its transformation as a state to emulate, which in turn would improve its status ranking in the global arena.

8

The Future

In December 2022, India assumed the rotating presidency of the G-20, the group consisting of the world's most powerful economies, for a year. The Narendra Modi government celebrated the occasion with several events across India, and the national media proclaimed it as a dramatic status elevation for the country. India used the opportunity to showcase its achievements when the actual summit took place in September 2023. During the September 9–10 meeting, leaders from 19 countries plus the European Union, as well as many observers, attended the multiple events in Delhi in a carnival-like atmosphere. The meeting produced a 34-page document containing declarations on climate change, global health, global governance, food security, financial institution reforms, and digital infrastructure. Although it made no mention of Russia's invasion of Ukraine, the resolution called for abjuring the use of force, in particular nuclear weapons. The key side deal was the India–Middle East–Europe Economic Corridor signed by the United States, Saudi Arabia, the United Arab Emirates, Germany, France, Italy, and the European Union, which is a clear challenge to China's BRI. India successfully projected itself as the protector of the interests of the Global South, and at India's behest, the meeting added the 55-nation African Union as the 21st member of the grouping.[1] For nine months prior to the summit, Indian streets were adorned by posters showing a logo of the meeting, which included pictures of a lotus, the electoral symbol of the BJP, and the prime minister himself, revealing the domestic dimensions of India's status pursuit.[2]

The Modi government has been astutely using international status symbols like the G-20 presidency for its own domestic political motives, exposing the multidimensional aspects of status politics in India today. At the Bali G-20 meeting in November 2022, India played a crucial role in obtaining a consensus document on Ukraine and announced plans to use the G-20 as a major platform for advancing the interests of the Global South countries, including the transparent transfer of environmental sustainability technologies and the building of digital economies across the world.[3] Indian diplomats have called for a consensus-driven G-20, replacing the poorly functioning, veto-ridden UN Security Council, as the final arbiter of peace and global security.[4]

In a previous episode, at the Glasgow climate change meeting (Cop-26) in November 2021, at the last minute, India forced a change in the final communique, altering the wording "phasing out coal" to "phasing down." India did this with the support of China, another leading coal-producing carbon emitter. This was universally condemned, and the conference chairman, Alok Sharma, an Indian expatriate in Britain, said: "they will have to explain to climate vulnerable countries why they did what they did."[5] More than a decade earlier, India had objected to some key provisions of the new Doha trade accord, virtually scuttling that process. In March 2022, India, along with China and three other countries, abstained from both the UN Security Council and General Assembly resolutions condemning Russia's aggression on Ukraine, to the chagrin of the United States and its Western allies, who were courting India to form a quasi-alliance with them against China and Russia through the Quad mechanism. While these episodes show that on many global collective-action decisions that require unanimous consent, India holds a veto power, partly due to its large size, the implications of which for global development, let alone India's own development, are yet to be properly assessed. Is this veto over global collective choices enough to claim major power status in the twenty-first century? Or is it better than nothing until Indian capabilities mature and a national consensus emerges as to what kind of major power India wants to be in the global order?[6] One thing is clear, in 76 years of independence, India has emerged as a leading power, and its status has definitely increased in the international arena from where it began in 1947. It is today viewed as a significant autonomous center of power, coveted for partnership by the United States and its Western allies such as Japan. It also has an ongoing strategic relationship with Russia, giving it a bridge-builder role, although it is questionable how much it can tangibly achieve with that role on serious security issues.

A popular Hindi song, *Sare jahaan se achha hindustan hamara* ("better than all the world is our India"), sums up the patriotic sensibility Indians have imbibed since the days of the freedom struggle. Written by the poet Iqbal, who also came up with the idea of the creation of an Islamic Pakistan, the song has become the epitome of aspirational power India has held for over 75 years. Despite the extraordinary challenges as a nation-state and a society that India has faced throughout its existence, many Indians cling to the expectation that India is an important power already and that it will only get better, destined one day to gain full status as a global power. Yet, the progress in obtaining international recognition of this aspirational idea has been slowly happening, especially since the economic liberalization of the 1990s. Indeed, as a latecomer to the post–World War II international order, India has made significant progress in enhancing its status peacefully, both perceptually and institutionally, especially in the post–Cold War era. Increasingly, though, the possibility of becoming a major balancing force against China as a swing state has become a factor in India's status aspirations. The peaceful accommodation of India as a major power will be a significant counter to the narrative built around European-era history of the rise and fall of great powers, which often were accompanied by major wars.

While India has achieved many milestone markers of international status, the durability, sustainability, and legitimacy of its ranking are still uncertain, as one's status is always relative to that of others. India is still the world's most unequal rising power, with a widening disparity in per capita income and massive discrepancies in rural and urban living standards, as well as between different communities, castes, and genders. The question often arises: Despite the high economic growth for nearly three decades, why has India not achieved significant status markers of a middle-income, quasi-developed country with clean water, decent healthcare, less polluted cities, and reliable infrastructure? Can India achieve its full potential as a major power of the twenty-first century without obtaining these developmental markers of status, even if it becomes a leading military and economic power in aggregate numbers? In 2023, the answers remain tentative. Hence, most likely India will remain a "truncated-major power," or a "partial power" in the short and medium terms and its elite at all levels—national, provincial, cities, and villages—needs to understand and appreciate this reality while taking remedial measures for inclusive growth on a war-footing. Moreover, relative status decline or stagnation due to negligence and complacency by the elite can happen, as status attainment is not a linear process. Also, similar to material decline, one can lose status quickly, especially in the competitive contexts of relative rankings.

Although great power status in the past was accorded to winners of major wars, in an era when such wars are unlikely to break out, social creativity, domestic economic and social development, and international economic presence have emerged as important pathways to achieve higher status. For both established and aspiring major powers, "spheres of influence" are not simply geopolitical constructs, but influence obtained through dynamic economic presence in different parts of the world. Although China was formally accorded the Permanent-5 (P-5) status in the UN Security Council in 1945 when its economic development was at the level of India, its recognition as a major contender for global leadership has occurred only in tandem with its massive economic progress and developmental achievements since the days of Deng Xiaoping's reforms. Since the 1980s, China has advanced far more rapidly, and today its economy is some five times larger than India's. In 2020, India's total foreign trade was $917 billion versus China's $5.76 trillion.[7] In social development indicators, tourism intake, energy consumption, and educational and scientific achievements, especially R&D, China is far ahead of India.[8] In response to this comparison, many Indians tend to defensively retort that China is an authoritarian state and democratic India cannot match the speed with which China has been able to reach this position. The assumption is that democracies are not all that good at development, whereas the record shows that this is not accurate. There have been many authoritarian states, some in India's neighborhood, that have not done any better than democratic India. The Chinese model is not easily replicable, and multiethnic India can never become like China. Democracy serves other functions in a diverse society, in particular giving representation and share of power to multitudes of castes, communities, and social groups. Further, an authoritarian India would be run by the same bureaucracy which shows little interest in achieving higher status through rapid economic and social development. In fact, in comparison with China, the global attractiveness of India is partially due to its democratic system, despite its flaws, and to its potential to become a key economic actor as a pluralistic and tolerant state.

India's Slow March toward Higher International Status

On many dimensions, the future is perhaps more promising than is generally acknowledged, especially if India can hold together as a democratic country. Despite facing a multitude of challenges, India still may have much higher chances of achieving major power status in the international arena by default, compared with almost all pivotal non-great-power states in the G-20 grouping, including Brazil. While China is perceived more as a revisionist power, India is not yet viewed as such by any of the great powers (except probably China), and this is a major advantage. It is the misrecognition of the assertive foreign policy of a rising power that often produces violent conflicts involving established powers. If the opposite happens, a rising power is recognized as legitimate, as in the case of the United States in the late nineteenth century. Germany in the first half of the twentieth century represents the opposite.[9] This is largely because raw indicators of status markers and power capabilities, as well as geostrategic location, matter for an aspiring state to fulfill its major power ambitions. Among the top of these markers is economic strength and long-term growth potential, as well as the country's importance in the global balance of power competition involving established great powers and rising powers. The emerging international system is likely to push India to a higher status due to the simple fact that after the United States, India is perhaps the only swing state that can challenge authoritarian China's rise in a sustained manner in the long run, especially in the Indian Ocean region. In other words, India is the pivotal state to prevent hegemony of any single state in the Indo-Pacific. Therefore, others threatened by China are likely to court India, and if it emerges as a strong, vibrant alternative power, its status will increase considerably. India, however, can become a valuable partner, if it is a tolerant, secular, and developmental state and one which can offer an alternative to the Chinese authoritarian model. In fact, India has grown out of its immediate region, South Asia, and has been modestly competing with China for influence and status in other regions, especially East and Southeast Asia, the Persian Gulf, and Africa, showing that it already possesses a significant marker of a rising power, a characteristic of which is exhibiting global influence versus regional influence.

The previous rising powers, starting in the twentieth century, became accepted to their higher position by (a) following a successful war against contending great powers (e.g., Japan after winning the 1904–1905 war with Russia); (b) accommodation by dominant states for balancing purposes (e.g., China in the 1970s by the United States to balance the Soviet Union); and (c) following an intense crisis when world order, especially key international institutions, were restructured (e.g., British acceptance of the United States as a great power after the Venezuelan crisis of 1895 between the two countries was resolved through arbitration, as per the demands of Washington). In India's case, the most probable routes are the last two, as a war in which India defeats another great power is less certain. Border skirmishes with China without a decisive victory are unlikely to produce such a systemic shift. Another military defeat at the hands of China could push back India's status elevation. However, succumbing to China's coercive tactics can also hurt India's status ambitions. The most likely routes are the United States' accommodation and acceptance of India as a consequential ally vis-à-vis China for reordering of global governing institutions. To reconfigure the world order, current international institutions have to fail massively, which in turn would create an urgent need for reform. Then rising powers like India can make a strong diplomatic push to get their positions accepted. Aligning with the United States can have favorable economic consequences, as evidenced by other U.S. allies, including Japan, Germany, South Korea, and China during the Deng era. Both Washington and New Delhi would have to be willing to open their markets further, and then India would have to adopt a viable economic and trading strategy that makes use of this structural opportunity. Geopolitical prominence need not always promote economic progress. While some allies in East Asia and Europe benefited from a U.S. geopolitical alliance, others failed to do so, including Pakistan, the Philippines, and Turkey, showing that U.S. support can have a reverse effect by creating a "geostrategic curse."[10] This happened as the elite squandered the geopolitical benefits by not making meaningful social, economic, and political adjustments.

Much depends on U.S.-China and U.S.-Russia relations and whether they evolve into a new cold war, and how India navigates the new structural fissures. Societal-level accommodation and acceptance are necessary for a deep-rooted relationship to emerge between the United States and India. The large-scale Indian diaspora community and the increasing trade and investment between the two countries have helped this process to an extent. However, this community is divided, and many espouse communal ideas in favor of creating a Hindu fundamentalist state back in India, despite living in liberal democracies and benefiting from the liberal freedoms offered to immigrants. They tend to forget that an intolerant and illiberal India, even if it maintains facades of electoral democracy, can lose its soft-power value for the world.[11] The challenge for India is that a rising power needs sustained achievements in both hard and soft power in order to become a pole of attraction. In India's case, hard power, especially in terms of economic growth and demographic advantages, is increasing, but these are yet to be fully tapped for status elevation.

The previous chapters identified the high potential of India which is unfulfilled due to certain weaknesses of the polity and the society at large, in particular in the developmental arena. A determined leadership with mobilizational capacity and an adaptive strategy can transform India and achieve a much higher status than it is accorded in the international arena today. In the third decade of the twenty-first century, the saga of India's status quest continues.

Status Markers That Set India Apart

As discussed in previous chapters, during the past two decades in particular India has made major strides in many hard-power indicators and some soft-power markers that have helped to increase its international status. Among the hard-power indicators, aggregate *economic growth rate* is indeed the major marker. In 2018, India emerged as the third-largest economy in the world in terms of purchasing power parity. In 2022, in nominal dollar terms, it became the fifth-largest global economy, and with the current growth rate India is poised to become the third-largest economy in dollar terms, behind China and the United States, by 2030. Economic reforms since 1991 produced sustained growth, albeit with brief periods of downturns. This growth has allowed an estimated 32 percent of the population (around 434 million) to have joined the ranks of the middle class by 2021.[12] Some major achievements in infrastructure, transportation (especially airports and airlines), improvement in poverty reduction and health and human services, as indicated by an increase in average life span, have all occurred. The service industry has shown much improvement, with shopping malls dotting many urban and semi-urban centers. Several Indian industrial houses have emerged as world class and are competing with multinational corporations in many domains.

Prime Minister Narendra Modi has been touting India's substantial economic growth rate as a major source of its status elevation. In 2018 he had announced a goal of doubling the Indian economy to $5 trillion by 2022, which it did not achieve, partly due to the COVID-19 pandemic.[13] Still, the projections on India reaching the third-largest economy are holding, and they assume a relative decline of China and the United States and India maintaining an average 7 percent growth rate for at least three decades. Many imponderables could hurt the prospects. The 2020–2022 coronavirus crisis put a big dent on these expectations, although all world economies were hurt by the pandemic. In the post-pandemic era, India has been growing better than most other significant states. Assuming that India achieves the status of a leading world economy in the next two decades, will this alter its status? It will definitely change in terms of a crucial marker. The next question is: Will the Indian economy have a key role to play in the global economy, especially in terms of trade and investment, stock markets, currency, technology innovations, and participation in leading international economic institutions? In 2022, despite being the fastest growing economy and becoming the fifth-largest economy, India's share in world market is small compared to China. This is partly because India is still a middle-range trading state registering moderate import-export levels. Also, its manufacturing capacity is not growing as rapidly, nor is it as diversified, as China's. It is also not part of any key trading groups and is still reluctant to embrace regional zonal trade agreements due to the fear of being overwhelmed by cheap Chinese imports. More importantly, will India translate its economic might to major parallel improvements in domestic living standards, quality of life, and infrastructure development on par with global standards? The answer is uncertain without substantial alterations in the attitudes of both the bureaucracy and the political elite.

The next key status marker is *military strength*. Having the second-largest standing army and the third-highest military spending in the world have been India's marker of status to some extent. India also has a nuclear capability, offering deterrence against a major assault by its adversaries. This status marker was legitimized to a limited extent with the 2005 India-U.S. nuclear accord. In 2022, Indian military spending was nearly $76.2 billion, placing it as the third-highest spender in the world.[14] Its conventional military capabilities have been increasing, despite the fact that 84.3 percent of conventional weapons were imported during the 2016–2020 period.[15] Russia accounted for the largest amount of imports, at 46 percent in 2017–2021, after topping at 69 percent during 2012–2017.[16] This reliance on Moscow has stymied India's ability to criticize globally detrimental aggressions like Russia's actions in Ukraine, denting its ability to be a shaper of the global security order. Silence or behind-doors diplomacy became the preferred option, as dependency on foreign weapons made criticisms of arms suppliers difficult to undertake. These massive imports do not help in the status domain, as a rising power needs to make a majority of its weapons capabilities at home if possible. Further, can these weapons deter and defend against adversaries only regionally, or beyond the region? Given the globalized nature of the weapons industry, some R&D can be obtained from others, but still one's own capabilities have to be much more indigenous because in a crisis, other sources of arms may not be readily available.

There are two major constraints that affect global status for the Indian military. First, India is sapped by the active two-front problem with Pakistan and China and the border challenges they present. This is only worsening, with the China border now requiring full attention and major deployment of a large number of Indian forces. And second, the military capability has been of limited value for global operations. The development of the navy is occurring, even though it is still largely focused on the Indian Ocean, a region that is increasingly becoming a pivotal one for great power contestation. India spent some 15 percent of its military budget on the navy. Possessing some key naval facilities in the Indian Ocean region, especially in the Andamans, a pivotal location for any operations in the Strait of Malacca, has increased the attractiveness of India for Western navies. However, the Indian Navy will require a substantial resource infusion if it wants to play any meaningful role beyond the Indian Ocean—in the Pacific, for instance.

A third hard-power marker of the progress of a rising power is in *science and technology*. Here the achievements of India are sectoral, rather than general or applied. India is indeed a leading space power, which now launches several satellites for other countries rather cheaply. Its spacecraft have reached the Moon and Mars, a milestone achievement. The successful landing of a vehicle on Moon's south pole in August 2023, the first country to do so, was a milestone event. The Indian IT industry has made major advancements as it emerged as a superpower in this area. A number of technology parks have been developed, and India has been exporting IT and IT services all over the world. The pharmaceutical industry also has been a major arena of success for India. Still, the pandemic showed that this industry is heavily dependent on foreign components and patent relaxation by giant pharmaceuticals in the West. Also, many cutting-edge technologies are missing in India's developmental ethos, as is evident in the poor state of applied technology in crucial areas such as infrastructure, healthcare, and urban planning. In critical areas such as AI and non-fissile energy sources, especially solar, there has been some progress, but India still relies heavily on coal and imported petroleum for its energy requirements. Telecommunications and IT have seen the largest growth and have further potential for advancement due to the demands from the rising middle class and international customers. Yet, the absence of university-corporate collaboration to develop new technologies, as well as the weaknesses of the corporate sector, barring a few industrial houses, to compete internationally are key challenges.

A fourth hard-power marker is the *demographic dividend* benefiting from a working-age group of 22–36 years constituting the largest percentage of the population. This demographic advantage has often been touted as India's great hope of extending economic growth and sustaining it beyond the abilities of other countries—including China—that do not command such a resource. However, there is general consensus that unless India utilizes its demographic dividend in the next 10–20-year period, it may lose that advantage as the robotic revolution will make extra low-skilled population less useful. A high-skilled workforce, with their own initiatives, will help boost the Indian economy and its position as a manufacturing and exporting hub. There is also likely mass migration of Indian youth to Western countries as they offer opportunities to skilled workers, which in turn will deplete India's own talent pool. Over time, the demographic dividend will also decrease as the percentage of the aging population increases. High unemployment among the youth is making it less productive than expected. As discussed in Chapters 2 and 6, the demographic dividend is not properly utilized in India due to the economic strategy that has paid limited attention to inclusive human development via education and skill enhancement. This constraint shows that India's aspirational goal of playing a larger role in the world is hampered by this internal factor more than the elite recognizes.

Many of the soft-power markers discussed in Chapter 3 have also seen some advancement in the past three decades. For instance, India's cultural attributes seem to have gained some global acceptance with globalization and the wide use of the internet. Bollywood, yoga, and its cuisines all have helped India's soft power, although tangible results for international status building are difficult to gauge. Yet the decline of its democratic and secular credentials has placed a major dent in the soft-power credentials that are valued by both the liberal West and the countries that India is attempting to court for security and status reasons. It is increasingly clear that the Hindutva ideology or model cannot replace democracy and secularism for increased international status, as there are no takers of this ideology anywhere else, even in the Hindu-majority state of Nepal.

World surveys still give a low rank to India on a crucial soft-power marker—democracy. Three such surveys show a marked decline in India's democratic credentials. Freedom in the World Index, EIU Democracy Index, and V-DEM indices place India as a flawed democracy, closer to what it was during the 1975 Emergency, affecting its ranking in World Bank's Worldwide Governance Indicators (WGI).[17] The WGI measures and ranks 215 countries on dimensions such as "voice and accountability," "political stability and absence of violence," "government effectiveness," "regulatory quality," "rule of law," and "control of corruption." In 2019, India's percentile score was 61.9

out of 100, "the lowest since the index was published in 2006."[18] However, the perceptions of Indians on their country's status are different. In a survey of a cross-national sample, Indians in large numbers believed their country's influence and image improved from 2016 to 2019.[19]

India's diplomatic achievements at the official level are perhaps more impressive. The "Look East" and "Act East" policies have generated substantial momentum in opening up relations with East and Southeast Asian states. Today, India is courted by the United States, Japan, ASEAN states, and some European countries such as France and the United Kingdom for economic and strategic partnerships. Unlike China, India has not created many enemies, beyond its traditional adversaries, Pakistan and China itself. The 2020 election of India as a non-permanent member of the UN Security Council almost unanimously was a major signpost of these diplomatic achievements. To some, it is the label "'responsible power' that has helped it greatly in obtaining status accommodation as a rising power."[20] The restraint in foreign policy adventures may well be a function of hard-power limitations and the elite's disproportionate focus on internal affairs most of the time. Further, within its immediate region of South Asia, China has made steady inroads, and India's own status is now contested and it has diminished as a result in some key countries such as Sri Lanka, Nepal, and Bangladesh. Yet, India's expanding activism and competition with China in Africa, the Middle East, and Southeast Asia show that it is no longer a South Asian power on par with Pakistan. Strong economic and soft-power bases are essential for legitimizing and sustaining status in the regions beyond South Asia. The possibility of the G-20 emerging as a key institutional mechanism supplanting the United Nations, especially the Security Council, the reforms of which are at an impasse, may provide India with a higher institutional profile than it now enjoys. India's reassertion as the champion of Global South interests, unlike during the Cold War era, has the blessings of the United States and the West, thanks largely to their competition with China. However, tactical victories like the consensus resolution at the 2023 Delhi G-20 meeting need not mean much strategically if follow-up action is missing. In addition, an intense zero-sum Cold War–like competition between the major powers, especially China and the United States, could divide the world again and weaken global institutions like G-20, which may also hamper India's status prospects.

The large diaspora has been both a major asset and a challenge to India's status advancement. Talented individuals, educated in Indian universities, have been migrating to the West in particular, and several today lead major

American corporations and university faculties. India thus offers a good basic education to a small segment of the population, who tend to excel when they are able to work in Western corporations and to be educated in the Western university system. However, many in this diaspora belonging to Hindu communities hold illiberal ideas and want to turn India into a Hindu state, providing a forum and a major source of financial support for leaders like Modi. They somehow assume that India's status advancement is possible only if it becomes a Hindu state, even though they are enjoying the fruits of liberal democracy in the West or job opportunities provided by majority-Muslim countries in the Persian Gulf region. The absence of liberal education may very well be the source of the attitudes of these otherwise intellectually high-caliber individuals. Some may be holding an intense desire for status rectification of humiliations suffered by Hindu India at the hands of foreign aggressors over the millennia, especially by the Muslim invaders and the Christian West.

The Indian elite have considered status as an intrinsic value and a right that derives from the size, civilizational position, and leadership role that India has been playing, in addition to its material capabilities, both realized and potential. Yet, it is often unclear what India will do with increased status. The BJP in particular has been wedded to a traditional definition of great power status, and it is vague as to what vision it has for international and regional orders. The inability to do much about Russian aggression on Ukraine showed the limitations of this vision. There has been little articulation of what kind of world India would like to see emerging, except for a multipolar order in which India holds a pivotal position. Nehru had a vision; even though it had flaws, there was leadership on some key issues, such as decolonization, disarmament, and peaceful coexistence, articulated through the Bandung process and the NAM. Newfound enthusiasm of the Modi government for championing the interests of the Global South may be a good thread if India can make concrete advances along with the West on that front.

India in the Emerging World Order

India's status adjustment will largely be facilitated by the emerging balance of power system and how India plays the balancing game globally. Further material advancement is crucial in this regard. However, the re-emergence of Asia, in particular the Indo-Pacific, as the most vibrant economic and strategic arena of the world is increasing India's status virtually by default.[21]

India's status accommodation will depend heavily on new configurations in global power structures, especially on how much existing powers will accommodate India. The United States and China play crucial roles in this scenario, and how India plays hard and soft balancing in the global structure will make a critical difference. In the past, new great powers were determined in postwar settlements, and although considerably weakened, the 1945 San Francisco system still continues. Herein lies the challenge for India's breaking into a lead state role with membership privileges in international institutions. The twenty-first-century balance of power provides India with a pivotal role. As Robert Kaplan argues: "As the United States and China become great power rivals, the direction in which India tilts could determine the course of geopolitics in Eurasia in the twenty-first century. India, in other words, looms as the ultimate pivot state."[22]

Despite systemic and domestic level constraints, India may still achieve higher international status by default. Being a leading economy will give it a larger role and potentially greater status as its economic indicators improve. In order for this to happen, global governance structures have to be reformed so that a large state like India could be placed in a leadership role. India needs to bridge the material gaps, especially in economic, military, and technological areas, with China if it ever wants to be a key balancing power. It also needs to improve its domestic conditions, in particular drastic reduction of poverty, creation of world-class infrastructure, and above all, maintaining a pluralistic, secular, and democratic order, if it wishes to be an alternative model to China. Throughout history, India was a victim of rapid technological changes and ambitious strategies of invaders that led to its conquest from the time of Alexander the Great onward. India as an independent pole of power and status is essential for preventing the entire Indo-Pacific from rapidly falling into the Chinese orbit, as multipolarity demands other attractive states in order to balance against a powerful actor. However, India is yet to recognize the connection between growth, inclusive development, and status advancement in the modern world. Durable status in the international arena requires three elements: legitimacy, competence, and dynamism.

Legitimizing Status

The durability of status of a major power will depend heavily on whether it has a legitimation mechanism, especially soft power and increasingly sharp power. It also requires using the internet and social media effectively. It is based on how important a power it is for global order, in both military and economic terms, and how progressive and inclusive it is, both externally and domestically. The United States has sustained its power for a longer period because of its willingness to accept enterprising individuals from around the world and offer them a chance to prosper, irrespective of class or creed. Despite waging many unnecessary wars, the United States has managed to acquire the status of a country where often the aspiring and hard-working individuals from almost any part of the world can succeed. Its soft-power credentials were key to its legitimacy as leader of the liberal order. A weakening of soft power did occur during the Trump era due to that administration's policies and the decline of its democratic credentials.

Imitating China's authoritarian model is not the way in which India can become an attractive alternate pole in the international system. India needs to defend liberal values and function as a liberal state if it wants to be an attractive model. As Larry Diamond argues: "Apologists for authoritarianism insist that people have a right to order—but without the rule of law, only the ruled are constrained, not the rulers. This kind of 'order' too readily descends into tyranny and fosters all of its worst consequences: torture, terror, mass imprisonment, and genocide."[23] Even in development and social progress, barring a few authoritarian cases, democracies have done better. Almost all of the 25 richest countries in the UN Development Index have been democracies.[24] There is an intrinsic relationship between internal legitimacy and external status legitimacy. Beyond legitimacy, competence and dynamism of the population at large matter tremendously for the world to perceive a country as a high-status achiever. This marker can happen only if a large segment of the population possesses a high level of skillsets and if the society is organized and functions as an efficient system, where the government and private sector offer services effectively and competently.

The Hindutva project, although highly ambitious on status acquisition for India on its own religious/nationalist terms, can be viewed as a status depreciator for India in many ways. Hinduism's virtues are many, but the BJP needs to adopt some of its nonviolent and reformist components if they want the rest of the world to respect Hindu values. They need to explore how early Hindu reformers such as Ramakrishna and Vivekananda achieved these goals, and how Gandhi elevated the nonviolent (Ahimsa) ideas from Hindu, Buddhist, and Jainist traditions as a viable strategy for the freedom struggle against the mighty British Empire. A fundamental reforming of the caste system, especially the abandonment of highly discriminatory ideas about lower castes and women enshrined in ancient archaic texts like *Manusmriti* (laws of Manu), is called for. It is incumbent on the BJP and the RSS to work toward changing these texts if their goal is to bring India to the twenty-first century as a modern state. This means that the political parties, especially the BJP, need to change, and the opposition Congress Party revitalizes itself as a modern-era, merit-oriented party stripped of its dynastic characteristics. The challenge of Indian political parties, especially the BJP and the regional parties in control of a myriad of state governments, is how to transform India to a modern state, even when they tout civilizational strengths as its base. Support of second-ranking states could increase if India maintained and strengthened its liberal-democratic space, that is, as a tolerant, multi-cultural, and multiethnic country, similar to the world order that they would like to see emerging internationally. How can India promote a multicultural order globally if it weakens its domestic liberal space and undermines its multiculturalism?

Why India Deserves a Place among the Major Powers

Skeptics may wonder why India deserves a place among the major powers or permanent membership in the UN and other forums. Some doubters state their opposition for geopolitical reasons (e.g., India won't be our ally) or low achievement in status markers (not near the level of China). Also, India is not solving domestic problems rapidly, especially endemic mass poverty, and until it settles conflicts such as Kashmir and it removes all the ills of a caste-ridden society, it should remain a non-great power. Or some turn to the sheer fact that great power ranking is an outmoded concept, arguing instead that democratic pluralism calls for equality of states, big or small. Others may hold unconscious biases given that an erstwhile subaltern non-Western country's elevation to great power status has been extremely difficult in the past. Some of these perceptual constraints may still linger. Nevertheless, several reasons can be stated in favor of India gaining a larger role in the global order:

- *Global governance*: India holds one-fifth of the world's population and recently overtook China as the globe's most populous country. Democratic global governance would require adequate representation to this large segment of humanity, even if the majority are poor.

In domestic democratic order, very few countries any longer restrict citizenship rights, including voting rights, on the basis of wealth, class, or gender. Arguably, the same values should govern global institutions for legitimacy and fairness reasons. "One state, one vote" in the UN General Assembly, for instance, was a Westphalian-inspired idea, only to be overshadowed by the hierarchy-oriented Security Council with special rights ascribed to the P-5 states. In reality, this has been a cover for existing great powers to retain their dominance and not allow any newcomers to enter the system. While this dual arrangement somewhat serves the smaller states' desire for juridical equality, they also expect the leading powers to solve collective-action problems, especially in times of crises.

- *Utilitarian*: To tackle many of the world's collective-action problems, be it trade liberalization, climate change, pandemics, or nuclear proliferation, the active participation of a large state such as India is necessary.
- *Grievance prevention*: It is recognized that it was the intense grievance that rising powers such as Germany and Japan perceived (which to some extent is felt by today's Russia and China) that led to their highly ambitious nationalism and status-seeking behavior through violence. India is yet to show immense grievance, unlike those rising powers. However, a prolonged period of status denial could generate ultra-religious nationalism in India, which is hardly conducive to domestic and international peace. Making India a responsible international stakeholder could temper the nationalism, especially of the Hindutva groups, since responsible membership would also require India to behave responsibly toward its minorities, for instance. The opposite can also happen, with parties such as the BJP exploiting India's improved international status for electoral gains and in turn suppressing minority rights.[25]
- *Removal of lingering racism*: India's status elevation can help improve the treatment of Indians and people of Indian origin abroad and help ameliorate the lingering racism and problems of unconscious bias that many Indians face abroad. In fact, India's improved economic and geopolitical position, thanks largely to its insertion into the globalized world economy, has helped to get Indians accepted as leaders of industry, especially in the IT sector. Lingering racism was evident in the manner in which Indian and African students fleeing from Russian bombings were denied transit at Ukraine's train stations in 2022.[26] Geopolitical status elevation and attendant economic progress have led Asians, in

particular Japanese and Koreans, to receive better international treatment. Geopolitical enmities can, however, take away the gains—witness what people of Chinese origin have faced in the wake of the Covid crisis and increasing U.S.-China tensions.

- *Great powers need not fully solve their domestic problems, but if they do, they gain durable status*: Historically, not all great powers obtained their status after removing all their domestic developmental problems or solving their conflicts with their neighbors. In fact, great powers are notorious for conflict with others, especially those that do not agree with them in their neighborhoods. Today's great powers, in particular the United States and Russia, exhibit high levels of social and economic inequalities and concentrated poverty. If they used a limited portion of the money spent on acquiring so-called status-enhancing weapons systems, they could solve many of their social ills. For instance, between 1940 and 1996, the United States spent some $5.5 trillion on nuclear weapons and associated programs,[27] and the number has since remained steady despite the end of the Cold War. In 2021 alone, the United States spent $44.2 billion on nuclear weapons, while all other nuclear states combined spent $38.2 billion.[28] According to a Brown University study, in the 20-year period since September 11, 2001, the United States spent some $8 trillion on wars, killing some 90,000 people.[29] Putin's Russia has prioritized military strength and the aggressive seizure of lost Soviet-era territories, and it is unlikely to sustain its status without substantial economic and social power. Granted, India's domestic challenges are much higher than those of these powers, but the argument that one becomes a great power only if one solves all its domestic problems is not a sound one, even though it intuitively is appealing. As I have shown, domestic challenges weaken a state's hard and soft power in tangible ways that also affect the country's status ranking.

Implications for Understanding International Status

The Indian case offers many insights for the study of status as a subject in international relations. The primacy of hard power, especially economic resources for status enhancement, is reaffirmed in this case. Whatever modest gains India has made in the status domain are due to its high economic growth since the liberalization in the 1990s and insertion into the global trading and investment arenas. In terms of military power, aggregate numbers are not sufficient (as in the case of India holding the rank of second-largest armed forces and third-largest military spender) because the forces need to be relevant beyond one's own immediate region. A modern navy is required to support one's economic interactions across regions. India's status marker in this respect is likely to be a strong navy, as its army and air forces are pinned down on two active fronts on the Pakistani and Chinese borders. Further, the value of demographic numbers is putative until a competent workforce emerges and propels the productivity level of the country to a higher level.

The central conclusion is that material markers are necessary but not sufficient conditions for obtaining major power status for a newcomer. However, the relationship between capabilities and major power status are intricately yet complexly related, but not in a straightforward manner. While a smaller power can obtain higher status in a specific domain like diplomacy, hard-power indicators are necessary for a state to attain higher leadership role in the international hierarchy. Even if a rising power achieves higher levels of material capabilities, deft diplomacy and favorable systemic conditions need to happen, especially in international institutional settings.

Other questions that emerge in this context include the following: How much status accommodation of a newcomer is possible if it involves the diminution of the ruling hegemon's status and possibly its power position? At what point does status recognition end? Or is it a continuing process? What are the relationships between growing material capabilities and changing status aspirations of and challenges by the rising power? When does accommodation turn into appeasement? When do social mobility, social creativity, and social competition become ideal strategies for status elevation? Can a rising power use all three strategies, or does it shift from one to the other? What determines the adoption of a strategy individually, or a shift from one to the other? The response of other great powers to one's status quest is also important. In this context, it is not just the hegemon that matters. Today, for instance, it is China that is blocking India's status elevation, not the United States. How to deal with the shifting policies of China, especially since the arrival of the Xi Jinping regime has been a challenge for India.

There is still an explanation needed as to why some countries become dissatisfied with status ascriptions and want to surpass others. A weakness of international relations scholarship is in understanding why some countries have been willing to go to war to achieve greater status while others do not.

Increasing hard-power capabilities could alter their motivations in favor of acquiring higher status is one common answer, but it is not fully convincing. The status mechanism that drives war behavior needs better answers. Why do we see war rarely in today's world, and what role do existing technologies/ weapons play in state calculations? If war is not an option, do countries use other creative instruments for status enhancement? Status is also a relative concept; states tend to look down upon their non-status equivalents seeking equality. The Chinese reactions during the 2017 Doklam crisis between China and India is an example. The Chinese commentators all emphasized the relative material weakness of India. They expected that India should behave like a lower-ranking power and not challenge Chinese policies, even if China's actions constitute a significant threat to Indian security. An interesting question is: When do these racial attitudes in the status domain change? Japan's winning against Russia (a European power) in 1905 helped bolster its position temporarily, but that was not sustained. Japan expected increased status and better indemnities at the Paris agreement after World War I, but they did not receive them.

Yet another pertinent question is as follows: When does the dominant state/group of states accept the rising power into a higher status ranking? Balance of power calculations are crucial here. China was accommodated by the Nixon administration for balance of power reasons. India was partially accommodated by the United States under the George W. Bush administration and its successors for balance of power reasons. The problem with the United States today is that it does not want to give equal status to either China or Russia, for fear of diminution of its own status. The underlying premise is that they do not have equal material strength and hence have no claim to it. The efforts by China to show economic and technological equality or superiority vis-à-vis the U.S. are based on an expectation that at some point these will bring higher status. Russia, on the other hand, believes military prowess without economic strength should offer it status equality. The variations in status calculations encourage them to behave differently.

India's status aspirations show the competitive nature of status politics in the international system. High-status nations in general are uneasy about accommodating an aspiring rising power unless that power is useful to their own status aspirations. If India's ascent and accommodation take place peacefully, it will challenge the dominant theoretical and empirical narrative that great power status is achieved only through spilling the blood of oneself and others. As the material markers of key states in the G-20 increase, along with many of the existing high-status states experiencing relative decline, more opportunities for status-driven conflict and cooperation will occur. Some form of shared status is a possibility for India in the interim, as no other regional state today possesses as much possibility as India does for a vital place in the world order, in particular in solving collective-action problems.

Notes

Chapter 1

1. The 16th round of commander-level talks in July 2022 produced a mutual force pull-back from one of the disputed areas, Gogra Hotsprings, but two other standoffs in Demchock and Depsang Plains continued. "Some Progress in the Border Dispute between China and India," *The Economist*, September 22, 2022, https://www.economist.com/china/2022/09/22/some-progress-in-the-border-dispute-between-china-and-india. The talks in August 2023 have produced limited progress but not full restoration of status quo ante. Manu Pubby, "India, China End Longest Border Talks on Positive Note," *The Economic Times*, August 25, 2023, https://economictimes.indiatimes.com/news/defence/india-china-end-longest-border-talks-on-positive-note/articleshow/103034353.cms?from=mdr

2. Ajay Banerjee, "34 Indian, 40 Chinese Soldiers Injured; Tawang Clash Was Building Up since October," *The Tribune*, December 13, 2022, https://www.tribuneindia.com/news/nation/34-indian-40-chinese-soldiers-injured-tawang-clash-was-building-up-since-oct-460697.

3. Vishnu Som, "Pics Expose China's Inroads Near Doklam," *NDTV*, July 20, 2022, https://www.ndtv.com/india-news/in-pics-chinas-bhutan-landgrab-in-bid-to-byp ass-indian-defences-3173358.

4. Pratik Jakhar, "India and China Race to Build along a Disputed Frontier," *BBC News*, July 30, 2020, https://www.bbc.com/news/world-asia-53171124.

5. Even though this number looks impressive, the per capita income of India in the same period was $2,500 versus Britain's $47,000, given the huge population differential. "India Overtakes U.K. to Become Fifth Largest Economy in the World," *The Hindu*, September 3, 2022, https://www.thehindu.com/news/national/india-overtakes-uk-to-become-fifth-largest-economy-in-the-world/article65844906.ece.

6. Rahul Sagar, *To Raise a Fallen People: The Nineteenth-Century Origins of Indian Views on International Politics* (New York: Columbia University Press, 2022), examines the writings of pre-independence Indian intellectuals who lamented the decline of India in economic, social, and political terms in the colonial era.

7. This strategy, however, has elicited criticism, especially in the West, as it is undermining India's democratic and secular credentials. See Mujib Mashal, "The New India: Expanding Influence Abroad, Straining Democracy at Home," *New York Times*, September 24, 2022, https://www.nytimes.com/2022/09/24/world/asia/india-democr acy.html.

8. On this, see Bibek Debroy, C. Rajamohan, and Ashley J. Tellis, *Grasping Greatness: Making India a Leading Power* (New Delhi: Penguin-Viking, 2023).

9. John W. Garver, *Protracted Contest: Sino-Indian Rivalry in the Twentieth Century* (Seattle: University of Washington Press, 2001); T. V. Paul, ed., *The China-India Rivalry in the Globalization Era* (Washington, DC: Georgetown University Press, 2018); Kanti Bajpai, Selina Ho, and Manjari Chatterjee Miller, eds., *Routledge Handbook of China-India Relations* (London: Routledge, 2020); Mohan Malik, *China and India: Great Power Rivals* (Boulder, CO, and London: First Forum Press, 2011); Jeff M. Smith, *Cold Peace: China-India Rivalry in the Twenty-First Century* (Lanham, MD: Lexington Books, 2014); Rajesh Basrur, Anit Mukherjee, and T. V. Paul, eds., *India-China Maritime Competition: The Security Dilemma at Sea* (London: Routledge, 2019); Kanti Bajpai, *India versus China: Why They Are Not Friends* (New Delhi: Juggernaut, 2021); and Sumit Ganguly, Manjeet S. Pardesi, and William R. Thompson, *The Sino-Indian Rivalry: Implications for Global Order* (Cambridge: Cambridge University Press, 2023).

10. Xiaoyu Pu, "Ambivalent Accommodation: Status Signaling of a Rising India and China's Response," *International Affairs* 93, no. 1 (January 2017): 147–163; Xiaoyu Pu, "Asymmetrical Competitors: Status Concerns and the China-India Rivalry," in Paul, ed., *The China-India Rivalry in the Globalization Era*, 62.

11. It must be recognized that this is a highly debated subject. It is contended that it was Nehru's "forward policy" of advanced patrolling of Indian troops over the contested Himalayan territory that led to the Chinese offensive. However, the manner in which China engaged in the offensive and retreated to pre-invasion areas in the Northeast sector showed that it was more of a "teaching a lesson" category of operation. On this debate, see Neville Maxwell, *India's China War* (New York: Random House, 2000); Mahesh Shankar, "Territory and the China-India Competition," in Paul, ed., *The China-India Rivalry in the Globalization Era*, 35–36; M. Taylor Fravel, *Strong Borders, Secure Nation: Cooperation and Conflict in China's Territorial Disputes* (Princeton, NJ: Princeton University Press, 2008), 190–197; John W. Garver, "China's Decision for War with India in 1962," in *New Directions in the Study of China's Foreign Policy*, ed. Alastair I. Johnston and Robert S. Ross (Stanford, CA: Stanford University Press, 2006), 86–130.

12. In his speech, Modi asked: "For how long will India be kept out of the decision-making structures of the United Nations? How long would a country have to wait particularly when the transformational changes happening in that country affect a large part of the world?" See, Arpan Rai, "Full Text of PM Modi's Address at 75th UNGA Session 2020," *Hindustan Times*, September 26, 2020, https://www.hindustantimes.com/india-news/full-text-of-pm-modi-s-address-at-75th-unga-session-2020/story-8sOpyLIDesleUtIhRYdIWJ.html.

13. "India Will Regain Importance in the World Order, Says PM Modi," *The Hindustan Times*, May 27, 2019, https://www.hindustantimes.com/india-news/after-poll-win-pm-modi-gets-big-welcome-in-ahmedabad/story-eoeVVCNSMsrvCoZPHWF8EK.html.

14. Jawaharlal Nehru, *The Discovery of India*, 8th ed. (New Delhi: Oxford University Press, 1989), 210.

15. Jawaharlal Nehru, *India's Foreign Policy: Selected Speeches, September 1946–April 1961* (New Delhi: Publications Division, Ministry of Information and Broadcasting, 1961), 13–15.

16. Manjeet Pardesi, "Is India a Great Power?," *Asian Security* 11, no. 1 (2015): 1–30.

17. A recent State Department fact sheet states: "The United States supports India's emergence as a leading global power and a vital partner in efforts to safeguard the Indo-Pacific as a region of peace, stability, and growing prosperity." See U.S. Department of State, "U.S. Relationsd with India," July 18, 2022, https://www.state.gov/u-s-relati ons-with-india/

18. "India Gets Support from 4 out of 5 UNSC Member Nations for Permnant Seat," *Livemint*, July 22, 2022, https://www.livemint.com/news/india/india-gets-support-from-4-out-of-5-unsc-member-nations-for-permanent-seat-11658497010584.html.

19. Yeshi Choedon, "India's Perspective on the UN Security Council Reform," *India Quarterly* 63, no. 4 (October 1, 2007): 16–17. On this, see M. S. Rajan, "India and the Making of the UN Charter," *International Studies* 12, no. 3 (July 1973): 430–459. The prevailing racialized world order was a major constraint in giving the colonized world a proper say in the formation of the United Nations. Amitav Acharya, "Race and Racism in the Founding of the Modern World Order," *International Affairs* 98, no. 1 (2022): 36.

20. Lanka Sundaram, "The International Status of India," *Journal of the Royal Institute of International Affairs* 9, no. 4 (July 1930): 452–466.

21. For my arguments on this, see T. V. Paul, "The Systemic Bases of India's Challenge to the Global Nuclear Order," *Non-Proliferation Review* 6, no. 1 (Fall 1998): 1–11.

22. Aseema Sinha, *Globalizing India: How Global Rules and Markets Are Shaping India's Rise to Power* (Cambridge: Cambridge University Press, 2016).

23. "IMF Cuts India's GDP Forecast to 9 Per Cent in FY22," *Economic Times*, January 25, 2022, https://economictimes.indiatimes.com/news/economy/indicators/imf-cuts-indias-gdp-forecast-to-9-per-cent-in-fy22/articleshow/89119752.cms?from=mdr.

24. This projection is based on a 2017 report by PWC, "The World in 2050," https://www.pwc.com/gx/en/research-insights/economy/the-world-in-2050.html. It appears to hold well.

25. For this comparison, see WorldData.info, https://www.worlddata.info/country-com parison.php?country1=CHN&country2=IND.

26. Xinhua Report, http://www.xinhuanet.com/english/2021-02/26/c_139767705.htm. According to a UN report, India is committed to eradicate extreme poverty by 2030. United Nations India, "Our Work on the Sustaibale Development Goals in India." https://india.un.org/en/sdgs/.

27. UNDP, Human Development Index, 2022, https://hdr.undp.org/data-center/speci fic-country-data#/countries/IND.

28. Jeffrey Gettleman and Kai Schultz, "Modi Orders 3-Week Total Lockdown for All 1.3 Billion Indians," *New York Times*, March 24, 2020, https://www.nytimes.com/ 2020/03/24/world/asia/india-coronavirus-lockdown.html; Hannah Ellis-Petersen and Manoj Chaurasia, "India Racked by Greatest Exodus since Partition due to

Coronavirus," *The Guardian*, March 30, 2020, https://www.theguardian.com/world/2020/mar/30/india-wracked-by-greatest-exodus-since-partition-due-to-coronavirus.

29. "The Covid Pandemic Pushed Millions of Indians into Poverty," *The Economist*, January 12, 2022, https://www.economist.com/graphic-detail/2022/01/12/the-covid-19-pandemic-pushed-millions-of-indians-into-poverty.

30. https://www.oxfam.org/en/india-extreme-inequality-numbers.

31. The World Inequality Report, https://wir2022.wid.world/www-site/uploads/2022/03/0098-21_WIL_RIM_RAPPORT_A4.pdf.

32. "Many of India's Billionaries Have Made Money by Their Proximity to Govt," *Times of India*, July 31, 2010, https://timesofindia.indiatimes.com/business/india-business/many-of-indias-billionaires-have-made-money-by-their-proximity-to-govt/articleshow/6239385.cms; Jean Drèze, *Sense and Solidarity: Jholawala Economics for Everyone* (Oxford: Oxford University Press, 2019); Jean Drèze and Amartya Sen, *An Uncertain Glory: India and Its Contradictions* (Princeton, NJ: Princeton University Press, 2013).

33. David R. Mares and Harold A. Trinkunas, *Aspirational Power: Brazil on the Long Road to Global Influence* (Washington, DC: Brookings Institution Press, 2016).

34. It can be argued that the United States has a similar racial inequality problem, but that did not prevent it from becoming a great power. Scholars find many similarities between the two systems of inequalities. See Isabel Wilkerson, *Caste: The Origins of Our Discontents* (New York: Random House, 2020). Note, the global rise of the United States occurred in the context of America winning two world wars, and before that, culturally and racially sympathetic Britain conceding it the dominant position in the Americas. Notably, the declines of Russia, the United Kingdom, and France are visible in material terms, but are partially offset by other soft power markers they possess, and in Russia's case, aggressive nationalist projection for status and redress of perceived humiliations by the West. In fact, today the relative decline of U.S. status may be happening due to deepening democratic recession and widening social and racial inequalities and resulting political divides.

35. "Current Health Expenditure (% of GDP)—India," *The World Bank*, January 30, 2022, https://data.worldbank.org/indicator/SH.XPD.CHEX.GD.ZS?locations=IN.

36. "China Data," *The World Bank*, August 30, 2022, https://data.worldbank.org/country/china?view=chart.

37. These states are classified in various reports for their performance in basic indicators of development; for instance, the Access [In]Equality Index in which healthcare, education, socioeconomic security, and access to justice are measured. See https://jgu.s3.ap-south-1.amazonaws.com/jslh/Access+(In)Equality+Index+Report+2021.pdf.

38. Madhvi Gupta and Pushkar, "Ethnic Diversity and the Demand for Public Goods: Interpreting the Evidence form Delhi," *Economic & Political Weekly* XLV, no. 43 (October 23, 2010): 64–72.

39. On the global inequality challenge, see Thomas Piketty, *Capital in the Twenty-first Century* (Cambridge, MA: Harvard University Press, 2014); Joseph E. Stiglitz, *The Great Divide: Unequal Societies and What We Can Do about Them*. 1st ed. (New York: W.W.

Norton, 2015); Branko Milanović, *Global Inequality: A New Approach for the Age of Globalization* (Cambridge, MA: Harvard University Press, 2016).

40. Jon Wilson, *The Chaos of Empire: The British Raj and the Conquest of India* (New York: Public Affairs, 2016), 274–275.

41. Ibid., 288.

42. To Mill, "The absorption of the conquerors in the less advanced people would be an evil: these must be governed as subjects, and the state of things is either a benefit or a misfortune, according as the subjugated people have or have not reached the state in which it is an injury not to be under a free government, and according as the conquerors do or do not use their superiority in a manner calculated to fit the conquered for a higher stage of improvement." John Stuart Mill, *Considerations on Representative Government* (New York: Harper & Brothers, 1862), 316. See also Edward W. Said, *Orientalism* (New York: Vintage, 1979), 14.

43. Shashi Tharoor, *An Era of Darkness: The British Empire in India* (New Delhi: Aleph, 2016), 215. Noted British historian Will Durant captures the "bleeding" of India by the British colonial rulers, in his *The Case for India* (New York: Simon and Shuster, 1930). It should be noted that Conservative voices like Edmund Burke had earlier argued strongly against the East India Company's rule even before the 1857 Revolt, and he was instrumental in the impeachment trial of Governor General Warren Hastings in 1877. In his speech in the British Parliament, Burke bitterly complained: "England has erected no churches, no hospitals, no palaces, no schools; England has built no bridges, made no high roads, cut no navigations, dug out no reservoirs." All it had bequeathed to India was an "oppressive, irregular, capricious, unsteady, rapacious, and peculating despotism." Burke, *Thoughts on the Cause of the Present Discontents*, in Works, I, 368–369; cited in Gertude Himmelfarb, *The Roads to Modernity: The British, French and American Enlightenments* (New York; Vintage Books, 2004), 8.

44. Quoted in Tharoor, *An Era of Darkness,* 218–219.

45. Myron Weiner, *The Child and the State in India* (Princeton, NJ: Princeton University Press, 1991), 5.

46. Nicholas B. Dirks, *Castes of Mind: Colonialism and the Making of Modern India* (Princeton, NJ: Princeton University Press, 2001), 14–15.

47. See Aakash Singh Rathore, *Ambedkar's Preamble: A Secret History of the Constitution of India* (New Delhi: Penguin-Random House India, 2020); Luis Carbera, *The Humble Cosmopolitan: Rights, Diversity and Trans-State Democracy* (New York: oxford University Press, 2020).

48. "An Evaluation of India's National Rural Employment Guarantee Act," *The World Bank*, https://www.worldbank.org/en/programs/sief-trust-fund/brief/an-evaluation-of-ind ias-national-rural-employment-guarantee-act#:~:text=In%202005%2C%20India%20 introduced%20a,year%20on%20public%20works%20projects.

49. Ayse Zarakol, *After Defeat: How the East Learned to Live with the West* (Cambridge: Cambridge University Press, 2011). On the problem of status immobility and its violent consequences, see Steven Ward, *Status and the Challenge of Rising Powers* (Cambridge: Cambridge University Press, 2020).

50. Brooke Anger, "India will Become the World's Most Populous Country in 2023," *The Economist*, November 14, 2022, https://www.economist.com/the-world-ahead/2022/11/14/india-will-become-the-worlds-most-populous-country-in-2023.

51. "HDI measures progress on 3 key dimensions of human development—a long and healthy life, access to education, and a decent standard of living. It is calculated using 4 indicators—life expectancy at birth, mean years of schooling, expected years of schooling, and the Gross National Income (GNI) per capita." *UNDP Human Development Report 2021–22*, https://www.undp.org/india/press-releases/india-ranks-132-human-development-index-global-development-stalls.

52. On the Chinese incentive program to attract diaspora talent and its constraints, see European Union Global Diaspora Facility, "Diaspora Engagement Mapping: China," https://diasporafordevelopment.eu/wp-content/uploads/2020/07/CF_China-v.4.pdf.

53. SIPRI Fact Sheet, March 2022, p. 6, https://www.sipri.org/sites/default/files/2022-03/fs_2203_at_2021.pdf.

54. Kumar Vikram, "India not Preferred Place for Firms Leaving China," *New Indian Express*, February 15, 2021, https://www.newindianexpress.com/nation/2021/feb/15/india-not-preferred-place-for-firms-leaving-china-2264146.html.

55. Daisuke Wakabayashi and Tripp Mickle, "Tech Companies Slowly Shift Production away from China," *Economic Times,* September 4, 2022, https://economictimes.indiatimes.com/small-biz/trade/exports/insights/tech-companies-slowly-shift-production-away-from-china/articleshow/93939739.cms.

56. On this, see W. G. Beasley, *The Meiji Restoration* (Stanford, CA: Stanford University Press, 2018).

57. On the relationship between the colonial drain and Western welfare state, see Utsa Patnaik and Prabhat Patnaik, *Capital and Imperialism: Theory, History, and the Present* (New York: Monthly Review Press, 2021); Gurminder K. Bhambra and John Holmwood, "Colonialism, Postcolonialism and the Liberal Welfare State," *New Political Economy* 23, no. 5 (2018): 574–587.

58. Sidney B. Fay, "Bismarck's Welfare State," *Current History* 18, no. 101 (January 1950): 1–7.

59. On this, see William E. Leuchtenberg, *Franklin D. Roosevelt and the New Deal: 1932–1940* (New York: Harper Perennial, 2009).

60. "India's Nuclear Weapons Program: Smiling Buddha: 1974," Nuclearweaponarchive.org, http://nuclearweaponarchive.org/India/IndiaSmiling.html.

61. The Whitehouse, "Remarks by the President to the Joint Session of the Indian Parliament in New Delhi, India," Washington, DC (November 8, 2010), https://obamawhitehouse.archives.gov/the-press-office/2010/11/08/remarks-president-joint-session-indian-parliament-new-delhi-india.

Chapter 2

1. Major works include: T. V. Paul, Deborah Welch Larson, and William C. Wohlforth, eds., *Status in World Politics* (Cambridge: Cambridge University Press, 2014);

Deborah Welch Larson and Alexei Shevchenko, *Quest for Status: Chinese and Russian Foreign Policy* (New Haven, CT: Yale University Press, 2019); Jonathan Renshon, *Fighting for Status: Hierarchy and Conflict in World Politics* (Princeton, NJ: Princeton University Press, 2017); Steven Ward, *Status and the Challenge of Rising Powers* (Cambridge: Cambridge University Press, 2017); Xiaoyu Pu, *Rebranding China: Contested Status Signaling in the Changing Global Order* (Stanford, CA: Stanford University Press, 2019); Rajesh Basrur and Kate Sullivan de Estrada, *Rising India: Status and Power* (London: Routledge, 2017); Thomas J. Volgy, Renato Corbetta, Keith A. Grant, and Ryan G. Baird, eds., *Major Powers and the Quest for Status in International Politics* (New York: Palgrave-MacMillan, 2011); Michelle Murray, *The Struggle for Recognition in International Relations: Status, Revisionism, and Rising Powers* (New York: Oxford University Press, 2019); Rohan Mukherjee, *Ascending Order: Rising Powers and the Politics of Status in International Institutions* (Cambridge: Cambridge University Press, 2022), 18.

2. Larson, Paul, and Wohlforth, "Status and World Order," in *Status in World Politics*, 7.

3. In some sense, for ruling elites, "symbiotically affirming superiority . . . confers positive valuation on the self at the expense of others," and what "social psychologists characterize as in-group positive stereotyping and favoritism vis-a-vis out-group negative stereotyping and discrimination"; Yong Deng, *China's Struggle for Status* (Cambridge: Cambridge University Press, 2008), 24. See also Henri Tajfel, *Human Groups and Social Categories: Studies in Social Psychology* (Cambridge: Cambridge University Press, 1981).

4. Larson and Shevchenko, *Quest for Status*, 3.

5. Ward, *Status and the Challenge of Rising Powers*, 208; Pu, *Rebranding China*, 17.

6. Cited in Ward, *Status and the Challenge of Rising Power*, 209.

7. Basrur and de Estrada, *Rising India: Status and Power*, 9.

8. Quote from Elias Gotz, "Status Matters in World Politics," *International Studies Review* 23, no. 1 (March 2021): 230. See also Yuen F. Khong, "Power as Prestige in World Politics," *International Affairs* 91, no. 1 (2019): 119–142; Larson and Shevchenko, *Quest for Status*.

9. Max Weber uses the term "status group" to refer to a group of people distinguished by honor, prestige, and power. Reinhart Bendix, *Max Weber: An Intellectual Portrait* (London: Heinemann, 1960), 105.

10. Murray Milner, *Status and Sacredness: A General Theory of Status Relations and Analysis of Indian Culture* (New York: Oxford University Press, 1994), 27–28.

11. In this respect, individuals can use both prestige-based and dominance-based strategies. The first "involve the cultivation of talents and skills that are valuable for others," whereas "dominance-based strategies, in contrast, involve the use of 'fear and intimidation' in order to get recognition from others"; Michael Bang Petersen, Mathias Osmundsen, and Alexander Bor, "Beyond Populism: The Psychology of Status Seeking and Extreme Political Discontent," in *The Psychology of Populism: The Tribal Challenge to Liberal Democracy*, ed. Joseph P. Forgas, William D. Crano, and Klaus Fiedler (London: Routledge, 2021), 63–64.

12. The "desire for recognition" (*thymos*) and the "desire to be recognized as superior to others" (*meglothymia*) have a deep pedigree in Western philosophy in Socrates, Machiavelli, Hobbes, Locke, and many liberal thinkers, as well as the framers of the U.S. Constitution, as expressed in the *Federalist*. See Francis Fukuyama, *The End of History and the Last Man* (New York: Avon Books, 1992), 187.

13. David Owen, "Machiavelli's *il Principe* and the Politics of Glory," *European Journal of Political Theory* 16, no. 1 (2017): 41–60.

14. Robert Gilpin, *War and Change in World Politics* (Cambridge: Cambridge University Press, 1981), 31.

15. The terms "prestige" and "status" are often used interchangeably, especially by authors like Gilpin. Differences exist between status and other associated concepts like "prestige," although some may overlap and covary. As we have discussed in an earlier work, status is "collective, subjective, and relative social relationship—involving hierarchy and deference." As such, it is different from "power," which is often defined as the ability to influence others' behavior. And "prestige refers to public recognition of admired achievements or qualities," while " 'honor' is a code of conduct associated with a status group." For a discussion of these cognate concepts and their relationships, see Larson, Paul, and Wohlforth, "Status and World Order," 13–16.

16. See BJP Election Manifesto 2019, http://library.bjp.org/jspui/bitstream/123456789/2988/1/BJP-Election-english-2019.pdf.

17. Diana C. Mutza, "Status Threat, Not Economic Hardship, Explains the 2016 Presidential Vote," *Proceedings of the National Academy of Sciences* 115, no. 19 (2018): 4330.

18. Stephen P. Cohen, *India: Emerging Power* (Washington, DC: Brookings, 2001), 22.

19. "China's Xi Jinping Lectures Justin Trudeau Over Alleged Leaks," *CNN* (November 17, 2022), https://www.cnn.com/2022/11/16/asia/china-xi-jinping-canada-justin-trudeau-g20-intl/index.html.

20. On this, see Bob Pease, *Undoing Privilege: Unearned Advantage in a Divided World* (London: Zed Books, 2010); Robin Diangelo, *White Fragility* (Boston: Beacon Press, 2018).

21. Edward W. Said, *Orientalism* (New York: Vintage Books, 1979), 226.

22. Pal Røren and Anders Wivel, "King in the North: Evaluating the Status Recognition and Performance of the Scandinavian Countries," *International Relations* 37, no. 2 (2023): 298–323.

23. A. F. K. Organski, *World Politics*, 2nd ed. (New York: Alfred A. Knopf, 1968), 364–366; Gilpin, *War and Change in World Politics*; Graham Allison, *Destined for War: Can America and China Escape the Thucydides's Trap* (New York: Houghton Mifflin Harcourt, 2017).

24. Ward, *Status and the Challenge of Rising Powers*, 2, 3.

25. Steve Chan, Huiyun Feng, Kai He, and Weixing Hu, *Contesting Revisionism: China, the United States and the Transformation of International Order* (Oxford: Oxford University Press, 2021).

26. I thank Manjeet Pardesi for this insight.

27. I use the terms "great power" and "major power" interchangeably.

28. Jack Levy, *War in the Modern Great Power System, 1495–1975* (Lexington: University Press of Kentucky, 1983), 16.

29. Samuel S. Kim, "China as a Great Power," *Current History* 96, no. 611 (September 1997): 246. Political economist Susan Strange puts more emphasis on the notion of structural power, which consists of four elements that a state holds: the "capacity to threaten, defend, deny, or increase the security of other states from violence; controls system of goods and services; determines structure of finance; and exerts the highest influence over acquisition and dissemination of knowledge"; Susan Strange, "The Persistent Myth of Lost Hegemony," *International Organization* 41, no. 4 (Autumn 1987): 565.

30. Baldev Raj Nayar and T. V. Paul, *India in the World Order: Searching for Major Power Status* (Cambridge: Cambridge University Press, 2000), 32.

31. Steven E. Lobell, Jeffrey W. Taliaferro, and Norrin M. Ripsman, "Grand Strategy between the World Wars," in *The Challenge of Grand Strategy*, ed. Taliaferro, Ripsman, and Lobell (Cambridge: Cambridge University Press, 2012), 15. Most definitions of grand strategy ignore status quest, and the emphasis has been on security. For instance, Barry Posen defines grand strategy as "a politico-military means-ends chain, a state's theory about how it can best cause security for itself"; Barry Posen, *The Sources of Military Doctrine: France, Britain and Germany between the World Wars* (Ithaca, NY: Cornell University Press, 1984), 13.

32. Larson and Shevchenko, *Quest for Status, 79.*

33. Iver B. Neumann, "Status Is Cultural: Durkheimian Poles and Weberian Russians Seek Great-Power Status," in *Status in World Politics*, ed. Paul, Larson, and Wohlforth, 85–112.

34. On this, see Robert Jervis, *The Meaning of the Nuclear Revolution* (Ithaca, NY: Cornell University Press, 1989).

35. Oriana Skylar Mastro, "The Stealth Superpower," *Foreign Affairs* 98, no. 1 (January–February 2019): 31–39; David Shambaugh, *China and the World* (New York: Oxford University Press, 2020).

36. A rising power in this context is defined as a "country that is rising to become a great power, should increase its relative military and economic power, begin to globalize its interest, and begin to gain recognition as a great power-to-be"; Manjari Chatterjee Miller, *Why Nations Rise: Narratives and Path to Great Power* (New York: Oxford University Press, 2021), 9. See also Mukherjee, *Ascending Order*, 18.

37. Chris Ogden, *China and India: Asia's Emergent Great Powers* (Cambridge: Polity Press, 2017), 12.

38. For these, see Paul Bairoch, "International Industrialization Level from 1750 to 1980," *Journal of European Economic History* 11 (Fall 1982): 269–334. Manas Chakravarthy, "World History by per Capita GDP," *LiveMint*, August 25, 2010, https://www.livem int.com/Opinion/Nb7KkZ3yOVSNW3vHf9K1oM/World-history-by-per-capita-GDP.html.

39. For these figures, see Bairoch, "International Industrialization Level from 1750 to 1980"; Paul Kennedy, *The Rise and Fall of the Great Powers* (New York: Random House, 1987), 149.

40. Amartya Sen, *The Argumentative Indian: Writings on Indian History, Culture and Identity* (New York: Farrar Straus and Giroux, 2005).

41. Roxanne Dunbar-Ortiz, *An Indigenous People's History of the United States* (Boston: Beacon Press, 2014).

42. Beverly Bossler and Ruby Lal, "Gender Systems: The Exotic Asian and Other Fallacies," in *What China and India Once Were*, ed. Sheldon Pollock and Benjamin Elman (New York: Columbia University Press, 2018), 95.

43. Gordon Andrew, *A Modern History of Japan: From Tokugawa Times to the Present* (New York: Oxford University Press, 2002); Donald Keene, *Emperor of Japan: Meiji and His World, 1852–1912* (New York: Columbia University Press, 2005).

44. For the role of maritime domination by the West, see K. M. Panikkar, *Asia and Western Dominance* (London: George Allen & Unwin, 1953).

45. Despite major expansion, the Mughal Empire was already declining during Aurangzeb's period, but subsequently other factors, such as Nadir Shah's attack and the rise of multiple kingdoms and principalities such as the Marathas, shrunk the empire. "Decline of the Mughal Dynasty," in *The Encyclopedia Britannica*, https://www.britannica.com/summary/Decline-of-the-Mughal-Dynasty.

46. The apostles of modernity, including early liberals, relegated these societies, including India, as not fitting into the "standards of civilization" set by European powers, and therefore in need of colonization and transformation. Andrew Linklater, "The Standard of Civilization in World Politics," *Social Character, Historical Processes* 5, no. 2 (July 2016), online publication, http://hdl.handle.net/2027/spo.11217607.0005.205. The European conception of modernity touted "enlightenment, progress, rationality, and self-interest," and in this exclusivist worldview, "non-members were denied basic rights such as contractual guarantees," and "were stigmatized as being inferior, backward, barbaric, effeminate, childish, despotic, and in need of enlightenment." Ayse Zarakol, *After Defeat: How the East Learned to Live with the West* (Cambridge: Cambridge University Press, 2011), 38, 51, 54.

47. M. S. Rajan, "India and the Making of the UN Charter," *International Studies* 12, no. 3 (July 1, 1973): 430–459.

48. Even today, historians lament this "forgotten army." *USA Today*, June 6, 2022, https://www.usatoday.com/story/opinion/voices/2022/06/06/d-day-world-war-ii-indian-soldiers/9831800002/?gnt-cfr=1; Srinath Raghavan, *India's War: The Making of Modern South Asia, 1939–1945* (New York: Basic Books, 2016).

49. Amitav Acharya, "Race and Racism in the Founding of the Modern World Order," *International Affairs* 98, no. 1 (2022): 36.

50. Lanka Sundaram, "The International Status of India," *Journal of the Royal Institute of International Affairs* 9, no. 4 (July 1930): 454.

51. Gilpin, *War and Change in World Politics*, 30–31.

52. Naoko Shimazu, *Japan, Race and Equality: The Racial Equality Proposal of 1919* (London: Routledge, 1998), 181–182.

53. https://www.mkgandhi.org/articles/inspiration.htm.

54. Manjari Chatterjee Miller, *Wronged by Empire: Imperial Ideology and Foreign Policy in India* (Stanford, CA: Stanford University Press), 2013. See also Deng, *China's Struggle for Status*.

55. For these strategies based on social identity theory, see Larson and Shevchenko, *Quest for Status*, 6–14.

56. It has been argued that leaders can engage in costly endeavors for status reasons, such as increasing their relative standing, even when they do not bring adequate material rewards. The examples studied include Ming Treasure fleets that were launched by the Yongle emperor of the Ming dynasty that sailed around the Indian Ocean to Africa in 1405 and Kennedy's Apollo missions in the 1960s; both were later abandoned by their successors. See Paul Musgrave and Daniel H. Nexon, "Defending Hierarchy from the Moon to the Indian Ocean: Symbolic Capital and Political Dominance in Early Modern China and the Cold War," *International Organization* 72, no. 3 (Summer 2018): 591–626.

57. To Xiaoyu Pu, status "signaling occurs when a holder of information takes observable action to make information available to others in order to shape a desired image." See his *Rebranding China*, 19.

58. Ibid., 23.

59. Increasing authoritarianism and religious intolerance in India are an examples. Manjari Chatterjee Miller, "India's Authoritarian Streak: What Modi Risks with His Divisive Populism," *Foreign Affairs* (May 2018), online publication, https://www.for eignaffairs.com/articles/india/2018-05-30/indias-authoritarian-streak. Pu talks of China emphasizing higher status for domestic consumption with a domestic audience, but diminishing its status at the international level. Pu, *Rebranding China*, ch. 4.

60. Joshua Freedman, "Status Insecurity and Temporality in World Politics," *European Journal of international Relations* 2, no. 4 (2016): 797–822.

61. Milner, *Status and Sacredness*, 31.

62. Ibid., 33.

63. Daniel Markey, "Developing India's Foreign Policy 'Software.'" *Asia Policy*, no. 8 (July 2009): 73–96.

64. See William C. Wohlforth, "Status Dilemmas and Interstate Conflict," in *Status in World Politics*, ed. Paul, Larson, and Wohlforth, 115–140. On security dilemma, see Robert Jervis, "Cooperation under the Security Dilemma," *World Politics* 30, no. 2 (January 1978): 167–214.

65. Milner, *Status and Sacredness*, 37.

66. See Ayse Zarakol, *Before the West: The Rise and Fall of Eastern World Orders* (Cambridge: Cambridge University Press, 2022).

67. Jon Terbush, "John McCain: Russia Is a Gas Station Masquerading as a Country," *The Week*, January 8, 2015, https://theweek.com/speedreads/456437/john-mccain-rus sia-gas-station-masquerading-country.

    After the end of the Cold War, Russia attempted to exert influence over post-Soviet states for international status reasons. Anne L. Clunan, *The Social Construction of Russia's Resurgence: Aspirations, Identity, and Security Interests* (Baltimore, MD: Johns Hopkins University Press, 2009); Andrej Krickovic and Yuval Weber, "What Can Russia Teach Us about Change? Status-Seeking as a Catalyst for Transformation in International Politics," *International Studies Review* 20, no. 2 (June 2018): 292–300.

68. John Glaser, "Status, Prestige, Activism and the Illusion of American Decline," *The Washington Quarterly* 41, no. 1 (2018): 176. See also Jonathan Mercer, "Illusion of International Prestige," *International Security* 41, no. 4 (Spring 2017): 133–168.

69. "Indians' Views of India," Pew Research Center, August 29, 2023, https://www.pewr esearch.org/global/2023/08/29/indians-views-of-india/.
70. T. V. Paul, *Restraining Great Powers: Soft Balancing from Empires to the Global Era* (New Haven, CT: Yale University Press, 2018), 89.
71. Joseph S. Nye, *The Future of Power* (New York: Public Affairs, 2011).
72. Gotz, "Status Matters in World Politics," 14.
73. Miller, *Why Nations Rise*, 25.
74. Miller, *Wronged by Empire*; Zheng Wang, "National Humiliation, History Education, and the Politics of Historical Memory: Patriotic Education Campaign in China," *International Studies Quarterly* 52, no. 4 (2008): 783–806; Zheng Wang, *Never Forget National Humiliation: Historical Memory in Chinese Politics and Foreign Relations* (New York: Columbia University Press, 2012).
75. Wang, *Never Forget*.

Chapter 3

1. "The poise with which *Chandrayaan-3*'s 'automatic landing sequence' brought the spacecraft down on to the Moon's surface was striking. The spacecraft's trajectory dropped smoothly from thousands of kilometers an hour to walking pace, before a last little cheeky hover as the system checked the landing site and then settled itself down onto the lunar surface. "India's Lunar Triumph," *The Economist*, August 23, 2023, https://www.economist.com/asia/2023/08/23/indias-lunar-triumph. Prime Minister Modi, who was attending the BRICS summit in South Africa, received much praise for the achievement. A prominent South African newspaper headlined it: "India's Modi Out of This World," *The Star*, August 24, 2023, https://www.iol.co.za/the-star/news/indias-modi-out-of-this-world-9edb5fb6-2d8a-489f-9aee-838bf ae20082. Modi himself stated, "We have reached where no other country could," Geeta Pandey, "Chandrayaan-3: India Makes Historic Landing Near Moon's South Pole," *BBC News*, August 23, 2023, https://www.bbc.com/news/world-asia-india-66594520.
2. India has some 50 communication and weather satellites in space. Exploring the Sun's impact on outer space objects will help their protection. Geeta Pandey, "Aditya-L1: India Successfully Launches Its First Mission of the Sun," *BBC News*, September 2, 2023, https://www.bbc.com/news/world-asia-india-66643805.
3. "PM Narendra Modi Hails Chandrayaan-2 Launch, Says Every Indian Immensely Proud," *India Today*, July 22, 2019, https://www.indiatoday.in/india/story/pm-naren dra-modi-hails-chandrayaan-2-launch-says-every-indian-immensely-proud-1572 274-2019-07-22.
4. Rahul Bedi, "India Launches Chandrayaan Spacecraft in Bid to Become Fourth Country on the Moon," *The Telegraph*, July 22, 2019, https://www.telegraph.co.uk/news/2019/07/22/india-launches-chandrayaan-spacecraft-bid-become-fourth-country/.

5. As Xiayou Pu argues, this is a form of "conspicuous consumption." See Pu, *Rebranding China: Contested Status Signaling in the Changing Global Order* (Stanford, CA: Stanford University Press, 2019), 9.

6. Manjari Chatterjee Miller, *Why Nations Rise: Narratives and the Path to Great Power* (New York: Oxford University Press, 2021), 135. Another case in Miller's study is late nineteenth-century Netherlands, which exhibited many parameters of great power capabilities, including possession of overseas colonies, yet chose not to seek great power status due to a small country mentality and the prevalence of non-imperial ideas. See ibid., 62. See also Sandra Destradi, *Reluctance in World Politics: Why States Fail to Act Decisively* (Bristol: Bristol University Press, 2023), ch. 4.

7. For a similar argument in the individual context, see Joe C. Magee and Adam D. Galinsky, "Social Hierarchy: The Self-Reinforcing Nature of Power and Status," *Academy of Management Annals* 2, no. 1 (2008): 364.

8. "Largest Armies in the World Ranked by Active Military Personnel in 2022," https://www.statista.com/statistics/264443/the-worlds-largest-armies-based-on-active-force-level/; International Institute of Strategic Studies (IISS), *The Military Balance*, December 31, 2022, 218, https://www.iiss.org/publications/the-military-balance.

9. Global Firepower, *Global Firepower 2023*, https://www.globalfirepower.com/countries-listing.php.

10. The standing is based on a weighted average of eight indicators of comprehensive power that include: economic capability, military capability, resilience, future resources, economic relationships, defense networks, diplomatic influence, and cultural influence. Lowy Institute, *Asia Power Index* (Sydney, 2021), https://power.lowyinstitute.org.

11. For these estimates, see Hans M. Kristensen and Matt Korda, "Nuclear Notebook: How Many Nuclear Weapons Does India Have in 2022?" *Bulletin of the Atomic Scientists* 78, no. 4 (July 11, 2022): 224–236..

12. "India's Conventional Military Capabilities," International Institute of Strategic Studies (IISS), London, *The Military Balance*, 2022, https://www.iiss.org/publications/the-military-balance.

13. On these, see "Army Day: Commands of Army, Navy, and Air Force with Headquarters," *India Today*, January 15, 2022, https://www.indiatoday.in/education-today/gk-current-affairs/story/army-day-commands-of-army-navy-and-air-force-with-headquarters-1900501-2022-01-15.

14. Anit Mukherjee, *The Absent Dialogue: Politicians, Bureaucrats and the Military in India* (New Delhi: Oxford University Press, 2020), 5.

15. International Institute of Strategic Studies (IISS), London, "India's Defense Transformation," *Strategic Comments*, October 2022, https://www.iiss.org/publications/strategic-comments/2022/indias-defence-transformation.

16. Snehesh Alex Philip, "India's Defence Budget Is Good News for Navy, BRO; Bad News for China. But There's a Catch," *The Print*, February 4, 2022, https://theprint.in/opinion/brahmastra/indias-defence-budget-is-good-news-for-navy-bro-bad-news-for-china-but-theres-a-catch/821090/.

17. P. K. Gautam, "The Cholas: Some Enduring Issues of Statecraft, Military Matters and International Relations," *Journal of Defence Studies* 7, no. 4 (2013): 54–55.

18. Nick Childs, "India's Aircraft Carrier Arrival: The Limits of Ambition?," *Military Balance Blog*, September 30, 2022, https://www.iiss.org/blogs/military-balance/2022/09/indias-aircraft-carrier-arrival-the-limits-of-ambition.

19. Stephen P. Cohen and Sunil Das Gupta, *Arming without Aiming: India's Military Modernization* (Washington, DC: Brookings Institution Press, 2010).

20. David Kinsella and Jugdep S. Chima, "Symbols of Statehood: Military Industrialization and Public Discourse in India," *Review of International Studies* 27, no. 3 (2001): 364.

21. *IDSA Journal* 4, no. 4 (April 1972), quoted in Raju G. C. Thomas, "The Armed Services and the Indian Defense Budget," *Asian Survey* 20, no. 3 (March 1980): 280–297.

22. "Aatmanirbhar in Defence Production: Where India Stands among Indo-Pacific Nations," *Indian Express*, October 18, 2022, https://indianexpress.com/article/explained/india-defence-production-exports-imports-capabilities-explained-8196801/; Saurav Anand, "India's Defence Exports Hit ₹14,000 Crore, Highest Ever," *The Mint*, December 10, 2022, https://www.livemint.com/news/india/indias-defence-exports-hit-14-000-crore-highest-ever-11670661555303.html.

23. *SIPRI Factsheet*, March 2022, 9, https://www.sipri.org/sites/default/files/2022-03/fs_2203_at_2021.pdf.

24. Dinakar Peri, "The Growth of India's Defence Exports," *The Hindu*, https://www.thehindu.com/news/national/the-growth-of-indias-defence-exports/article37966675.ece.

25. "GDP (Current US$)," *World Bank*, September 1, https://data.worldbank.org/indicator/NY.GDP.MKTP.CD

26. Morgan Stanley, "India's Impending Economic Boom," November 8, 2022, https://www.morganstanley.com/ideas/investment-opportunities-in-india.

27. Sarojit Gupta, "Nearly 1 in 3 Indians Middle Class, to Double in 25 Years: Report," *Times of India*, November 22, 2022, https://timesofindia.indiatimes.com/business/india-business/middle-class-nearly-1/3rd-of-indias-population-to-be-2/3rds-by-2047-report/articleshow/95239621.cms.

28. On this, see Sanjaya Baru, *1991: How P.V. Narasimha Rao Made History* (New Delhi: Alph Book, 2016); Vinay Sitapati, *The Man Who Remade India: A Biography of P.V. Narasimha Rao* (New York: Oxford University Press, 2018). On the reforms, see Jagdish Bhagwati and Arvind Panagariya, *Reforms and Economic Transformation in India* (New York: Oxford University Press, 2012); Rahul Mukherjee, *Political Economy of Reforms in India* (New Delhi: Oxford University Press, 2014).

29. India Brand Equity Foundation, "Foreign Direct Investment (FDI)," December 2022, https://www.ibef.org/economy/foreign-direct-investment.

30. "Imports Hit Record $610 bn. in 2021–22," *The Hindu*, April 4, 2022, https://www.thehindu.com/business/Economy/imports-hit-record-610-bn-in-2021-22/article65290161.ece.

31. Sunil Mani, "High Technology Manufacturing in India," in *CTEIR Handbook: Technology and Innovation in India*, 2021, 33–38, http://www.ctier.org/handbook2021.html.

32. Pritam Deuskar, "India—A 1 Trillion Manufacturing Export Market by 2030," *The Mint*, December 1, 2022, https://www.livemint.com/economy/india-a-1-trillion-manufacturing-export-market-by-2030-11669800286004.html.

33. "GDP Growth (Annual %)—India," *World Bank*, September 1, 2022, https://data.worldbank.org/indicator/NY.GDP.MKTP.KD.ZG?end=2021&locations=IN&name_desc=false&start=1961&view=chart.

34. See Sunil Mani and Chidambaran G. Iyer, eds., *India's Economy and Society: Lateral Explorations* (Heidelberg: Springer, 2021).

35. See Andrew B. Kennedy and Darren J. Lim, "The Innovation Imperative: Technology and US–China Rivalry in the Twenty-First Century," *International Affairs* 94, no. 3 (May 2018): 553–572.

36. There is debate on the actual meaning of Krishna's exhortation to Arjuna to wage war against his cousins, who represented evil forces, in the name of Dharma (universal duty) as "irrespective of what Arjuna does, everything is in the hands of the divine," while the literal translation is not 'death' but 'world destroying time.'" James Temperton, "'Now I Am Become Death, the Destroyer of Worlds': The Story of Oppenheimer's Infamous Quote," *Wired* (September 8, 2017), https://www.wired.co.uk/article/manhattan-project-robert-oppenheimer.

37. T. V. Paul, "Great Equalizers or Agents of Chaos? Weapons of Mass Destruction and the Emerging International Order," in *International Order and the Future of World Politics*, ed. T. V. Paul and John A. Hall (Cambridge: Cambridge University Press, 1999), 373–374.

38. George Perkovich, *India's Nuclear Bomb: The Impact on Global Proliferation* (Berkeley: University of California Press, 1999), 6. To Itty Abraham, nuclear acquisition was the "post-colonial state's project of modernity." See his *The Making of the Indian Atomic Bomb: Science, Secrecy and the Post-Colonial State* (London: Zed Books, 1980), 3.

39. Perkovich, *India's Nuclear Bomb*, 8.

40. Perkovich, *India's Nuclear Bomb*, 59. Homi J. Bhabha was the first chairman of the Indian Atomic Energy Commission and is considered the father of the Indian atomic energy program.

41. Perkovich, *India's Nuclear Bomb*, 457.

42. A. Vinod Kumar, "Between Idealism, Activism, and the Bomb: Why Did India Reject the NPT?," in *Negotiating the Nuclear Non-Proliferation Treaty: Origins of the Nuclear Order*, ed. Roland Popp, Liviu Horovitz, and Andreas Wenger (London: Routledge), 142–143.

43. T. V. Paul, "The Systemic Bases of India's Challenge to the Global Nuclear Order," *The Non-Proliferation Review* 6, no. 1 (Fall 1998): 1–11.

44. "Statement by the Indian Representative [Trivedi] to the First Committee of the General Assembly: Nonproliferation of Nuclear Weapons, October 31, 1966," quoted in Rajesh Basrur and Kate Sullivan de Estrada, *Rising India: Status and Power* (London: Routledge, 2017), 70.

45. Perkovich, *India's Nuclear Bomb*, 168.

46. Cited in ibid., 105.

47. Cited in ibid., 520.
48. Interagency Intelligence Memorandum, "Prospects for an Indian Nuclear Force," June 19, 1974, Secret, https://nsarchive.gwu.edu/document/29500-document-15-interagency-intelligence-memorandum-prospects-indian-nuclear-force-19.
49. Ashis Nandy, "Between Two Gandhis: Psychopolitical Aspects of the Nuclearization of India," *Asian Survey* 14, no. 11 (November 1974): 966–970.
50. Basrur and de Estrada, *Rising India*, 74.
51. Nixon in particular was skeptical of non-proliferation efforts, especially the NPT. See James Cameron and Or Rabinowitz, "Eight Lost Years? Nixon, Ford, Kissinger and the Non-Proliferation Regime, 1969–1977," *Journal of Strategic Studies* 40, no. 6 (2017): 839–866.
52. Nuclear Non-Proliferation Act of 1978, Public Law 95-242, March 10, 1978.
53. Quoted in *India Abroad*, May 22, 1998, 10.
54. Jaswant Singh, "Against Nuclear Apartheid," *Foreign Affairs* 77, no. 5 (September–October 1998): 44–45.
55. T. T. Poulose, *The CTBT and the Rise of Nuclear Nationalism in India* (New Delhi: Lancers Books, 1996).
56. Statement by Arundhati Ghose, Plenary of the Conference of Disarmament (June 20, 1996), in *Statements by India on Comprehensive Test Ban Treaty (1993–1996)*, Government of India, Ministry of External Affairs, 105.
57. James Risen, Steven Lee Myers and Tim Weiner, "U.S. May Have Helped India Hide Its Nuclear Activity," *New York Times*, May 25, 1998, A3.
58. Craig R. Whitney, "Top U.N. Members Urge India and Pakistan to End Arms Race," *New York Times*, June 5, 1998), A8.
59. Nicola Leveringhaus and Kate Sullivan de Estrada, "Between Conformity and Innovation: China's Quest for Status as Responsible Nuclear Powers, " *Review of International Studies* 44, no. 3 (2018): 483.
60. Manoj Kumar Patairiya, "Why India Is Going to Mars," *New York Times*, November 22, 2013, https://www.nytimes.com/2013/11/23/opinion/india-must-go-to-mars.html?hp&rref=opinion/internationalize.
61. For a comprehensive assessment of the achievements in space, see Sunil Mani, V. K. Dadhwal, and C. S. Shajumon, "India's Space Economy, 2011–12 to 2020–21: Its Size and Structure," *Space Policy* (November 19, 2022), https://www.sciencedirect.com/science/article/abs/pii/S0265964622000509.
62. "List of International Customer Satellites Launched by ISRO," https://web.archive.org/web/20221024134415/https://www.isro.gov.in/media_isro/pdf/ForeignSatellites/381_foreign_satellites.pdf.
63. Kiran Stacey and Aliya Ram, "India Launches World Record 104 Satellites on a Single Rocket," *Financial Times*, February 15, 2017, https://www.ft.com/content/2159e098-86d4-11e6-bcfc-debbef66f80e.
64. "Foreign Media on India's Record of 104 Satellites Launched by ISRO on one Rocket," *NDTV*, February 16, 2017, https://www.ndtv.com/india-news/foreign-media-on-indias-record-of-104-satellites-launched-by-isro-on-one-rocket-1659797.

65. Badar Bashir, "2023 to Be India's Space Year with Launch of Chandrayaan-3, Gaganyaan," *The Sunday Guardian*, January 8, 2023, https://www.sundayguardianl ive.com/news/2023-indias-space-year-launch-chandrayaan-3-gaganyaan.

66. Geeta Pandey, "Aditya-L1: India Successfully Launches Its First Mission of the Sun," *BBC News*, September 2, 2023, https://www.bbc.com/news/world-asia-india-66643805.

67. "Moon Mission Done, ISRO Aims for the Sun with Aditya-L1 Launch on September 2," *The Indian Express*, August 28, 2023, https://indianexpress.com/article/technol ogy/science/isros-solar-mission-aditya-l1-to-be-launched-on-september-2-says-space-agency-8913266/.

68. Ashley J. Tellis, "India's ASAT Test: An Incomplete Success," Carnegie Endowment for International Peace, April 15, 2019, https://carnegieendowment.org/2019/04/15/ india-s-asat-test-incomplete-success-pub-78884; Jeffrey Gettleman and Hari Kumar, "India Shot Down a Satellite, Modi Says, Shifting Balance of Power in Asia," *New York Times*, March 27, 2019, https://www.nytimes.com/2019/03/27/world/asia/india-weat her-satellite-missle.html.

69. "First Time Lucky," *The Economist*, September 24, 2014, https://www.economist.com/ babbage/2014/09/24/first-time-lucky.

70. "India to Become a Developed Nation by 2020: Kalam," *Times of India*, March 2, 2003, https://timesofindia.indiatimes.com/india/india-to-become-a-developed-nation-by-2020-kalam/articleshow/39070278.cms.

71. Singh Rahul Sunilkumar, "Rajiv Gandhi Birth Anniversary: Ex-PM's 5 Contribution to India's Tech Prowess," *Hindustan Times*, August 20, 2022, https://www.hindustanti mes.com/technology/rajiv-gandhi-birth-anniversary-ex-pm-s-5-contribution-to-india-s-tech-prowess-101660970997819.html.

72. Shivani Shinde, "Indian IT Crosses $200-bn Revenue Mark, Hits $227 bn in F722: Nasscom," *Business Standard*, February 15, 2022, https://www.business-stand ard.com/article/companies/indian-it-crosses-200-bn-revenue-mark-hits-227-bn-in-fy22-nasscom-122021500828_1.html.

73. "Huawei and ZTE Left Out of India's 5G Trials," *BBC News*, May 5, 2021, https://www. bbc.com/news/business-56990236.

74. McKinsey Global Institute, *Digital India*, March 2019, https://www.mckinsey.com/ capabilities/mckinsey-digital/our-insights/digital-india-technology-to-transform-a-connected-nation.

75. Morgan Stanley, "India's Impending Economic Boom."

76. Ibid.

77. "Indian Pharmaceutical Industry," India Brand Equity Foundation, August 2022, https://www.ibef.org/industry/pharmaceutical-india.

78. "Indian Pharma Industry Likely to Grow to $130 bn by 2030, Says IPA," *Business Standard*, September 15, 2022, https://www.business-standard.com/article/compan ies/indian-pharma-industry-likely-to-grow-to-130-bn-by-2030-says-ipa-1220915 00656_1.html.

79. See Serum Institute of India, https://www.seruminstitute.com/about_us.php.

80. Olivia Choo, "How This Millennial CEO Steered the World's Largest Vaccine Maker during the Pandemic," *CNBC*, December 16, 2022, https://www.cnbc.com/2022/12/16/how-this-millennial-ceo-steered-serum-institute-of-india-during-covid.html.

81. Nitin Pai, "India Must Dominate the Game of Chips—Through Its Human Resources," *The Mint*, October 24, 2022, https://www.livemint.com/opinion/columns/india-must-invest-in-manpower-to-succeed-in-the-game-of-chips-11666539909289.html.

82. T. C. A. Sharad Raghavan, "India's Made Big Strides on Renewable Energy , but It's Still Set to Miss 2022 Target of 175 GW," *The Print*, November 19, 2022, https://theprint.in/economy/indias-made-big-strides-on-renewable-energy-but-its-still-set-to-miss-2022-target-of-175-gw/1222231/.

83. Alec Pronk, "WIPO Report: China Sees Massive Surge in IP Filings across the Board," *IPwatchdog*, November 22, 2022, https://ipwatchdog.com/2022/11/26/wipo-report-china-sees-massive-surge-ip-filings-across-board/id=153536/.

84. Anand JC, "India's R&D Spends amongst the Lowest in the World: NITI Aayog Study," *The Economic Times*, July 22, 2022, https://economictimes.indiatimes.com/news/india/indias-rd-spends-amongst-the-lowest-in-the-world-niti-aayog-study/articleshow/93024586.cms?from=mdr.

85. Nitin Nohria, "Innovation: India Inc.'s Next Challenge," in *Reimagining India*, ed. McKinsey & Company (New York: Simon & Schuster, 2013),125.

86. Cameron G. Thies and Mark David Nieman, *Rising Powers and Foreign Policy Revisionism: Understanding BRICS Identity and Behavior through Time* (Ann Arbor: University of Michigan Press, 2017).

Chapter 4

1. *The Hindu*, January 4, 1946, quoted in V. Suryanaryayan, *Dialogue* 9, no. 1 (July–September 2007): 7.

2. Note that I am using the concept of "civilization" as a composite and pluralistic idea and not as the "homogeneous cultural units" often found in religious-nationalist narratives in India and elsewhere.

3. On this, see Becky Little, "How Martin Luther King Jr. Took Inspiration from Gandhi on Nonviolence," *Biography*, January 19, 2021, https://www.biography.com/news/martin-luther-king-jr-gandhi-nonviolence-inspiration.

4. "Freedom in the World 2022: India," *Freedom House*, https://freedomhouse.org/country/india/freedom-world/2022.

5. Arend Lijphart, "The Puzzle of Indian Democracy: A Consociational Interpretation," *American Political Science Review* 90, no. 2 (1996): 258–268.

6. Joseph S. Nye, *Soft Power: The Means to Success in World Politics* (New York: Pacific Affairs, 2004): x.

7. On this, see James Pomfret, "Opinion of China in Advanced Economies Sours 'Precipitously' under Xi–Pew," *Reuters*, September 29, 2022, https://www.reuters.com/world/china/opinion-china-advanced-economies-sours-precipitously-under-xi-pew-2022-09-29/.

8. For different perspectives on India's soft power, see Christian Wagner, "From Hard Power to Soft Power? Ideas, Interaction, Institutions, and Images in India's South Asia Policy," *Heidelberg Papers in South Asian and Comparative Politics*, no. 26, South Asia Institute, University of Heidelberg (March 2005); Jacques E. Hymans, "India's Soft Power and Vulnerability," *India Review* 8, no. 3 (July–September 2009): 234–265; Bibek Debroy, "India's Soft Power and Cultural Influence," in *Challenges of Economic Growth, Inequality and Conflict in South Asia*, ed. Tan Tai Yong (Singapore: World Scientific, 2010), 107–126.

9. Deborah Welch Larson and Alexei Shevchenko, *Quest for Status: Chinese and Russian Foreign Policy* (New Haven, CT: Yale University Press, 2019), 12.

10. Joseph S. Nye, "The Information Revolution and American Soft Power," *Asia-Pacific Review* 9, no. 1 (2002): 70; Nye, *Soft Power*, 11. The challenge for Nye is that his markers are all Western/liberal, and the assumption that these norms hold sway is contested by some rising powers, especially Russia and China.

11. See "Angkor Wat," *Encyclopedia Britannica*, https://www.britannica.com/topic/Angkor-Wat.

12. Peter J. Katzenstein, "A World of Plural and Pluralist Civilizations: Multiple Actors, Traditions and Practices," in *Civilizations in World Politics: Plural and Pluralist Perspectives*, ed. Peter Katzenstein (London: Routledge, 2010), 18.

13. Samuel P. Huntington, *The Clash of Civilizations and the Remaking of World Order* (New York: Simon & Schuster, 1996), 45.

14. Srisurang Poolthupya, "The Influence of the Ramayana on Thai Culture: Kingship, Literature, Fine Arts and Performing Art," Paper Presented at the 2nd International Ramayana Conference, University of Northern Illinois (July 2005); "Ramakian," *The Wonders of the World*, https://www.wonders-of-the-world.net/Temple-of-the-emerald-Buddha/Ramakian.php. On Indian religious and cultural influences in Southeast Asia, see George Coedes and Walter F. Vella, eds., *The Indianized States of Southeast Asia*, trans. Susan Brown Cowing (Honolulu: University of Hawaii Press, 1970); R. C. Majumdar, *India and Southeast Asia* (Delhi: B. R. Publishing, 1979).

15. Amit Singh and Amit Sarval, "Paraspara, Encounters, and Confluences: India's Soft Power Objective in the Indo-Pacific Region," *Politics & Policy* 45, no. 5 (2017): 733–761.

16. See A. L. Bashama, ed., *A Cultural History of India* (Oxford: Oxford University Press, 1975).

17. Amartya Sen, *The Argumentative Indian* (New York: Farrar, Straus and Giroux, 2005), xii.

18. Jawaharlal Nehru, *The Discovery of India*, 8th impression (New Delhi: Oxford University Press, 1989), 128.

19. T. N. Madhan, "Religion in India," *Daedalus* 118, no. 4 (Fall 1989): 115–146.

20. Susanne Hoeber Rudolph, "Four Variants of Indian Civilization," in Katzenstein, *Civilizations in World Politics*, 148.

21. Shashi Tharoor, *The Elephant, The Tiger and the Cell Phone* (New York: Arcade, 2007), 8.

22. Kishore Mahbubani, *The New Asian Hemisphere: The Irresistible Shift of Global Power to the East* (New York: Public Affairs, 2008), 173.

23. Rob Cain, "No Hollywood Film Has Topped 'Dangal' in China since May Except 'Transformers 5,'" *Forbes* 14 (October 2017), https://www.forbes.com/sites/robcain/ 2017/10/14/no-hollywood-film-has-topped-dangal-in-china-since-may-but-trans formers-5/?sh=5276c636198b; Pradeep Taneja, "Bilateral Economic Relations and Trade and Trust Deficits," in *Routledge Handbook of China-India Relations*, ed. Kanti Bajpai, Selina Ho, and Manjari Chatterjee Miller (London: Routledge, 2020), 299.

24. Yong Deng, *China's Struggle for Status* (Cambridge: Cambridge University Press, 2008), 78–79.

25. Ian Hall, *Modi and the Reinvention of Indian Foreign Policy* (Bristol: Bristol University Press, 2019), 19.

26. "Elections in India an Inspiration around the World: US," *The Statesman*, May 24, 2019, https://www.thestatesman.com/world/elections-india-inspiration-around-world-us- 1502758341.html.

27. Sunil Khilnani, *The Idea of India* (New York: Farrar, Straus and Giroux, 1999), 78.

28. Asuthosh Varshney, "India's Democratic Longevity and Its Troubled Trajectory," in *Democracy in Hard Places*, ed. Scott Mainwaring and Tarek Masoud (New York: Oxford University Press, 2022), 34–72; Milan Vaishnav, *When Crime Pays: Money and Muscle in Indian Politics* (New Delhi: Harper Collins, 2018).

29. *New York Times* columnist Thomas Friedman noticed this exceptionalism in India. See his "No Way, No How, Not Here," *New York Times*, February 17, 2009, https:// www.nytimes.com/2009/02/18/opinion/18friedman.html.

30. Compiled by Sen, *The Argumentative Indian*, 297–300.

31. Vinayak Damodar Savarkar, *Essentials of Hindutva* (first published in 1923, inde- pendently published 2019), 55.

32. See Christophe Jaffrelot, *The Hindu Nationalist Movement in India* (New York: Columbia University Press, 1993); Thomas Blom Hansen, *The Saffron Wave: Democracy and Hindu Nationalism in Modern India* (Princeton, NJ: Princeton University Press, 1999); Christophe Jaffrelot, *Modi's India: Hindu Nationalism and the Rise of Ethnic Democracy* (translated by Cynthia Schoch) (Princeton, NJ: Princeton University Press, 2021); Thomas Blom Hansen and Srirupa Roy, eds., *Saffron Republic: Hindu Nationalism and State Power in India* (Cambridge: Cambridge University Press, 2022).

33. Patrick J. Geary, *The Myth of Nations: The Medieval Origins of Europe* (Princeton, NJ: Princeton University Press, 2003).

34. Stephen P. Cohen, *India: Emerging Power* (Washington, DC: Brookings Institution Press, 2001), 119–120.

35. I am indebted to Manjeet Pardesi for suggesting this point.

36. Brendan O'Leary, "What States Can Do with Nations: An Iron Law of Nationalism and Federation?," in *The Nation-State in Question*, ed. T. V. Paul, G. John Ikenberry, and John A. Hall (Princeton, NJ: Princeton University Press, 2003), 68.

37. Although imperfect, such a model in Malaysia, which offers some political power to minority Chinese and Indian populations along with the majority Malays, is considered to be peace-preserving in the largely Muslim country. The absence of such a model is viewed as the cause of Sri Lanka's continued political and social unrest. On such a comparison, see Barbara Morris, "The Dynamics of Governmental Structure and the Advancement of Women: A Comparison of Sri Lanka and Malaysia,"

Journal of Asian African Studies 34, no. 4 (1999): 403–426. For the original model, see Arend Lijphart, "Consociational Democracy," *World Politics* 21, no. 2 (January 1969): 207–225.

38. Lijphart, "The Puzzle of Indian Democracy."

39. T. V. Paul, ed., *South Asia's Weak State: Understanding the Regional Insecurity Predicament* (Stanford, CA: Stanford University Press, 2010).

40. https://freedomhouse.org/country/india/freedom-world/2022.

41. Matthew Kroening, *The Return of Great Power Rivalry: Democracy versus Autocracy from the Ancient World to the US and China* (Oxford: Oxford University Press, 2020), 15–35.

42. Barry Posen, *The Sources of Military Doctrine* (Ithaca, NY: Cornell University Press, 1984), 25.

43. George K. Tanham, *India's Strategic Thought: An Interpretative Essay* (Santa Monica, CA: Rand, 1992), 17. On counter points, see Kanti P. Bajpai and Amitabh Mattoo, eds., *Securing India: Strategic Thought and Practice* (New Delhi: Manohar, 1996).

44. Arzan Tarapore, "Zone Balancing: India and the Quad's New Strategic Logic," *International Affairs* 99, no. 1 (January 2023): 239–257; Rajesh Rajagopalan, "Evasive Balancing: India's Unviable Indo-Pacific Strategy," *International Affairs* 96, no. 1 (2020): 75–93.

45. A. P. Rana, "The Intellectual Dimensions of India's Nonalignment," *Journal of Asian Studies* 28, no. 2 (February 1969): 307.

46. Zorawar Daulet Singh, *Power and Diplomacy: India's Foreign Policies during the Cold War* (Oxford: Oxford University Press, 2019), 14.

47. See Seng Tan and Amitav Acharya, *Bandung Revisited: The Legacy of the 1955 Asian-African Conference for International Order* (Singapore: NUS Press, 2008); Lorenz M. Luthi, *Cold Wars: Asia, the Middle East, Europe* (Cambridge: Cambridge University Press, 2020), 261.

48. On India's diplomatic role in Korea, see K. P. Fabian, "The Less Known Truth about Nehru & Korean War," *Madras Courier*, August 7, 2023, https://madrascourier.com/opinion/the-less-known-truth-about-nehru-the-korean-war.

49. Amitav Acharya, "Can Asia Lead? Power Ambitions and Global Governance in the Twenty-First Century," *International Affairs* 87, no. 4 (July 2011): 854.

50. To Basrur and Estrada, "India's temporary status gains through its normative innovation were undermined by its weak levels of associational status, that is through an absence of power." Rajesh Basrur and Kate Sullivan de Estrada, *Rising India: Status and Power* (London: Routledge, 2017), 26.

51. C. Raja Mohan, *Crossing the Rubicon* (New York: Palgrave-Macmillan, 2003).

52. John Lee, India's Edge over China: Soft Power," *Bloomberg Businessweek*, July 17, 2012, https://www.bloomberg.com/news/articles/2010-06-17/indias-edge-over-china-soft-power#xj4y7vzkg.

53. Kristen Hopewell, *Breaking the WTO: How Emerging Powers Disrupted the Neoliberal Project* (Stanford, CA: Stanford University Press, 2016); Amrita Narlikar, ed., *Deadlocks in Multilateral Negotiations: Causes and Solutions* (Cambridge: Cambridge University Press, 2010), 142–163.

54. Amrita Narlikar, "All That Glitters Is Not Gold: India's Rise to Power," *Third World Quarterly* 28, no. 5 (2007): 983–984.

55. Aseema Sinha, "Partial Accommodation without Conflict: India as a Rising Link Power," in *Accommodating Rising Powers: Past, Present and Future*, ed. T. V. Paul (Cambridge: Cambridge University Press, 2016), 222–245.

56. Shashank Matto, "India Still Punches Below Its Weight in Global Affairs, says Brahma Chellaney," *The Mint*, November 16, 2022, https://www.livemint.com/news/india/india-still-punches-below-its-weight-in-global-affairs-says-brahma-chellaney-116 68593724358.html

    The Mint, November 16, 2022.

57. On this, see Shyam Saran, *How India Sees the World: Kautilya to the 21st Century* (New Delhi: Juggernaught, 2018). See also Subrata K. Mitra, Markus Pauli, and Jivanta Schottli, *India: Statecraft and Foreign Policy* (Nomos: Baden-Baden, 2021).

58. Arijit Mazumdar, "India's Soft Power Diplomacy under the Modi Administration: Buddhism, Diaspora and Yoga," *Asian Affairs* 49, no. 3 (2018): 482.

59. Mazumdar, "India's Soft Power Diplomacy under the Modi Administration," 87.

60. Nicolas Blarel, "India: The Next Superpower?: India's Soft Power: From Potential to Reality?" *IDEAS Reports: Special Reports*, ed. Nicholas Kitchen. SR010. London: LSE IDEAS, London School of Economics and Political Science, 2012. http://eprints.lse.ac.uk/43445/.

61. Hall, *Modi and the Reinvention of Indian Foreign Policy*, 20, 39.

62. "G-20 New Delhi Leaders' Declaration," September 9–10, 2023, *The Hindu*, https://www.thehindu.com/news/national/67288583-G20-New-Delhi-Leaders-Declaration.pdf.

63. Zoya Mateen, "Delhi G20: How India is Asserting its Global Presence at G20 Summit," *BBC News*, September 6, 2023, https://www.bbc.com/news/world-asia-india-66682770.

64. United Nations, Department of Economic and Social Affairs, *International Migration*, 2020, 16, https://www.un.org/development/desa/pd/sites/www.un.org.development.desa.pd/files/undesa_pd_2020_international_migration_highlights.pdf.

65. "Placement Scenario: What IITians Do Post College," *Topper*, November 15, 2016, https://www.toppr.com/bytes/iitians-post-college/.

66. "Three-fourths of H1B Visa Holders in 2018 Are Indians: US Report," *The Economic Times*, October 20, 2018, https://economictimes.indiatimes.com/nri/visa-and-immigration/three-fourths-of-h1b-visa-holders-in-2018-are-indians-us-report/articleshow/66289772.cms.

67. "Indians in US Wealthier with Average Household Earning of $123,700: Report," *The Economic Times*, August 25, 2021, https://economictimes.indiatimes.com/nri/migrate/indians-in-us-wealthier-with-average-household-earning-of-123700-report/articleshow/85623601.cms?from=mdr.

68. "Nadella, Pichai, Narasimhan: Indian-origin CEOs at the Helm of American Cos," *Business Standard*, September 2, 2022, https://www.business-standard.com/article/current-affairs/nadella-pichai-narasimhan-indian-origin-ceos-at-the-helm-of-american-cos-122090200444_1.html.

69. *ICEF Monitor*, Forecast Projects 1.8 Million Indian Students Abroad by 2024, August 31, 2022, https://monitor.icef.com/2022/08/forecast-projects-1-8-million-indian-students-abroad-by-2024/.

70. Devesh Kapur, "Indian Diaspora as a Strategic Asset," *Economic and Political Weekly* 38, no. 5 (February 1–7, 2003): 447.

71. It must be noted that this program has generated suspicions in the United States, especially under the Trump administration. On this, see "China's Thousand Talents Plan to Entice Researchers Home Boosted Their Output," *Nature*, January 5, 2023, https://www.nature.com/articles/d41586-023-00012-5.

72. Rohan Mukherjee, "The False Promise of India's Soft Power," *Geopolitics, History, and International Relations* 6, no. 1 (2014): 46–62.

73. Christian Wagner, "India's Soft Power Prospects and Limitations," *India Quarterly* 66, no. 4 (2010): 341.

Chapter 5

1. Graham T. Allison, *Destined for War: Can America and China Escape Thucydides's Trap?* (Boston, MA: Houghton Mifflin Harcourt, 2017). For cases of successful accomodatitons, see T. V. Paul, ed., *Accommodating Rising Powers: Past, Present and Future* (Cambridge: Cambridge University Press, 2016).

2. John Vasquez, *The War Puzzle Revisited* (Cambridge: Cambridge University Press, 2009), 90.

3. Kyle M. Lascurettes, *Orders of Exclusion: Great Powers and the Strategic Sources of Foundational Rules in International Relations* (New York: Oxford University Press, 2020), ch. 7. For a liberal perspective on inclusive order building, see G. John Ikenberry, *After Victory* (Princeton, NJ: Princeton University Press, 2000).

4. M. S. Rajan, *India and International Affairs* (New Delhi: Lancers Books, 1999), 6–7.

5. See, for instance, Foreign Minister S. Jayashankar's *The India Way: Strategies for an Uncertain World* (New Delhi: Harper Collins India, 2022).

6. Dennis Kux, *India and the United States: Estranged Democracies* (Washington, DC: National Defense University Press, 1993).

7. "Dulles Declares Neutrality Pose Is Obsolete Idea," *New York Times*, June 10, 1956, 1.

8. Author's interview with Selig Harrison, Washington, DC, December 16, 1999.

9. Selig S. Harrison, "A Nuclear Bargain with India," Paper presented at the conference, "India the Crossroads," Southern Methodist University, Dallas, Texas, March 27, 1998, 6–8.

10. Dominic Wilson and Rupa Purushothaman, "Dreaming with BRICS: The Path to 2020," *Global Economics Paper* no. 99 (October 2003), https://www.goldmansachs.com/intelligence/archive/brics-dream.html

11. Robert J. McMahon, *Cold War in the Periphery: The United States, India and Pakistan* (New York: Columbia University Press, 1994), 64.

12. Strobe Talbott, *Engaging India: Diplomacy, Democracy and the Bomb* (Washington, DC: Brookings Institution Press, 2004), 7.

13. Ibid., 7.

14. Even before independence, Nehru described his antipathy toward opposing alliances. In a radio address in September 7, 1946, Nehru, as external affairs minister in the

interim Indian government, stated: "We propose so far as possible, to keep away from the power politics of groups, aligned against one another, which have led in the past to world wars and which may again lead to disasters on an even vaster scale." Jawaharlal Nehru, *India's Foreign Policy: Selected Speeches, September 1946–April 1961* (New Delhi: Publications Division, Ministry of Information and Broadcasting, Government of India, 1961), 2.

15. John Fricker, *Battle for Pakistan: The Air War of 1965* (Shepperton: Ian Allan, 1979), 11, 13

16. Bruce Riedel, *JFK's Forgotten Crisis: Tibet, the CIA, and the Sino-Indian War* (Washington, DC: Brookings Institution Press, 2017), 158–159.

17. Nabarun Roy, "In the Shadow of Great Power Politics: Why Nehru Supported PRC's Admission to the Security Council," *International History Review* 40, no. 2 (May 2017): 1–21.

18. The Editorial Department of the Renmin Ribao, "More on Nehru's Philosophy in the Light of the Sino-Indian Boundary Question," *China Deconstructs, Special Supplement* (December 1962), 15.

19. Baldev Raj Nayar, *Superpower Dominance and Military Aid: A Study of Military Aid to Pakistan* (New Delhi: Manohar, 1991).

20. For the text of the report, see National Security Archives, Washington, DC, https://nsarchive2.gwu.edu/NSAEBB/NSAEBB1/nhch7_1.htm.

21. Chester Bowles, *Promises to Keep: My Years in Public Life, 1941–1969* (New York: Harper Collins, 1971), 525.

22. Baldev Raj Nayar and T. V. Paul, *India in the World Order: Searching for Major Power Status* (Cambridge: Cambridge University Press, 2000), 169.

23. Gary J. Bass, *The Blood Telegram: Nixon, Kissinger, and a Forgotten Genocide* (New York: Alfred A. Knopf, 2013), 255.

24. Ibid.

25. Conversation among President Nixon, the President's Assistant for National Security Advisor (Kissinger), and the President's Assistant (Haldeman), November 5, 1971, Foreign Relations of the United States, 1969–1976, Vol E-7, Documents on South Asia, 1969–1972, https://history.state.gov/historicaldocuments/frus1969-76ve07/d150.

26. For an extensive list of documents on this, see William Burr, ed., *Beijing–Washington Backchannel and Henry Kissinger's Secret Trip to China, September 1970–July 1971* (Washington, DC: National Security Archive Electronic Briefing Book), No. 66 (February 27, 2002).

27. Mark Hibbs, "Pakistan's Bomb," *Non-Proliferation Review* 15, no. 2 (2008): 381–391.

28. See Indian Ambassador to the Conference on Disarmament in Geneva, Arundhati Ghose's statement, January 26, 1996, CD/PV.722; C. Uday Bhaskar, "India and the CTBT: Implications," *Strategic Analysis* 22, no. 8 (July 2008): 1237–1241.

29. Talbott, *Engaging India*, 27.

30. On this, see C. Rajamohan, *Crossing the Rubicon* (New York: Palgrave-Macmillan, 2004); Ian Hall, ed., *The Engagement of India* (Washington, DC: Georgetown University Press), 2014.

31. Talbott, *Engaging India*, 84.

32. Ibid., 85.

33. Bruce Riedel, "How the Kargil War Redefined US-India Ties," Washington, DC: Brookings Institution, July 2019, https://www.brookings.edu/blog/order-from-chaos/2019/07/24/how-the-1999-kargil-conflict-redefined-us-india-ties/.

34. Jane Perlz, "Clinton Decides to Visit Pakistan, After All," *New York Times*, March 8, 2000, https://www.nytimes.com/2000/03/08/world/clinton-decides-to-visit-pakistan-after-all.html.

35. Condoleezza Rice, *No Higher Honor: A Memoir of My Years in Washington* (New York: Crown, 2011), 262.

36. Dinshaw Mistry, *The US-India Nuclear Agreement: Diplomacy and Domestic Politics* (Delhi: Cambridge University Press, 2014), 2.

37. Ashley J. Tellis, *Atoms for War? US-India Nuclear Cooperation and India's Nuclear Arsenal* (Washington, DC: Carnegie Endowment for International Peace, 2006), 52.

38. C. Rajamohan, "India and the Balance of Power," *Foreign Affairs* 85, no. 4 (July–August 2006): 17; Harsh V. Pant, "The US-India Nuclear Deal: The Beginning of a Beautiful Relationship?," *Cambridge Review of International Affairs* 20, no. 3 (September 2007): 455–472.

39. U.S. Department of State, "US Security Cooperation with India," *Fact Sheet*, January 20, 2021, https://www.state.gov/u-s-security-cooperation-with-india/.

40. India Country Commercial Guide, U.S. Department of Commerce, September 7, 2022, https://www.trade.gov/knowledge-product/exporting-india-market-overview.

41. Rudra Chaudhuri, "The US and India Are Stepping up Tech Collaborations," *Hindustan Times*, January 15, 2023, https://www.hindustantimes.com/opinion/the-us-and-india-are-stepping-up-tech-collaborations-101673793203101.html.

42. C. Raja Mohan, "The Rediscovery of Geopolitics," in *Facets of India's Security: Essays for C. Uday Bhaskar*, ed. P. R. Kumaraswamy (London: Routledge, 2022), 5–7. See also "Indo-Pacific over 'Asia-Pacific' Reflects India's Rise: US Official," https://economicti mes.indiatimes.com/news/defence/indo-pacific-over-asia-pacific-reflects-indias-rise-us-official/articleshow/61519684.cms.

43. Rory Medcalf, *Indo-Pacific Empire* (Manchester: Manchester University Press, 2020), 4.

44. Chidanand Rajghatta, "Biden Singles Out India for 'Shaky' Response to Russia's Aggression," *Times of India*, March 23, 2022, https://timesofindia.indiatimes.com/world/us/biden-singles-out-india-for-shaky-response-to-russias-aggression/articles how/90381570.cms.

45. For the text of the memorandum of understanding, see White House, September 9, 2023, https://www.whitehouse.gov/wp-content/uploads/2023/09/Project-Gateway-Multilateral-MOU.pdf.

46. Nadeen Ebrahim, "New US-Backed India-Middle East Trade Route to Challenge China's Ambitions," *CNN*, September 1, 2023, https://www.cnn.com/2023/09/11/mid dleeast/us-india-gulf-europe-corridor-mime-intl/index.html.

47. Ian Hall, "The Engagement of India," in *The Engagement of India*, ed. Ian Hall (Washington, DC: Georgetown University Press, 2014), 8, 13.

48. Sushanta Mallik and Brigitte Granville, "What Does India Want from Russia?," *Project Syndicate*, August 12, 2022, https://www.project-syndicate.org/commentary/india-using-russia-to-gain-strategic-autonomy-by-sushanta-mallick-and-brigitte-granvi lle-2022-08?barrier=accesspaylog .

49. Memorandum of Conversation between Mao Zedong and Henry Kissinger, November 12, 1973, Wilson Center Archive, https://digitalarchive.wilsoncenter.org/document/memorandum-conversation-between-mao-zedong-and-henry-kissinger.

50. Xiaoyu Pu, "Asymmetrical Competitors: Status Concerns and the China-India Rivalry," in *The China-India Rivalry in the Globalization Era*, ed. T. V. Paul (Washington, DC: Georgetown University Press, 2018), 62.

51. On this, see Manjari Chatterjee Miller, "China, India, and Their Differing Conceptions of International Order," in Paul, *The China-India Rivalry in the Globalization Era*, 75–93.

52. Bérénice Guyot-Réchard, *Shadow States: India, China and the Himalayas, 1910–1962* (Cambridge: Cambridge University Press, 2017), 3–4.

53. "Comparing China and India by Economy," *Statistics Times*, May 16, 2021, https://statisticstimes.com/economy/china-vs-india-economy.php.

54. Amitav Acharya, *East of India, South of China: Sino-Indian Encounters in Southeast Asia* (Delhi: Oxford University Press, 2017), ch. 4.

55. Riedel, *JFK's Forgotten Crisis*, 112.

56. Rudolf G. Wagner, "China and India Pre-1939," in *Routledge Handbook of China-India Relations*, ed. Kanti Bajpai, Selina Ho, and Manjari Chatterjee Miller (London: Routledge, 2020), 35 and 58.

57. John W. Garver, "China's Decision for War with India in 1962," in *New Directions in the Study of China's Foreign Policy*, ed. Alastair I. Johnston and Robert S. Ross (Stanford, CA: Stanford University Press, 2006), 86–130.

58. Simon Shen and Debasish Roy Chowdhury, "The Alien Next Door: Media Images in China and India," in Bajpai, Ho, and Miller, *Routledge Handbook of China-India Relations*, 120. See also Shyam Saran, *How China Sees India and the World* (New Delhi: Juggernaut, 2022).

59. Kanti Bajpai, *India versus China: Why They Are Not Friends* (New Delhi: Juggernaught, 2021). On Chinese perceptions of India, see also Ananth Krishnan, *India's China Challenge: A Journey through China's Rise and What It Means for India* (New Delhi: Harper Colins, 2020).

60. Yong Deng, *China's Struggle for Status* (Cambridge: Cambridge University Press, 2008), 111.

61. Rush Doshi, *The Long Game: China's Grand Strategy to Displace American Order* (New York: Oxford University Press, 2021), 3.

62. In response to Indian Army Chief General Bipin Rawat's statement that "India was ready to take on China, Pakistan and internal security issues," a Chinese PLA spokesperson Wu Qian stated: "India should learn lessons from its defeat in 1962 and stop clamouring for a war." Sutirtho Patranobis, "China's PLA Warns India: 'Learn Lessons from 1962 Defeat, Stop Clamouring for War,'" *Hindustan Times*, July 5, 2017, https://www.hindustantimes.com/world-news/china-warns-india-to-remember-1962-stop-clamouring-for-war/story-SsjgL5nMONHpZ50dvdwuCP.html.

63. On two occasions, in November 2020 and February 2022, India banned several Chinese apps. Sherisse Pham, "India Bans More Chinese Apps as Tensions Remain High," *CNN Business*, November 20, 2020, https://edition.cnn.com/2020/11/25/tech/india-bans-chinese-apps-hnk-intl/index.html; "India Bans 54 Chinese Apps,

Including Those of Tencent, Alibaba and NetEase, on Security Concerns, Report Says," *South China Morning Post*, February 14, 2022, https://www.scmp.com/tech/big-tech/article/3166950/india-bans-54-chinese-apps-including-those-tencent-alibaba-and.

64. The Ministry of National Defense, Beijing, Whitepapers, http://eng.mod.gov.cn/publications/node_48467.htm.

65. See for instance, Qian Feng, "India's China Policy Entangled by Four Complex Mindsets," *Global Times*, December 15, 2022, https://www.globaltimes.cn/page/202212/1281952.shtml.

66. Larry Diamond, *Ill Winds: Saving Democracy from Russian Rage, Chinese Ambition, and American Complacency* (New York: Penguin, Press, 2019), 131.

67. Diamond, *Ill Winds*, 177.

68. *BBC News*, September 4, 2023, https://www.bbc.com/news/world-asia-china-66704059.

69. Neville Maxwell's book, *India's China War* (New York: Random House, 2000), pitting the blame largely on Nehru's policies, has been a dominant work for several decades since its original publication in 1970 and is said to have influenced the views of Chou Enlai, Kissinger, and Nixon, who used its contents during their diplomatic engagement in the early 1970s. This revisionist account's biggest weakness is its entire reliance on Indian documents. Opposite views or more balanced accounts are presented in books such as Steven A. Hoffmann, *India and the China Crisis* (Berkeley: University of California Press, 1990); John W. Garver, *Protracted Contest: Sino-Indian Rivalry in the 20th Century* (Seattle: University of Washington Press, 2002).

70. Sen, *The Argumentative Indian*, 164.

71. Ibid., 161.

72. Pu, "Asymmetrical Competitors," 63.

73. Susan L. Shirk, "One-Sided Rivalry: China's Perceptions and Policies toward India," in *The India–China Relationship: What the United States Needs to Know*, ed. Francine R. Frankel and Harry Harding (New York: Columbia University Press, 2004), 94.

74. Ibid., 94.

75. Asley J. Tellis, "China and India in Asia," in Frankel and Harding, *The India–China Relationship: What the United States Needs to Know*, 140.

76. Sumit Ganguly, Manjeet S. Pardesi, and William R. Thompson, *The Sino-Indian Rivalry: Implications for Global Order* (Cambridge: Cambridge University Press, 2023).

77. Record of Conversation between Indira Gandhi and Kosygin, May 6, 1969, Subject File 258, P. N. Haskar papers (III Installment), Nehru Memorial Museum and Library, New Delhi, quoted in Srinath Raghavan, *1971: A Global History of the Creation of Bangladesh* (Cambridge, MA: Harvard University Press, 2013), 112.

78. Mohammed Ayoob, "India in South Asia: The Quest for Regional Predominance," *World Policy Journal* 7, no. 1 (Winter 1989): 111.

79. Harsh V. Pant, "India Russia Ties and India's Strategic Culture: Dominance of a Realist Worldview," *India Review* 12, no. 1 (2013): 6.

80. Stephen P. Cohen, *India: Emerging Power* (Washington, DC: Brookings, 2001), 85.

81. On this, see Sameer Lalwani, "Will India Ditch Russia: Debating the Future of an Old Friendship," *Foreign Affairs* (January 24, 2023), https://www.foreignaffairs.com/india/will-india-ditch-russia; and Happymon Jacob, "Russia Is Losing India," *Foreign Affairs* (September 22, 2022), https://www.foreignaffairs.com/india/russia-losing-india.

82. Ashley J. Tellis, "What Is in Our Interests: India and the Ukraine War," Carnegie Endowment for International Peace, April 25, 2022 https://carnegieendowment.org/2022/04/25/what-is-in-our-interest-india-and-ukraine-war-pub-86961. See also, on the Indian popular support for India's abstaining from the UN Security Council vote condemning Russia, Sunainaa Chadha, "6 in 10 Indians Satisfied with India's Decision of Not Voting on UN Resolution against Russia: Survey," *Times of India*, March 3, 2022, https://timesofindia.indiatimes.com/business/india-business/6-in-10-indians-satisfied-with-indias-decision-of-not-voting-on-un-resolution-against-russia-survey/articleshow/89968765.cms.

83. Andrew Wyatt, "India and the United Kingdom: Finding a New Equilibrium," in *Engaging the World: Indian Foreign Policy since 1947*, ed. Sumit Ganguly (New Delhi: Oxford University Press, 2016), ch. 8.

84. Alexander A. Davis, *India and the Anglosphere: Race, Identity and Hierarchy in International Relations* (New York: Routledge, 2018), 162.

85. Pramit Pal Choudhury, "Brexit and India-UK Relations," in *India and European Union in a Turbulent World*, ed. Rajendra K. Jain (Singapore: Springer, 2020), 91–107.

86. David Scott, "The Rise of India: UK Perspectives," *International Affairs* 93, no. 1 (2017): 165–188.

87. Vidhi Doshi, "How the East India Company Became a Weapon to Challenge UK's Colonial Past," *The Guardian*, May 7, 2017, https://www.theguardian.com/world/2017/may/06/east-india-company-british-businessman.

88. See, for instance, William Dalrymple, *The Anarchy: The East India Company, Corporate Violence, and the Pillage of an Empire* (London: Bloomsbury, 2019).

89. Jean-Luc Racine, "The Indo-French Strategic Dialogue: Bilateralism and World Perceptions," *Journal of Strategic Studies* 25, no. 4 (2002): 151.

90. Jean-Luc Racine, "India's Foreign Policy toward France: A Strategic Partnership First," in Ganguly, *Engaging the World*, 246.

91. Rajeshwari Pillai Rajagopalan, "Strengthening the France-India Partnership," *The Diplomat*, May 16, 2022, https://thediplomat.com/2022/05/strengthening-the-france-india-partnership/.

92. Dietmar Rothermund, "Indo-German Relations: From Cautious Beginning of Robust Partnership," *India Quarterly* 66, no. 1 (March 2010): 1–12.

93. Gurjit Singh, "The Role of Perceptions in India–Germany Relations," New Delhi: Observer Research Foundation, Occasional Papers, August 17, 2022, https://www.orfonline.org/research/the-role-of-perceptions-in-india-germany-relations/.

94. Shairee Malhotra, "EU-India Summit 2021: Pushing Ahead with the 4Cs," *The Diplomat*, May 11, 2021, https://thediplomat.com/2021/05/eu-india-summit-2021-pushing-ahead-with-the-4-cs/.

95. European Commission, "India," https://policy.trade.ec.europa.eu/eu-trade-relationships-country-and-region/countries-and-regions/india_en.

96. Christophe Jaffrelot, "The Europe-India Balance Sheet," *India Forum*, December 14, 2021, https://www.theindiaforum.in/article/europe-india-balance-sheet.

97. "Tokyo Declaration for India-Japan Special Strategic and Global Partnership," *Times of India*, September 1, 2014, https://timesofindia.indiatimes.com/india/tokyo-decl aration-for-india-japan-special-strategic-and-global-partnership/articleshow/ 41433328.cms.

98. "Japan PM Kishida Announces $42 Billion Investment in India," *Reuters*, March 19, 2022, https://www.reuters.com/world/india/japan-pm-kishida-announces-42-bill ion-investment-india-2022-03-19/.

99. T. N. Raghunatha, "Bullet Train Project: JICA Announces 3rd Tranche Loan of '6,000 cr,'" *The Pioneer*, July 26, 2022, https://www.dailypioneer.com/2022/india/ bullet-train-project--jica-announces-3rd-tranche-loan-of--6-000-cr.html.

100. G. V. C. Naidu and Ishida Yasuyuki, "India–Japan Defence Ties: Building a Strategic Partnership," *Strategic Analysis* 43, no. 1 (2019): 13–27.

101. Manjeet S Pardesi, "India's Relations with Japan and South Korea," in Ganguly, *Engaging the World*, 303–325.

102. Rohan Mukherjee, "Japan's Strategic Outreach to India and the Prospects of a Japan-India Alliance," *International Affairs* 94, no. 4 (2018): 844.

103. Rohan Mukherjee, "India and Japan's Grand Bargain in the Context of China's Rise," in *India's Great Power Politics*, ed. Rohan Mukherjee (New Delhi: Routledge India), 248.

104. Muchkund Dubey, "The Historic Importance of G-77," *UN Chronicle*, vol. 1 (May 2014), https://www.un.org/en/chronicle/article/historic-importance-g-77.

105. Heather Stewart, "Tariffs: WTO Talks Collapse after India and China Clash with America over Farm Products," *The Guardian*, July 30, 2008, https://www.theguard ian.com/world/2008/jul/30/wto.india.

106. Shubhajit Roy, "Global South Has Always Shown Middle Path, Says Jaishankar," *Indian Express*, January 14, 2023, https://indianexpress.com/article/india/global- south-has-always-shown-middle-path-says-jaishankar-8380751/.

107. Andrew F. Cooper, "China, India and the Pattern of G20/BRICS Engagement: Differentiated Ambivalence between 'Rising' Power Status and solidarity with the Global South," *Third World Quarterly* 42, no. 9 (2021): 1945–1962.

Chapter 6

1. George McGhee, *Envoy to the Middle World: Adventures in Diplomacy* (New York: Harper & Row, 1983), 91. See also Husain Haqqani, *Magnificent Delusions: Pakistan, the United States and an Epic History of Misunderstanding* (New York: Public Affairs, 2013), 45.

2. See the key works, T. V. Paul, Deborah Welch Larson, and William C. Wohlforth, eds., *Status in World Politics* (Cambridge: Cambridge University Press, 2014); Deborah Welch Larson and Alexei Shevchenko, *Quest for Status: Chinese and*

Russian Foreign Policy (New Haven, CT: Yale University Press, 2019); Jonathan Renshon, *Fighting for Status: Hierarchy and Conflict in World Politics* (Princeton, NJ: Princeton University Press, 2017).

3. William R. Thompson, "Status Conflict, Hierarchies and Interpretation Dilemmas," in Paul, Larson, and Wohlforth, *Status in World Politics*, 219–245.

4. June Tuefel Dreyer, "The 'Tianxia Trope': Will China Change the International System?," *Journal of Contemporary China* 24, no. 96 (April 2015): 1015.

5. On this, see Manjari Chatterjee Miller, "China, India and Their Differing Conceptions of International Order," in *China-India Rivalry in the Globalization Era*, ed. T. V. Paul (Washington, DC: Georgetown University Press, 2018), 75–94; Sarah C. M. Paine, *Imperial Rivals: China, Russia and Their Disputed Frontier* (Armonk, NY: M. E. Sharpe, 1996), 50.

6. Fei-Ling Wang "From *Tianxia* to Westphalia: The Evolving Chinese Conception of Sovereignty and World Order," in *America, China, and the Struggle for World Order*, ed. G. J. Ikenberry, Zhu Feng, and Wang Jisi (New York: Palgrave-Macmillan, 2015), 43–68; David C. Kang, *China Rising* (New York: Columbia University Press, 2007), 43–44.

7. Yuen Foong Khong, "The American Tributary System," *Chinese Journal of International Politics* 6, no. 1 (2013): 1.

8. Quoted in Mohammed Ayoob, "India in South Asia: The Quest for Regional Predominance," *World Policy Journal* 7, no. 1 (Winter 1989): 124.

9. Mohammed Ayoob, "India as Regional Hegemon: External Opportunities and Internal Constraints," *International Journal* 46, no. 3 (Summer 1991): 421–422.

10. Ayoob, "India in South Asia: The Quest for Regional Predominance," 109. It is also based on a spatial image which is simultaneously cultural and state-centric. Shibashis Chatterjee, *India's Spatial Imaginations of South Asia* (New Delhi: Oxford University Press, 2019).

11. Riya Sinha and Niara Sareen, "India's Limited Trade Connectivity with South Asia," Brookings Institution, May 26, 2020, https://www.brookings.edu/research/indias-limited-trade-connectivity-with-south-asia/. According to the World Bank, in 2018 India's $19 billion trade in the region was 3 percent of its total trade and $43 billion below its potential. With Pakistan the formal trade was only $2 billion, even though there is some amount of informal trade. "South Asia Should Remove Trade Barriers for Mutual Economic Gains: New World Bank Report," World Bank, September 24, 2018, https://www.worldbank.org/en/news/press-release/2018/09/24/south-asia-remove-trade-barriers-mutual-economic-gains-report.

12. As a Pakistani scholar puts it: "India and Pakistan are both hostages to stubborn fixations—one of a rising power seeking its place in the sun, and the other of a nation, seeking parity with its mightier neighbor; in the process both have lost their bearings and caused the drift on their relationship." Feroz Hassan Khan, *Subcontinent Adrift: Strategic Futures of South Asia* (Amherst, NY: Cambria Press, 2022), xi.

13. Sunil Chander, "Congress-Raj Conflict and the Rise of the Muslim League in the Ministry Period, 1937–39," *Modern Asian Studies* 21, no. 2 (1987): 303–328.

14. Haqqani, *Magnificent Delusions*, 26.

15. Stephen P. Cohen, "Arms and Politics in Bangladesh, India and Pakistan," *Special Studies* 49 (New York: Council on International Studies, State University of New York at Buffalo, 1973), 26.

16. Henry Kissinger, *White House Years* (Boston: Little Brown, 1979), 861.

17. Jorg Friedrichs, "An Intercultural Theory of International Relations: How Self-Worth Underlies Politics among Nations," *International Theory* 28, no. 1 (2016): 630–696.

18. Ibid., 686.

19. Margaret Bourke-White, *Halfway to Freedom: A Report on the New India in the Words and Photographs of Margaret Bourke-White* (New York: Simon & Schuster, 1949), 92–93.

20. McGhee, *Envoy to the Middle World*, 91.

21. Haqqani, *Magnificent Delusions*, 345.

22. Memorandum of Conversation between Kissinger and Air Marshall Nur Khan, Lahore, Pakistan, August 1, 1969, FRUS E-7 (1969–1976), 1–3, cited in Haqqani, *Magnificent Delusions*, 137.

23. Haqqani, *Magnificent Delusions*, 137.

24. Studies show that an "unexpected military failure can seriously threaten the status of the defeated state, leading it to engage in aggressive actions in an attempt to bolster its image in the eyes of others." Joslyn Barnhart, "The Consequences of Defeat: The Quest for Status and Morale in the Aftermath of War," *Journal of Conflict Resolution*, 65, no. 1 (2021): 196. See also Russell J. Leng, "Realpolitik and Learning in the India-Pakistan Rivalry," in *The India-Pakistan Conflict: An Enduring Rivalry*, ed. T. V. Paul (Cambridge: Cambridge University Press, 2005), 103–130.

25. Quoted in Feroze Hassan Khan, *Eating Grass: The Making of the Pakistani Bomb* (Stanford, CA: Stanford University Press, 2012), 87.

26. John Ward Anderson and Kamran Khan, "Pakistan Sets off Nuclear Blasts," *Washington Post*, May 29, 1998, https://www.washingtonpost.com/archive/politics/1998/05/29/pakistan-sets-off-nuclear-blasts/be94cba3-7ffc-4ecc-9f67-ac6ddfe2a94c/?utm_term=.53178b4dc38e.

27. Haqqani, *Magnificent Delusions*, 209.

28. C. Christine Fair, *Fighting to the End: The Pakistan Army's Way of War* (New York: Oxford University Press, 2014).

29. Steve Coll, *Ghost Wars: The Secret History of the CIA, Afghanistan, and Bin Laden, from the Soviet Invasion to September 10, 2001* (New York: Penguin, 2004); Jeffrey W. Taliaferro, *Defending Frenemies* (Oxford: Oxford University Press, 2019), 116–117.

30. Owen L. Sirrs, *Pakistan's Inter-Services Intelligence Directorate: Covert Action and Internal Operations* (New York: Routledge, 2018).

31. On this, see Paul Kapur, *Jihad as Grand Strategy: Islamist Militancy, National Security, and the Pakistani State* (New York: Oxford University Press, 2016).

32. "Why Is Pakistan's Government Asking People to Drink Less Tea?," *The Economist*, June 21, 2022, https://www.economist.com/the-economist-explains/2022/06/21/why-is-pakistans-government-asking-people-to-drink-less-tea.

33. T. J. S. George, "Why Do Neighbors Dislike India?," *New Indian Express*, April 1, 2018, https://www.newindianexpress.com/opinions/columns/t-j-s-george/2018/apr/01/why-do-neighbours-dislike-india-1795288.html.

34. Asoke Mukerji, "A Diplomatic Narrative of the 1971 War," *The Wire*, December 18, 2021, https://thewire.in/diplomacy/a-diplomatic-narrative-of-the-1971-war.

35. Padmaja Murthy, "The Gujral Doctrine and Beyond," *Strategic Analysis* 23, no. 4 (July 1999): 639–652.

36. Sinha and Sareen, "India's Limited Trade Connectivity with South Asia."

37. Constantino Xavier, "Converting Convergence into Cooperation: The United States and India in South Asia," *Asia Policy* 14, no. 1 (January 2019): 19–50; Walter C. Ladwig III and Anit Mukherjee, "India and the United States: The Contours of an Asian Partnership," *Asia Policy* 14, no. 1 (January 2019): 3–18.

38. Gurpreet S. Khurana, "China's 'String of Pearls' in the Indian Ocean and Its Security Implications," *Strategic Analysis* 32, no. 1 (2018): 1–22; John W. Garver, "The Diplomacy of a Rising China in South Asia," *Orbis* 56, no. 3 (2012): 391–411.

39. Obja Borah Hazarika and Vivek Mishra, "Soft Power Contestation between India and China in South Asia," *Indian Foreign Affairs Journal* 11, no. 2 (April–June 2016): 144–145.

40. Maya Chaddha, "Rebellion and State Formation in Nepal, Implications for South Asian Security," in *South Asia's Weak States: Understanding the Regional Insecurity Predicament*, ed. T. V. Paul (Stanford, CA: Stanford University Press, 2010), 280.

41. Ibid., 280.

42. Ibid., 282.

43. Galen Murton, Austin Lord, and Robert Beazley, "A Handshake across the Himalayas: Chinese Investment, Hydropower Development, and State Formation in Nepal," *Eurasian Geography and Economics* 57, no. 3 (2016): 403–432.

44. Biswas Baral, "India's 'Blockade' Has Opened the Door for China in Nepal," *The Wire*, March 2, 2016, https://thewire.in/diplomacy/indias-blockade-has-opened-the-door-for-china-in-nepal>

45. Harsh V. Pant, "China's Moment in Nepal: Implications for India," *The Diplomat*, December 27, 2017, https://thediplomat.com/2017/12/chinas-moment-in-nepal-implications-for-india/.

46. "As Nepal Elects New Govt, Political Pundits Emphasise on Strong India-Nepal Relations," *Businessline*, December 22, 2022, https://www.thehindubusinessline.com/news/world/as-nepal-elects-new-govt-political-pundits-emphasise-on-strong-india-nepal-relations/article66307561.ece.

47. Mahua Venkatesh, "India—Sri Lanka's 2nd Largest Trading Partner—Worried as Economic Crisis Hits Island Nation," *Daijiworld.com*, September 4, 2021, https://www.daijiworld.com/news/newsDisplay?newsID=869900.

48. "Sri Lanka Formally Hands Over Hambantota Port on 99-year Lease to China," *The Hindu*, December 9, 2017, https://www.thehindu.com/news/international/sri-lanka-formally-hands-over-hambantota-port-on-99-year-lease-to-china/article61847422.ece

49. "India to Help Sri Lanka with USD 2.4 Billion to Overcome Financial Crisis: Report," *The Statesman*, January 20, 2022 . https://www.thestatesman.com/world/india-help-sri-lanka-usd-2-4-billion-overcome-financial-crisis-report-1503039923.html.

50. Ayeshea Perera, "Sri Lanka: Why Is the Country in an Economic Crisis?," *BBC News*, July 14, 2022, https://www.bbc.com/news/world-61028138.

51. Mohammad Hossain, "How Huge China Investment in Bangladesh Affects Region," *Anadolu Agency* (November 10, 2016), https://www.aa.com.tr/en/analysis-news/opinion-how-huge-china-investment-in-bangladesh-affects-region/683065.

52. *ORF Occasional Paper*, July 13, 2017, https://www.orfonline.org/research/the-2015-india-bangladesh-land-boundary-agreement-identifying-constraints-and-exploring-possibilities-in-cooch-behar/.

53. See, on this, https://bimstec.org.

54. Anu Anwar, "As US, China Fight over Bangladesh, India Is the Real Winner," *The Diplomat*, January 21, 2023, https://thediplomat.com/2023/01/as-us-china-fight-over-bangladesh-india-is-the-real-winner/.

55. Sudha Ramachandran, "The China-Maldives Connection," *The Diplomat*, January 25, 2018, https://thediplomat.com/2018/01/the-china-maldives-connection/.

56. "Maldives-China Relations," Globalsecurity.org, September 2, 2018, https://www.globalsecurity.org/military/world/indian-ocean/mv-forrel-prc.htm.

57. "Different Narratives: On India-Maldives Ties," *The Hindu*, April 23, 2022, https://www.thehindu.com/opinion/editorial/different-narratives-the-hindu-editorial-on-india-maldives-ties/article65345414.ece.

58. Dennis Hardy, "Will India Try Again for a Military Base in Seychelles?" *The Diplomat*, July 26, 2022, https://thediplomat.com/2022/07/will-india-try-again-for-a-military-base-in-seychelles/.

59. Vinita Singh Chetri, "Bilateral Relations between Seychelles and India," *Diplomacy & Beyond*, August 31, 2022, https://diplomacybeyond.com/bilateral-relation-between-seychelles-and-india/.

60. Samuel Bashfield, "Agalega: A Glimpse of India's Remote Island Military Base," *The Interpreter*, March 2, 2021, https://www.lowyinstitute.org/the-interpreter/agalega-glimpse-india-s-remote-island-military-base.

61. See Leo E. Rose, "Bhutan's External Relations," *Pacific Affairs* 47, no. 2 (Summer,1974): 192–208.

62. Rose, "Bhutan's External Relations," 193.

63. Royal Bhutanese Embassy, New Delhi, "Bhutan-India Hydro Power Relations," https://www.mfa.gov.bt/rbedelhi/bhutan-india-relations/bhutan-india-hydropower-relations/ (undated).

64. Sudha Ramachandran, "China Advances into Bhutan's Dokhlam: India Watches," *The Diplomat*, July 30, 2022, https://thediplomat.com/2022/07/china-advances-into-bhutans-doklam-india-watches/.

65. Ubeer Naqushbandi, "Would India Invest in Afghanistan under Taliban? Memories of 1999 IAF Hijacking Remain Fresh," *Outlook India*, December 4, 2022, https://www.outlookindia.com/national/would-india-invest-in-taliban-s-afghanistan-with-which-it-has-horrifying-iaf-1999-hijacking-experience--news-242301.

66. Tripti Lahiri and Rajesh Roy, "India Takes Cautious Steps towards Ties with Taliban," *Wall Street Journal*, September 4, 2022, https://www.wsj.com/articles/india-takes-cautious-steps-toward-ties-with-taliban-11662296400.

67. Shashank Joshi, "Indian Power Projection, Ambition, Arms and Influence," *Whitehall Paper* 85 (2015): 44.

68. David Scott, "India's 'Extended Neighborhood' Concept: Power Projection for a Rising Power," *India Review* 8, no. 2 (2009): 107–143.

69. Julie McCarthy, "With U.S. Focused on Defense, China's Trade and Infrastructure Sweep Southeast Asia," *NPR*, January 20, 2022, https://www.npr.org/2022/01/20/107 3764647/us-china-southeast-asia-trade-defense.

70. Niranjan Marjani, "India, ASEAN Elevating Ties to a Comprehensive Strategic Partnership," *The Diplomat*, November 11, 2022, https://thediplomat.com/2022/11/india-asean-elevating-ties-to-a-comprehensive-strategic-partnership.

71. Narinder Chauhan, "The Contrasting Role of India and China in Africa," *Financial Express*, January 18, 2022, https://www.financialexpress.com/defence/the-contrast ing-role-of-india-and-china-in-africa/2409400/.

72. International Institute of Sustainable Development, "India Seeks to Strengthen Its Longstanding Ties with Africa," September 25, 2022, https://www.iisd.org/articles/news/india-strengthen-ties-africa.

73. "India-UAE Trade Set to Surpass $88 Billion after Signing of Free Trade Deal," *Hindustan Times*, November 22, 2022, https://www.hindustantimes.com/india-news/indiauae-trade-set-to-surpass-88-billion-after-signing-of-free-trade-deal-10166912 2288088.html; India has a historic relationship with the UAE dating to ancient times, largely through maritime trade and two-way migration. See Venu Rajamony, *India and the UAE: In Celebration of a Legendary Friendship* (New Delhi: Lustre Press, 2008).

74. Md. Muddassir Quamar, "The Changing Nature of the Pakistan Factor in India-Gulf Relations: An Indian Perspective," *Asian Affairs* 49, no. 4 (2018): 625–644.

75. "India's Bilateral Trade with Gulf Council Grows at Rapid Pace, Data Shows," *Business Standard*, June 7, 2022, https://www.business-standard.com/article/economy-policy/india-s-bilateral-trade-with-gulf-council-grows-at-rapid-pace-data-shows-1220606 00615_1.html.

76. N. Janardhan, "India's 'Think West' Matches Gulf's 'Look East' Policy," in *The Arab Gulf's Pivot to Asia*, ed. N. Janardhan (Berlin: Gerlach Press, 2020), 81–95.

77. Sumitha Narayan Kutty, "Dealing with Differences: The Iran Factor in India-US Relations," *Asia Policy* 14, no. 1 (January 2019): 95–118.

78. Suhasini Haidar, "India's Catch-22 Dilemma on Relations with Iran," *The Hindu*, September 29, 2022, https://www.thehindu.com/opinion/op-ed/indias-catch-22-dile mma-on-relations-with-iran/article65949504.ece.

79. In many respects, India's behavior is akin to that of a major power, as its interests and activities are very wide in the different regions, unlike other regional powers. Manjeet S. Pardesi, "Is India a Great Power? Understanding Great Power Status in Contemporary International Relations," *Asian Security* 11, no. 1 (2015): 1–30. To Buzan, the ability to operate in more than one region is a key criterion for a major power status. Barry Buzan, "Great Powers," in *The Oxford Handbook of International Security*, ed. Alexandra Gheciu and William C. Wohlforth (New York: Oxford University Press, 2018), ch. 43.

Chapter 7

1. UNDP, *Human Development Index*, 2022, https://hdr.undp.org/data-center/specific-country-data#/countries/IND.
2. Soutik Biswas, "Why India's Covid Death May Never Be Known," *BBC News*, May 5, 2022, https://www.bbc.com/news/world-asia-india-60981318.
3. According to one estimate, the middle class was shrunk by some 32 million in 2020, and some 70 million have joined the ranks of the poor earning less than $2 a day. Pew Research Center, March 18, 2021, https://www.pewresearch.org/fact-tank/2021/03/18/in-the-pandemic-indias-middle-class-shrinks-and-poverty-spreads-while-china-sees-smaller-changes/; see also *Assessing Impact of the COVID-19 Pandemic on the Socio-economic Situation of Vulnerable Populations through Community-Based Monitoring* (New Delhi: UNICEF and IHD Report, 2021), https://www.unicef.org/india/media/6761/file/Assessing%20impact%20of%20the%20COVID-19%20pandemic%20.pdf.
4. Maja Pašović, Katherine Leach-Kemon, Christopher Troeger, Theo Vos, and Rafael Lozano, "Countries Hit Hardest by Covid-19" (Washington, DC: Institute for Health Metrics and Evaluation, November 17, 2021), https://www.thinkglobalhealth.org/article/countries-hit-hardest-covid-19.
5. Soutik Biswas, "Inequality in India Can Be Seen from Outer Space," *BBC News*, May 26, 2018, https://www.bbc.com/news/world-asia-india-44193144.
6. According to Selina Ho, different types of social contracts that exist between the citizens and the state in the two countries explain this variation; the Chinese model emphasizes performance, while the Indian model is a form of rigid bureaucratic socialism mixed with ad hoc populist measures. See her *Thirsty Cities: Social Contracts and Public Goods Provisions in China and India* (Cambridge: Cambridge University Press, 2019).
7. Prasun Sonwalkar, "8 Indian States = 25 African Nations: Oxford Study on Poverty," *The Hindustan Times*, June 26, 2015, https://www.hindustantimes.com/india/8-indian-states-25-african-nations-oxford-study-on-poverty/story-ys7Oths8HIzK21WWdB8AnL.html.
8. Shekhar Gupta, "Sub-African India: Much of Africa is Richer than Us, has Better Indicators, while we Diminish," *The Print*, June 5, 2021, https://theprint.in/national-interest/sub-african-india-much-of-africa-is-richer-than-us-has-better-indicators-while-we-diminish/672235/.
9. According to a report based on India's Ministry of Statistics and Program Implementation, in 2019, "South Indian states have higher GDP per capita than India's average. Bihar, Uttar Pradesh, Jharkhand, Manipur, and Assam are the top five poorest states." See "Indian States by GDP Per Capita," *Statistics Times*, March 1, 2021, https://statisticstimes.com/economy/india/indian-states-gdp-per-capita.php.
10. "Life Expectancy up: The Best Place to be Born, Work, and Retire in India," *The Times of India*, June 13, 2022, https://timesofindia.indiatimes.com/india/where-in-india-will-you-live-the-longest-and-where-shortest/articleshow/92178313.cms.

11. See World Bank Databank, 2023, https://data.worldbank.org/indicator/SP.DYN. LE00.MA.IN?locations=RU.

12. "Why India Is So Low on the Global Hunger Index," *Times of India*, October 17, 2022, https://timesofindia.indiatimes.com/india/why-india-is-so-low-on-the-global-hunger-index/articleshow/87100798.cms.

13. Esha Roy, "Over 35.5% Kids Stunted, Govt Releases Target to Curb Malnutrition," *Indian Express*, July 28, 2022, https://indianexpress.com/article/india/over-35-5-kids-stunted-govt-releases-target-to-curb-malnutrition-8055777/.

14. "Viewpoint: Modi's Currency Gamble Damaged Indian Economy," *BBC News*, November 8, 2017, https://www.bbc.com/news/world-asia-india-41896865.

15. The 2022 World Inequality Report, World Inequality Lab 2022, https://wir2022.wid. world.

16. Kamini Mathai, "Hurun Rich List 2022: India Has 221 Billionaires," *Times of India*, September 21, 2022, http://timesofindia.indiatimes.com/articleshow/94357215. cms?utm_source=contentofinterest&utm_medium=text&utm_campaign=cppst.

17. Chetan Bhattacharji, "63 Indian Cities in 100 Most Polluted Places on Earth: Report," *NDTV*, March 23, 2022, https://www.ndtv.com/india-news/delhi-is-worlds-most-polluted-capital-for-2nd-straight-year-report-2836028. See the IQR world air quality report, 2021, https://www.iqair.com/us/world-air-quality-report.

18. United Nations Development Program, "271 Million Fewer Poor People in India," September 20, 2018, https://www.undp.org/india/271-million-fewer-poor-people-india.

19. Bangladesh, marginally higher at 129, and Sri Lanka, at 73, are much higher than India's 131 out of 191 countries; "India's Rank Falls in Human Development Index; see Pakistan, China, Sri Lanka's Ranks," *Editorji*, September 11, 2022, https://www. editorji.com/india-news/india-s-rank-falls-in-human-development-index-see-pakistan-china-sri-lanka-s-ranks-1662715622736.

20. Aparna Pande, *Making India Great: The Promise of a Reluctant Global Power* (New Delhi: Harper Collins, 2021).

21. Transparency International, *Corruption Perceptions Index 2021*, https://www.transparency.org/en/cpi/2021.

22. Edward Luce, *In Spite of the Gods: The Strange Rise of Modern India* (New York: Doubleday, 2006), 73.

23. As Edward Luce states: "To the poor the state is both an enemy and a friend. It tantalizes them with an order that promises to lift them out of poverty, but it habitually kicks them in the teeth when they turn to it for help. It inspires both fear and promise. To India's poor the state is like an abusive father whom you can never abandon. It is through you that his sins are likely to live on." Luce, *In Spite of the Gods*, 84.

24. Rajesh Basrur, *Subcontinental Drift: Domestic Politics and India's Foreign Policy* (Washington, DC: Georgetown University Press, 2022).

25. T. V. Paul, "State Capacity and South Asia's Perennial Insecurity Problems," in *South Asia's Weak States: Understanding the Regional Insecurity Predicament*, ed. T. V. Paul (Stanford, CA: Stanford University Press, 2010), 5.

26. Joel S. Migdal, *Strong Societies and Weak States* (Princeton, NJ: Princeton University Press, 1988), 4–5.

27. Robert I. Rothberg, ed., *State Failure and State Weakness in a Time of Terror* (Washington, DC: Brookings Institution Press, 2003).
28. Paul, "State Capacity and South Asia's Perennial Insecurity Problems," 3–27.
29. A. Ksheerasagr, "Why Do So Few Individuals in India Pay Income Tax?," *LiveMint*, August 8, 2022, https://mintgenie.livemint.com/news/markets/why-do-so-few-indi viduals-in-india-pay-income-tax-151659927408731.; *Finshots*, "Why Do Only 5% of Indians Pay Income Tax?." https://finshots.in/archive/why-do-only-5-of-indians-pay-income-tax/.
30. "The Clogged State of the Indian Judiciary," *The Hindu*, May 10, 2022, https://www.thehindu.com/news/national/indian-judiciary-pendency-data-courts-statistics-expl ain-judges-ramana-chief-justiceundertrials/article65378182.ece.
31. India, Ministry of External Affairs, March 2022, https://www.mea.gov.in/Images/CPV/lu3820-1-mar-25-22.pdf.
32. Anshul Singhal, "1.8 Million Indian Students Would Be Studying Abroad by 2024," *Y-Axis*, October 15, 2022, https://www.y-axis.com/news/1-8-million-indian-stude nts-would-be-studying-abroad-by-2024/.
33. Pratap Bhanu Mehta, "UGC Guidelines on Foreign Universities: The University Gimmicks Commission," *Indian Express*, January 7, 2023, https://indianexpress.com/article/opinion/columns/ugc-guidelines-foreign-universities-in-india-pratap-bhanu-mehta-opinion-8367022/.
34. "Budget Allocation on Education Sector Crosses Rs 1 lakh Crore for the First Time: MoS Education," *Economic Times*, March 23, 2022, https://economictimes.ind iatimes.com/news/india/budget-allocation-on-education-sector-crosses-rs-1-lakh-crore-for-the-first-time-mos-education/articleshow/90397232.cms?from=mdr.
35. To Amartya Sen, "this state of affairs is the result of the continuation of British im-perial neglect of mass education, which has been reinforced by India's traditional elitism, as well as upper class dominated contemporary politics except in parts of India, such as Kerala, where anti-upper-caste movements have tended to concentrate on education as a great leveler." Sen, *The Argumentative Indian* (New York: Farrar, Straus and Giroux, 2005), 116.
36. Rebecca Leung, "Imported from India," *60 Minutes*, CBS News, https://www.cbsnews.com/news/imported-from-india/.
37. University Grants Commission, List of Private Universities, November 25, 2022, https://www.ugc.ac.in/oldpdf/Private%20University/Consolidated_List_Private_Universities.pdf; "Number of Universities across India from 2015 to 2021," *Statista*, December 2022, https://www.statista.com/statistics/1102334/india-number-of-universities/.
38. QS World University Ranking, 2023, https://www.universityrankings.ch/en/results/QS/202?ranking=QS&year=202&region=&q=India.
39. Ismat Ara, "JNU Profs Allege 'Gross' Irregularities in New Hiring, Seek President's Intervention," *The Wire*, November 27, 2020, https://thewire.in/education/jnu-irr egularities-hiring-professors-ram-nath-kovind-jagadesh-kumar.
40. Ritika Trikha, "The Interdependency of Stanford and Silicon Valley," *TechCrunch*, September 9, 2015, https://techcrunch.com/2015/09/04/what-will-stanford-be-with out-silicon-valley/.

41. See William E. Odom, *The Collapse of the Soviet Military* (New Haven, CT: Yale University Press, 2008).

42. *QS University Ranking 2023*, https://www.universityrankings.ch/results?ranking= QS&region=World&year=2023&q=China.

43. LEAD, *National Education Policy 2020*, https://leadschool.in/school-owner/national- education-policy-nep-2020/.

44. "Total Length of National Highways Increases to about 1,40,937 km till November End: Nitin Gadkari," *The Times of India*, December 15, 2021, https://timesofindia.ind iatimes.com/india/total-length-of-national-highways-increases-to-about-140937- km-till-november-end-nitin-gadkari/articleshow/88299372.cms.

45. Ashish Kumar Chauhan, "India Is Not Producing Enough Town Planners to Make Our Cities More Livable," *DownToEarth*, December 14, 2022, https://www.down toearth.org.in/blog/governance/india-is-not-producing-enough-town-planners-to- make-our-cities-more-livable-86564.

46. World Bank Data, 2021, https://data.worldbank.org/indicator/SP.URB.TOTL. IN.ZS?locations=IN.

47. For a list of Indian entrepreneurs in the Persian Gulf region, see "Revealed: Arabian Business' Indian Power List 2022," *Arabian Business*, April 8, 2022, https://www.arab ianbusiness.com/gcc/uae/revealed-arabian-business-indian-power-list-2022.

48. Tom Hancock, "How China Plans to Spend $1trn on Infrastructure to Boost Economy," *Business Standard*, August 26, 2022, https://www.business-standard.com/ article/international/how-china-plans-to-spend-1-trn-on-infrastructure-to-boost- economy-122082600185_1.html.

49. On this, see EPW Research Foundation, Mumbai, NABARD Research Study, no. 13, July 2021, https://www.nabard.org/auth/writereaddata/tender/1007211141NRS-13- %20Construction%20of%20State-wise%20RII%20%26%20Scheme%20of%20R IDF%20Allocation.pdf.

50. The World Health Organization, "India: A Push to Vaccinate Every Child, Everywhere, Ended Polio in India," April 7, 2021, https://www.who.int/india/news/feature-stories/ detail/a-push-to-vaccinate-every-child-everywhere-ended-polio-in-india.

51. The World Health Organization, *The Global Tuberculosis Report 2022*, https://worldhe althorg.shinyapps.io/tb_profiles/?_inputs_&entity_type=%22country%22&lan= %22EN%22&iso2=%22IN%22.

52. On the positives of the reforms, see Urvashi Sahni, "India's National Education Policy 2020A Reformist Step Forward?," *Brookings*, October 2, 2020, https://www.brooki ngs.edu/blog/education-plus-development/2020/10/02/indias-national-education- policy-2020-a-reformist-step-forward/.

53. United Nations, Department of Economic and Social Affairs, "Swachh Bharat Abhiyan (Clean India Mission)," https://sdgs.un.org/partnerships/swachh-bharat- abhiyan-clean-india-mission.

54. IQAir, Air Quality index, 2022, https://www.iqair.com/ca/india; Energy Policy Institute, University of Chicago, The Air Quality Life Index, 2020, https://aqli.epic. uchicago.edu/the-index/.

55. Charles Rajesh Kumar and M. A. Majid, "Renewable Energy for Sustainable Development in India: Current Status, Future Prospects, Challenges, Employment, and Investment Opportunities," *Energy, Sustainability and Society* 10, no. 1 (2020): 1–36.

56. Chalmers Johnson, *MITI and the Japanese Miracle: The Growth of Industrial Policy, 1925–1975* (Stanford, CA: Stanford University Press, 1982). See also Meredith Woo-Cummings, ed., *The Developmental State* (Ithaca, NY: Cornell University Press, 1999), especially the chapter by Donald J. Herring, "Embedded Particularism: India's Failed Developmental State," 306–334.

57. To Atul Kohli, the creation of effective states mattered in how variations of industrialization took place in the post-colonial states. See his *State-Directed Development: Political Power and Industrialization in the Global Periphery* (Cambridge: Cambridge University Press, 2004).

58. Surinder S. Jodhka, *Caste in Contemporary India*, 2nd ed. (London: Routledge, 2018), 15.

59. Luce, *In Spite of the Gods*, 156.

60. Larry Diamond, *Ill Winds: Saving Democracy from Russian Rage, Chinese Ambition, and American Complacency* (New York: Penguin, Press, 2019), 16.

61. Lingling Wei and Jonathan Cheng, "Why Xi Jinping Reversed his Zero-Covid Policy in China," *Wall Street Journal*, January 4, 2023, https://www.wsj.com/articles/why-xi-jinping-reversed-his-zero-covid-policy-in-china-11672853171.

62. *US News and World Report*, "Quality of Life," 2023, https://www.usnews.com/news/best-countries/rankings/quality-of-life.

63. Yasheng Huang, "Overtaking the Dragon," in *Reimagining India*, ed. McKinsey & Company (New York: Simon & Schuster, 2013), 75.

Chapter 8

1. Clement Tan, "G20 Welcomes African Union as Permanent Member at Delhi Summit," *CNBC*, September 9, 2023, https://www.cnbc.com/2023/09/09/g20-african-union-au.html.

2. Zoya Mateen, "Delhi G20: How India Is Asserting Its Global Presence at G20 Summit," *BBC News*, September 6, 2023, https://www.bbc.com/news/world-asia-india-66682770.

3. Narendra Modi, "One Earth, One Family, One Nature," *Indian Express*, December 1, 2022, https://indianexpress.com/article/opinion/columns/prime-minister-narendra-modi-writes-indias-agenda-during-its-g20-presidency-will-be-inclusive-ambitious-action-oriented-and-decisive-8299143/. To mark the occasion, the Modi government illuminated 100 monuments and planned to host some 200 meetings across the country. "India to Assume G20 Presidency from Today; 100 Monuments to Be Illuminated for a Week," *The Mint*, December 1, 2022, https://www.livemint.com/

news/india/india-to-assume-g20-presidency-from-today-100-monuments-to-be-illuminated-for-a-week-11669851915398.html.

4. See T. P. Sreenivasan, "The G-20 Can Be the UN Security Council Alternative," *The Hindu*, December 10, 2022, https://www.thehindu.com/opinion/op-ed/the-g-20-can-be-the-un-security-council-alternative/article66244029.ece.

5. Fiona Harvey and Rowena Mason, "Alok Sharma 'deeply Frustrated' by India and China over Coal," *The Guardian,* November 14, 2021, https://www.theguardian.com/environment/2021/nov/14/alok-sharma-deeply-frustrated-by-india-and-china-over-coal.

6. Critics argue that India's negotiating style is often "defensive," "prickly," and "obstructionist" and that "India has fallen short when it comes to addressing salient Global governance challenges." Karthik Nachiappan, *Does India Negotiate* (Oxford: Oxford University Press, 2019), 4.

7. For these see, World Bank, *World Integrated Trade Solution*, December 2022, https://wits.worldbank.org/CountryProfile/en/Country/IND/Year/2020/Summary.

8. The World Bank, *Data for China and India*, https://data.worldbank.org/?locations=CN-IN.

9. On this, see Michelle Murray, *The Struggle for Recognition in International Relations: Status, Revisionism, and Rising Powers* (New York: Oxford University Press, 2019).

10. On this, see T. V. Paul, *The Warrior State: Pakistan in the Contemporary World* (New York: Oxford University Press, 2014).

11. Ashley J. Tellis, "If India Keeps Diluting Its Liberal Character, the West Will Be a Less Eager Partner," *The Print*, September 23, 2020, https://theprint.in/opinion/if-india-keeps-diluting-its-liberal-character-the-west-will-be-a-less-eager-partner/506160/.

12. "One out of Every Three Indians 'Middle Class'; to Double by 2047: Report," *Business Standard*, November 2, 2022, https://www.business-standard.com/article/current-affairs/every-one-in-three-indians-middle-class-to-double-by-2047-report-122110200522_1.html>

13. "India's Economy to Double in Size to $5 Trillion by 2022: PM Modi," *Business Standard*, January 4, 2018, https://www.business-standard.com/article/economy-policy/india-s-economy-to-double-in-size-to-5-trillion-by-2022-pm-modi-118092000665_1.html.

14. The International Institute for Strategic Studies (IISS), The Military Balance 2022 and Stockholm International Peace Research Institute (SIPRI), Arms Transfers Database, 2022.

15. Amit Cowshish, "SIPRI's Assessment of India's Quest for Self-Reliance in Defence Production," *Financial Express*, October 12, 2022, https://www.financialexpress.com/defence/sipris-assessment-of-indias-quest-for-self-reliance-in-defence-production/2707740/.

16. "Russia's Share of Arms Import to India Fell from 69% in 2012–17 to 46% in 2017–21: Report," *The Hindu*, March 15, 2022, https://www.thehindu.com/news/national/russias-share-of-arms-import-to-india-fell-from-69-in-2012-17-to-46-in-2017-21-report/article65226945.ece.

17. Sanjeev Sanyal and Aakanksha Arora, "Why India Does Poorly on Global Perception Indices," Economic Advisory Council to the PM, November 2022, https://eacpm.gov.in/wp-content/uploads/2022/11/Global-perception-indices_Final_22_Nov.pdf.

18. Anisha Datta, "Govt Flagged Low Score in World Bank's Governance Indicators," *Indian Express*, May 19, 2022, https://indianexpress.com/article/india/govt-flagged-low-score-in-world-banks-governance-index-7924696/ .

19. *Statista*, "Public Opinion on India's Global Influence and Image 2016–2019," September 12, 2022, https://www.statista.com/statistics/986091/public-opinion-on-india-s-global-image/.

20. Rajesh Basrur and Kate Sullivan de Estrada, *Rising India: Status and Power* (London and New York: Routledge, 2017), 2.

21. On India's engagement in the region, see Shivshankar Menon, *India and Asian Geopolitics* (Washington, DC: Brookings Institution Press, 2021).

22. Robert D. Kaplan, *The Revenge of Geography* (New York: Random House, 2012), 228. In this vein, Indian scholars call for smart balancing in South Asia, by making accommodation with Pakistan and focus on China while Keeping Russia from falling into a full embrace with Beijing. See Happymon Jacob, "The Role of the China Test in India's Grand Strategy," *The Hindu*, December 12, 2012, https://www.thehindu.com/opinion/lead/the-role-of-the-china-test-in-indias-grand-strategy/article66252325.ece.

23. Larry Diamond, *Ill Winds: Saving Democracy from Russian Rage, Chinese Ambition, and American Complacency* (New York: Penguin Books, 2019), 6.

24. Ibid., 32.

25. Rahul Sagar, "State of Mind: What Kind of Power Will India Become?," *International Affairs* 85, no. 4 (2009): 801–816.

26. Stephanie Busari, Nimi Princewill, Shama Nasinde, and Mohammed Tawfeeq, "Foreign Students Fleeing Ukraine Say They Face Segregation, Racism at Border," *CNN*, March 4, 2022, https://edition.cnn.com/2022/02/28/europe/students-allege-racism-ukraine-cmd-intl/index.html.

27. Stephen I. Schwartz, "The Hidden Costs of Our Nuclear Arsenal," Brookings Institution, June 20, 1998, https://www.brookings.edu/the-hidden-costs-of-our-nuclear-arsenal-overview-of-project-findings/.

28. International Campaign to Abolish Nuclear Weapons (ICAN) Report, *Squandered: 2021 Global Nuclear Weapons Spending*, https://assets.nationbuilder.com/ican/pages/2873/attachments/original/1655145777/Spending_Report_2022_web.pdf?1655145777.

29. Watson Institute of International Affairs, Brown University, *Costs of War Project*, September 1, 2021, https://www.brown.edu/news/2021-09-01/costsofwar.

Index

For the benefit of digital users, indexed terms that span two pages (e.g., 52–53) may, on occasion, appear on only one of those pages.

Figures are indicated by *f* following the page number